Essential tables

RATES OF INCOME TAX
(ITA 2007, Pt 2, Ch 2)

Taxable income £	Rate %	Tax £	Cumulative £
2012–13			
0–34,370	20	6,874.00	6,874.00
34,371–150,000	40	46,251.60	53,125.60
Over 150,000	50	–	–
2011–12			
0–35,000	20	7,000.00	7,000.00
35,001–150,000	40	46,000.00	53,000.00
Over 150,000	50	–	–
2010–11			
0–37,400	20	7,480.00	7,480.00
37,401–150,000	40	45,040.00	52,520.00
Over 150,000	50	–	–
2009–10			
0–37,400	20	7,480.00	7,480.00
Over 37,400	40	–	–
2008–09			
0–34,800	20	6,960.00	6,960.00
Over 34,800	40	–	–
2007–08			
0–2,230	10	223.00	223.00
2,231–34,600	22	7,121.40	7,344.40
Over 34,600	40	–	–
2006–07			
0–2,150	10	215.00	215.00
2,151–33,300	22	6,853.00	7,068.00
Over 33,300	40	–	–

See further **Personal Taxation**, p 1.

Essential tables

PERSONAL ALLOWANCES AND RELIEFS

(*ITA 2007, Pt 3*)

	2012–13 £	2011–12 £	2010–11 £	2009–10 £
Personal allowance (under 65 years)	8,105	7,475	6,475	6,475
Age allowance				
Personal allowance (age 65–74)	10,500	9,940	9,490	9,490
Personal allowance (age 75 and over)	10,660	10,090	9,640	9,640
Income limit for age-related allowances	25,400	24,000	22,900	22,900
Married couple's allowance				
Basic allowance	2,960	2,800	2,670	2,670
Age 75 or over	7,705	7,295	6,965	6,965
Blind person's allowance	2,100	1,980	1,890	1,890
Rent-a-room relief	4,250	4,250	4,250	4,250

See further **Personal Taxation**, p 3.

RATES OF CORPORATION TAX

(*CTA 2010, Pt 2, Ch 2, 3; Pt 3*)

	Financial Year commencing 1 April		
	2012	2011	2010
Small Profits Rate	20%	20%	21%
Small Profits Rate can be claimed by qualifying companies with profits at a rate not exceeding	£300,000	£300,000	£300,000
Marginal Relief Lower Limit	£300,000	£300,000	£300,000
Marginal Relief Upper Limit	£1,500,000	£1,500,000	£1,500,000
Standard fraction	1/100	3/200	7/400
Main rate of Corporation Tax	24%	26%	28%

	2009	2008	2007	2006
Small Profits Rate	21%	21%	20%	19%
Small Profits Rate can be claimed by qualifying companies with profits at a rate not exceeding	£300,000	£300,000	£300,000	£300,000
Marginal Relief Lower Limit	£300,000	£300,000	£300,000	£300,000
Marginal Relief Upper Limit	£1,500,000	£1,500,000	£1,500,000	£1,500,000
Standard fraction	7/400	7/400	1/40	11/400
Main rate of Corporation Tax	28%	28%	30%	30%

See further **Taxation of Companies**, p 70.

CGT RATES AND ANNUAL EXEMPTIONS

(TCGA 1992, ss 3, 4, Sch 1)

Tax Year	Annual exempt amount		Rate	
	Individuals, personal representatives (PR's) and trusts for mentally disabled	General trusts	Individuals	Trustees and PR's
	£	£	%	%
2012–13	10,600	5,300		
– Standard rate			18	28
– Higher rate			28	
2011–12	10,600	5,300		
– Standard rate			18	28
– Higher rate			28	
2010–11 (23 June 2010 to 6 April 2011) – Standard rate – Higher rate	10,100 (whole tax year	5,050 (whole tax year)	18 28	28
2010–11 (6 April to 22 June 2010)	10,100 (whole tax year)	5,050 (whole tax year)	18	18
2009–10	10,100	5,050	18	18
2008–09	9,600	4,800	18	18
2007–08	9,200	4,600	10/20/40	40
2006–07	8,800	4,400	10/20/40	40

See further **Capital Gains Tax**, p 86.

Key Tax Dates

Monthly

- 19th – Non-electronic payments of PAYE, Class 1 NIC and CIS deductions for the period ended 5th of the month should reach HMRC's Accounts Office by this date (*SI 2003/2682, reg 69(1)(b); SI 2005/2045, reg 7(1)(b)SI 2001/1004, Sch 4, reg 10(1)*).
- 22nd – Electronic payments of PAYE, Class 1 NIC and CIS deductions for the period ended 5th of the month should clear into HMRC's bank account by this date (*SI 2003/2682, reg 69(1)(a); SI 2001/1004, Sch 4, reg 10(1); SI 2005/2045, reg 7(1)(a)*).

3 May 2012

- Employers must submit Form P46 (Car) if appropriate to report changes affecting car benefits during the quarter to 5 April 2012.

19 May 2012

- Employers must submit 2011–12 end of year PAYE returns (forms P35 and P38A, including 'nil' returns if appropriate, and P14) to HMRC by this date (*SI 2003/2682, regs 73, 74*).

31 May 2012

- Employers have until 31 May 2012 to provide a 2011–12 form P60 to each employee who worked for them at 5 April 2012, and from whom the employer was required to deduct tax from relevant payments at any time during the tax year (*SI 2003/2682, reg 67*).

5 July 2012

- PAYE Settlement Agreements (PSAs) for 2011–12 must be agreed with HMRC by this date (*SI 2003/2682, reg 112*).

6 July 2012

- Deadline for employers to submit returns of benefits and expenses (forms P11D and P9D) to HMRC for 2011–12 (*SI 2003/2682, reg 85*).
- Returns of Class 1A NICs (forms P11D(b)) for 2011–12 must reach HMRC by this date (*SI 2001/1004, reg 80*).
- Employers must supply relevant employees with P11D(b), P11D and P9D information for 2011–12 by this date (*SI 2003/2682, reg 94*).

Key Tax Dates

- Form 42 (or equivalent) dealing with employment-related securities and options and reportable events for the tax year ended 5 April 2012 must normally reach HMRC by this date (*ITEPA 2003, s 421J*). This is also the normal due date for 2011–12 end of year return forms 34, 35, 39 and 40, in respect of employee share schemes.

19 July 2012

- Employer non-electronic payments of Class 1A NICs for 2011–12 on benefits returned on a declaration of expenses and benefits (form P11D(b)) must reach HMRC by this date. The payment date is extended to 22 July for payments made by an approved electronic payment method (*SI 2001/1004, reg 71*).

31 July 2012

- The second payment on account of self assessment income tax (and Class 4 NIC, if appropriate) by individuals for 2011–12 must reach HMRC no later than this date, if late payment interest charges are to be avoided (*TMA 1970, s 59A(2)*).

1 August 2012

- Most individual taxpayers who have not paid their remaining tax liabilities (and Class 4 NIC, if appropriate) for 2010–11 by this date face a further 5% penalty, in addition to the 5% penalty suffered on amounts outstanding at 1 March 2012 (*FA 2009, Sch 56, para 3; SI 2011/702, art 3*).

2 August 2012

- Employers must submit Form P46 (Car) if appropriate to report changes affecting car benefits during the quarter to 5 July 2012.

31 August 2012

- If HMRC have not issued a 2011–12 income tax self assessment notice to file until after this date, the normal submission deadline of 31 October 2012 to ensure that HMRC will calculate the tax (and, if applicable, Class 4 NIC) due is extended to two months after the date on which the notice is issued (*TMA 1970, s 9(2)(b)*).

5 October 2012

- Any person chargeable to income tax or CGT for 2011–12 who has not received a notice to file a self assessment return must notify HMRC by this date that they are so chargeable (*TMA 1970, s 7(1)*).

19 October 2012

- Employer non-electronic payments of income tax in respect of PAYE settlement agreements (PSAs) for 2011–12 should reach HMRC Accounts Office by this date (*SI 2003/2682, reg 109(2)*) (nb the due date is extended to 22 October 2012 for payments made by an approved electronic payment method). This is also the normal due date for payment of Class 1B NIC liabilities in respect of PSAs for 2011–12 (or 22 October 2012 for electronic payments) (*SI 2001/1004, Sch 4 reg 13(1)*).

Key Tax Dates

31 October 2012

- Paper (non-electronic) income tax self-assessment returns for 2011–12 must generally be filed no later than this date (or, if later, three months after the date on which HMRC issue a notice to file a tax return). This applies to individuals, (*TMA 1970, s 8(1D)–(1F)*), trustees (*TMA 1970, s 8A(1B)–(1D)*) and partnerships which include one or more individuals (*TMA 1970, s 12AA(4A)–(4D)*).
- If HMRC do not issue a notice to file a 2011–12 self-assessment income tax return until after 31 October 2012, the return must be filed within three months from the date of the notice, whether the return is electronic or paper (*TMA 1970, ss 8(1G), 8A(1E), 12AA(4E)*).
- A self assessment taxpayer is relieved of the obligation to calculate their tax (and, if applicable, Class 4 NIC) for 2011–12, and HMRC will calculate it instead and notify the taxpayer before the 31 January payment deadline, if the return is filed on paper by 31 October 2012. However, if HMRC did not issue a notice to file the return until after 31 August 2012, this deadline is extended to two months after the date on which the notice is issued (*TMA 1970, s 9(2)(b)*). If the deadline is missed, in practice HMRC will generally still make the calculations but cannot guarantee doing so by the due date for payment.
- An employed taxpayer who submits a paper self assessment return for 2011–12 must do so by 31 October 2012 if they wish HMRC to collect a tax underpayment of less than £3,000 by adjustment to their future PAYE code where possible (ITEPA 2003, s 684(3A); SI 2003/2682, reg 186(4)). This limit was £2,000 for 2010–11.

2 November 2012

- Employers must submit Form P46 (Car) if appropriate to report changes affecting car benefits during the quarter to 5 October 2012.

30 December 2012

- An employed taxpayer who submits an electronic self assessment return for 2011–12 must do so by 30 December 2012 if they wish HMRC to collect a tax underpayment of less than £3,000 by adjustment to their future PAYE code where possible (ITEPA 2003, s 684(3A); SI 2003/2682, reg 186(4)). This limit was £2,000 for 2010–11.

31 January 2013

- Electronic income tax self-assessment returns for 2011–12 must normally be filed by this date, and any balancing payment of tax due for that year received by HMRC. However, if the notice to file was issued after 31 October 2011, the deadline for filing the return (whether electronically or on paper) is extended to three months from the date of issue of that notice (*TMA 1970, ss 8(1D)(b), 8(1G); 8A(1B)(b), 8A(1E); 12AA(4B), 12AA(4E)*).
- Any balancing payment of self assessment income tax (and Class 4 NIC, if applicable) for 2011–12 plus any capital gains tax for that year is normally payable by 31 January 2013. However, for 2011–12 tax returns where HMRC was notified of chargeability to tax by 5 October 2012 and the notice to file was issued after 31 October 2012, the payable date is extended to three months after the date on which the notice to file was issued (TMA 1970, s 59B(3), (4)).

Key Tax Dates

- If a first payment on account is required for the tax year 2012–13, the payment of tax (and Class 4 NIC, if applicable) must reach HMRC by 31 January 2012 (*TMA 1970, s 59A(2)(a)*).

1 February 2013

- Most individual taxpayers who have not paid their remaining tax liabilities (and Class 4 NIC, if appropriate) for 2010–11 by this date face a further 5% penalty, in addition to the 5% penalties suffered on amounts outstanding at 1 March 2012 and 1 August 2012 (*FA 2009, Sch 56, para 3; SI 2011/702, art 3*).

2 February 2013

- Employers must submit Form P46 (Car) if appropriate to report changes affecting car benefits during the quarter to 5 January 2013.

1 March 2013

- Most individual taxpayers who have not paid their tax liabilities (and Class 4 NIC, if appropriate) for 2011–12 by this date face a 5% penalty (*FA 2009, Sch 56, para 3; SI 2011/702, art 3*).

5 April 2013

- The end of tax year 2012–13, and a crucial day for deciding whether to take particular action either before or after 5 April 2013 (eg utilising personal allowances, the CGT and IHT annual exemptions, etc).

30 April 2013

- Payment of IHT on lifetime transfers between 6 April and 30 September 2012 is due by this date (*IHTA 1984, s 226(1)*).

3 May 2013

- Employers must submit Form P46 (Car) if appropriate to report changes affecting car benefits during the quarter to 5 April 2013.

19 May 2013

- Employers must submit 2012–13 end of year PAYE returns (forms P35 and P38A, including 'nil' returns if appropriate, and P14) to HMRC by this date (*SI 2003/2682, regs 73, 74*).

31 May 2013

- Employers have until 31 May 2013 to provide a 2012–13 form P60 to each employee who worked for them at 5 April 2013, and from whom the employer was required to deduct tax from relevant payments at any time during the tax year (*SI 2003/2682, reg 67*).

Note

The above list is for general information purposes only, and is not exhaustive.

Bloomsbury's Tax Rates and Tables 2012/13

Budget edition

Compiled by:

Donald Drysdale CA CTA (Fellow) TEP MBCS CITP

Contributing Editor:

Mark McLaughlin CTA (Fellow) ATT TEP

Welcome to *Tax Rates and Tables 2012/13* (Budget edition), published by Bloomsbury Professional.

Following very positive feedback in last year, we are again producing this publication twice – in Budget and Finance Act editions. This Budget edition of *Tax Rates and Tables 2012/13* retains the successful format already established, but contains a significant amount of new material – having been updated to reflect measures announced in the Budget of 21 March 2012 and the subsequent Finance Bill. Everyone involved in this book is constantly striving for improvements in content and format. We would welcome your constructive comments or suggestions for future editions.

The publishers, Bloomsbury Professional, have retained *Tax Rates and Tables 2012/13* (Budget edition) at a very attractive and competitive price. I hope you will agree that it provides excellent value for money for tax professionals and taxpayers alike.

Sincere thanks are due to my colleague Donald Drysdale of Taxing Words Ltd for all his hard work and commitment towards bringing this edition together. Many thanks as well to everyone at Bloomsbury Professional who was involved in the publication, particularly Jane Bradford for her considerable skill and professionalism in bringing all the material together.

Finally, thank you for acquiring *Tax Rates and Tables 2012/13* (Budget edition).

I hope that you find it very useful and practical.

Mark McLaughlin CTA (Fellow) ATT TEP
Contributing Editor
April 2012

Bloomsbury Professional

Bloomsbury Professional Ltd, Maxwelton House, 41–43 Boltro Road, Haywards Heath, West Sussex, RH16 1BJ

© Bloomsbury Professional Ltd 2012
Bloomsbury Professional is an imprint of Bloomsbury Publishing Plc

All rights reserved. No part of this publication may be reproduced in any material form (including photocopying or storing it in any medium by electronic means and whether or not transiently or incidentally to some other use of this publication) without the written permission of the copyright owner except in accordance with the provisions of the Copyright, Designs and Patents Act 1988 or under the terms of a licence issued by the Copyright Licensing Agency Ltd, Saffron House, 6–10 Kirby Street, London, England EC1N 8TS. Applications for the copyright owner's written permission to reproduce any part of this publication should be addressed to the publisher.

Whilst every care has been taken to ensure the accuracy of the content of this work, no responsibility for loss occasioned to any person acting or refraining from action as a result of the material in this publication can be accepted by the author or by the publisher.

Warning: The doing of an unauthorised act in relation to a copyright work may result in both a civil claim for damages and criminal prosecution.

Crown copyright material is reproduced with the permission of the Controller of HMSO and the Queen's Printer for Scotland. Any European material in this work which has been reproduced from EUR-lex, the official European Communities legislation website, is European Communities copyright

A CIP Catalogue record for this book is available from the British Library.

ISBN 978 1 84766 973 5

Typeset by Phoenix Photosetting, Chatham, Kent
Printed and bound in Great Britain by Hobbs the Printers, Totton, Hampshire

1

Personal Taxation

RATES OF INCOME TAX

(ITA 2007, Pt 2, Ch 2)

Taxable income £	Rate %	Tax £	Cumulative £
2012–13			
0–34,370	20	6,874.00	6,874.00
34,371–150,000	40	46,251.60	53,125.60
Over 150,000	50	–	–
2011–12			
0–35,000	20	7,000.00	7,000.00
35,001–150,000	40	46,000.00	53,000.00
Over 150,000	50	–	–
2010–11			
0–37,400	20	7,480.00	7,480.00
37,401–150,000	40	45,040.00	52,520.00
Over 150,000	50	–	–
2009–10			
0–37,400	20	7,480.00	7,480.00
Over 37,400	40	–	–
2008–09			
0–34,800	20	6,960.00	6,960.00
Over 34,800	40	–	–
2007–08			
0–2,230	10	223.00	223.00
2,231–34,600	22	7,121.40	7,344.40
Over 34,600	40	–	–
2006–07			
0–2,150	10	215.00	215.00
2,151–33,300	22	6,853.00	7,068.00
Over 33,300	40	–	–

Notes

(1) The additional rate of income tax for 2013–14 will be reduced from 50% to 45% (Budget, 21 March 2012; *FB 2012, cl 1*).

(2) The basic rate limit is to be reduced from £34,370 (for 2012–13) to £32,245 (for 2013–14) in order to claw back 75% of the benefit of the increase in the personal allowance from those with incomes at or above that limit (Budget, 21 March 2012).

1 Personal Taxation

TAX RATES FOR SAVINGS AND DIVIDENDS

(ITA 2007, ss 10–19)

Non-dividend savings income rates	2012–13	2011–12	2010–11	2009–10	2008–09	2007–08
Starting Rate	10% up to £2,710	10% up to £2,560	10% up to £2,440	10% up to £2,440	10% up to £2,320	10% up to starting rate limit
Basic Rate	20%	20%	20%	20%	20%	20%
Higher Rate	40%	40%	40%	40%	40%	40%
Additional Rate	50%	50%	50%	–	–	–

Notes

(1) *Savings income* – From 2008–09, a 10% starting rate of income tax applies to savings income only. If non-savings income exceeds this limit, the 10% starting rate for savings does not apply. If savings income does not exceed the basic rate limit, there is no additional tax to pay on savings income from which 20% tax has been deducted, but higher rate taxpayers are liable to income tax at 40% or (from 2010–11) 50% to the extent that savings income exceeds the higher or additional rate thresholds.

(2) *Dividend income* – If gross dividend income does not exceed the basic rate threshold, the income tax rate is 10%. For the years 2010–11 to 2012–13, higher rate or additional rate taxpayers are liable to income tax at 32.5% or 42.5%, to the extent that dividend income exceeds the higher or additional rate thresholds.

(3) The additional rate of income tax for 2013–14 will be reduced from 50% to 45%, and the additional rate for dividend income for 2013–14 will be 37.5% (Budget, 21 March 2012; *FB 2012, cl 1*).

The 10% non-repayable tax credit on dividends from UK resident companies can be calculated by applying a fraction of 1/9th to the net amount. In addition, from 6 April 2008 a non-repayable tax credit of 1/9th of the net dividend is available in respect of non–UK resident companies where the taxpayer's shareholding is less than 10%, if certain conditions are satisfied. The availability of a tax credit was extended to taxpayers with shareholdings of 10% or more, with effect from 22 April 2009 (*ITTOIA 2005, ss 397–397C*).

TRUST RATES

(ITA 2007, s 9)

	Trust rate	Dividend trust rate
2010–11 to 2012–13	50%	42.5%
2004–05 to 2009–10	40%	32.5%

Notes

(1) A 'standard rate band' applies to the first £1,000 of taxable income arising in 2006–07 and later years (for 2005–06, the starting rate band was £500). Income within this band is not taxable at the above trust rates, but is generally taxable at the

(non-trust) rates applicable to the particular source of income (eg 10% for dividend income, or 20% for other savings income or non-savings income (eg rental and business profits). In the case of trusts made by the same settlor, the standard rate band is divided by the number of such trusts, subject to a minimum starting rate band of £200 (*ITA 2007, ss 491, 492*).

(2) The above trust rates broadly apply to accumulated or discretionary trust income (*ITA 2007, s 479*). Trustees of an interest in possession trust are generally liable to income tax (for 2010–11 to 2012–13) at 10% in respect of dividend income, or 20% on other savings income or non-savings income), although certain capital receipts for trust law purposes are liable at the above trust rates (*ITA 2007, ss 481, 482*).

(3) The trust rate of income tax for 2013–14 will be reduced from 50% to 45%, and the dividend trust rate for 2013–14 will be 37.5% (Budget, 21 March 2012; *FB 2012, cl 1*).

PERSONAL ALLOWANCES AND RELIEFS

(*ITA 2007, Pt 3*)

	2012–13 £	2011–12 £	2010–11 £	2009–10 £
Personal allowance (under 65 years)	8,105	7,475	6,475	6,475
Age allowance				
Personal allowance (age 65–74)	10,500	9,940	9,490	9,490
Personal allowance (age 75 and over)	10,660	10,090	9,640	9,640
Income limit for age-related allowances	25,400	24,000	22,900	22,900
Married couple's allowance				
Basic allowance	2,960	2,800	2,670	2,670
Age 75 or over	7,705	7,295	6,965	6,965
Blind person's allowance	2,100	1,980	1,890	1,890
Rent-a-room relief	4,250	4,250	4,250	4,250

Notes

(1) *Reduction in personal allowances* – From 2010–11 onwards, personal allowances are reduced if 'adjusted net income' (as defined in *ITA 2007, s 58*) exceeds £100,000, by £1 for every £2 above the £100,000 threshold, irrespective of the taxpayer's age (*ITA 2007, s 35*).

(2) *Personal allowances, 2013–14* – Legislation will be introduced in the *Finance Bill 2013* to set the personal allowance for 2013–14 at £9,205 for those aged under 65.

(3) *Abatement of age-related allowances* – The age-related personal and married couple's allowances are subject to abatement to the extent that income exceeds the income limit, by £1 for every £2 of income above the limit. For tax years before 2010–11, allowances cannot be reduced below the basic personal allowance (or minimum amount of married couple's allowance) (*ITA 2007, ss 36, 37, 45*).

1 Personal Taxation

However, from 2010–11 personal allowances for individuals aged 65–74 or 75 and over can be reduced below the basic personal allowance if income exceeds £100,000.

(4) *Phasing out of age-related allowances* – From 2013–14, the age-related personal allowances will not be increased and their availability will be restricted to people born on or before:

- 5 April 1948 for the allowance worth £10,500; and
- 5 April 1938 for the allowance worth £10,660.

People born on or after 6 April 1948 will be entitled to the personal allowance of £9,205 for 2013–14 (Budget, 21 March 2012; *FB 2012, cl 4*).

(5) *Married couple's allowance* – The rate of tax relief for the married couple's allowance is 10% (*ITA 2007, s 45*). The marriage must have taken place before 5 December 2005 and at least one party to the marriage must have been born before 6 April 1935.

CAP ON UNLIMITED TAX RELIEFS

Legislation will be introduced in the *Finance Bill 2013* to apply a cap on income tax reliefs claimed by individuals with effect from 6 April 2013. The cap will apply only to reliefs which are currently unlimited. For anyone seeking to claim more than £50,000 in reliefs, the cap will be set at the greater of £50,000 and 25% of income (Budget, 21 March 2012).

OLYMPIC, PARALYMPIC AND COMMONWEALTH GAMES

HMRC are concerned to ensure compliance with UK tax law by all those involved in the London 2012 Olympic and Paralympic Game. A limited range of tax exemptions are available (*SI 2010/2913*). Details can be found at www.hmrc.gov.uk/2012games/intro.htm.

The Government has also announced that the *Finance Bill 2013* will bring forward provisions for a limited tax exemption in connection with the Glasgow 2014 Commonwealth Games. UK-resident athletes will pay income tax in the UK as normal. Non-resident competitors will be exempt from UK tax on any income arising from their appearance in the Commonwealth Games, but will remain liable to tax in their home country (HM Treasury Press Release, 26 January 2012; Budget, 21 March 2012).

SELF ASSESSMENT TAX RETURN FILING DATES: INDIVIDUALS AND TRUSTEES

(*TMA 1970, ss 8, 8A*)

Paper returns – Non-electronic returns must be filed by 31 October following the end of the tax year (*ss 8(1D)(a), 8A(1B)(a)*).

Electronic returns – Electronically submitted returns must be submitted by 31 January following the end of the tax year (*ss 8(1D)(b), 8A(1B)(b)*).

The above filing dates are subject to the following exceptions:

- Return (or notice to file) issued after 31 July but before 31 October following the end of the tax year – the filing date is 3 months from the date of the return/notice for paper returns, or 31 January for electronic returns (*ss 8(1F), 8A(1D)*).
- Return (or notice to file) issued after 31 October following the end of the tax year – the filing date is 3 months from the date of the return/notice (whether paper or electronic) (*ss 8(1G), 8A(1E)*).

Notes

(1) Individuals filing returns electronically who owe tax of less than £3,000 and wish HMRC to collect the liability through a reduction in their PAYE coding for the next tax year must file their tax return online by 30 December, instead of 31 January. This coding threshold was increased from £2,000 on 20 July 2011 and the new limit generally applies only to returns for 2010–11 and later years

(2) The above filing dates also apply to partnerships with individual members (*TMA 1970, s 12AA(4)–(4E)*). Separate provisions apply in the case of partnerships involving one or more companies (*s 12AA(5)–(5E)*).

SELF ASSESSMENT: DUE DATES FOR PAYMENT OF TAX

(*TMA 1970, ss 59A, 59B*)

1st payment on account – On or before 31 January in the tax year.

2nd payment on account – On or before 31 July following the end of the tax year.

Balancing payment – On or before 31 January next following the tax year of assessment. This is also the due date for any capital gains tax (for which payments on account are not required). However, if a return (or a notice to file) was not issued until after 31 October following the end of the tax year and the taxpayer has notified chargeability by 5 October, the due date for the final payment (including any capital gains tax) is 3 months from the issue of the return/notice (*TMA 1970, s 59B(3), (4)*).

Notes

(1) Payments on account are not required where:
  - More than 80% of the previous year's tax liability was covered by tax deducted at source and dividend tax credits; or
  - the previous year's liability (net of tax deducted at source) was less than £1,000 (2009–10 onwards, previously £500) (*SI 1996/1654, SI 2008/838*).

1 Personal Taxation

SELF ASSESSMENT PENALTY PROVISIONS

(TMA 1970, ss 59A(6), 93, 93A; FA 2007, s 97, Sch 24; FA 2008, s 113, Sch 36; s 115, Sch 37; s 123, Sch 41; FA 2009, s 106, Sch 55; FA 2009, s 107, Sch 56; FA 2011, s 86, Sch 23)

Late payments: 2010–11 and later tax years

(FA 2009, s 107, Sch 56)

Length of delay	Penalty
30 days	5% of the unpaid tax
6 months	5% of the unpaid tax (additional)
12 months	5% of the unpaid tax (additional)

Notes

(1) *General* – The penalty regime for failure to make payments on time was introduced in *FA 2009, s 107, Sch 56*. The above penalties apply to late balancing payments of income tax and late payments of capital gains tax under self-assessment (ie based on tax returns for individuals or trustees etc, and in certain other circumstances) with effect from 6 April 2011, in relation to 2010–11 and later tax years, following its entry into force by Treasury order (*SI 2011/702, art 3*).

The above penalties replace the surcharge provisions on unpaid income tax and capital gains tax (*TMA 1970, s 59C*), which apply to balancing payments for tax years up to 2009–10 (see *Surcharges* below).

(2) *Assessments and appeals* – HMRC must assess the late payment penalty, and notify the person liable. The penalty notice must state the period to which the penalty relates. The penalty is payable within 30 days from the day on which the penalty notice is issued. There is a right of appeal against both the imposition of a penalty, and the amount involved (*FA 2009, Sch 56, paras 11, 13*).

(3) *Penalty reduction and suspension* – HMRC may reduce a late payment penalty in 'special circumstances', which does not include inability to pay (*FA 2009, Sch 56, para 9*). In addition, a defence of 'reasonable excuse' may be available (*Sch 56, para 16*).

Surcharges (up to 2009–10)

(TMA 1970 s 59C)

Tax Overdue	Surcharge amount
28 days following the due date	5% of the unpaid tax
6 months following the due date	5% of the unpaid tax (additional)

Notes

(1) *General* – Surcharges apply to any balancing payment of income tax (and class 4 NIC) or capital gains tax payable for a tax year, in respect of personal tax returns up to 2009–10 inclusive. Surcharges attract interest if paid late.

(2) *Appeals* – An appeal against a surcharge can be made within 30 days of the date on which the surcharge was imposed.

(3) *Exceptions* – A surcharge is not imposed if a penalty has been incurred based on the same tax, or if agreement has been reached with HMRC in advance to pay the tax by instalments, where those instalments are duly paid in accordance with the agreement.

(4) *New regime* – As to penalties for the late payment of income tax and capital gains tax for 2010–11 and later years, see **Late payments: 2010–11 and later tax years** above.

Late returns: 2010–11 and later tax years

(FA 2009, s 106, Sch 55)

Period	Penalty	Notes
Up to 3 months late	£100	Fixed penalty
More than 3 months late	£10 per day	• Daily penalties apply for up to 90 days (maximum £900). • Payable only if HMRC give notice of the penalty, and the notice specifies the date from which the penalty is payable.
More than 6 months late	Greater of: • 5% of tax liability; and • £300	'Tax liability' refers to any tax which would have been shown in the return in question.
More than 12 months late: Any case except below	Greater of: • 5% of tax liability; and • £300	
Information withheld Deliberate but not concealed	Greater of: • Relevant % of tax liability; and • £300	See percentages below
Deliberate and concealed	Greater of: • Relevant % of tax liability; and • £300	See percentages below

Information withheld deliberately	Unprompted disclosure		Prompted disclosure	
	Max. Penalty	Min. Penalty	Max. Penalty	Min. Penalty
Category 1 information				
Deliberate but not concealed	70%	20%	70%	35%
Deliberate and concealed	100%	30%	100%	50%

continued

1 Personal Taxation

Period	Penalty		Notes	
Category 2 information				
Deliberate but not concealed	105%	30%	105%	52.5%
Deliberate and concealed	150%	45%	150%	75%
Category 3 information				
Deliberate but not concealed	140%	40%	140%	70%
Deliberate and concealed	200%	60%	200%	100%

Notes

(1) *General* – The above penalty regime for the late filing of income tax self-assessment returns (and certain others returns etc) introduced in *FA 2009, s 106, Sch 55* was brought into force by Treasury order (*SI 2011/702; see also CH61120*).

The *FA 2009, s 106, Sch 55* provisions were introduced with effect from 6 April 2011, in respect of returns for 2010–11 and later years, and were subsequently amended in respect of the offshore income penalty regime (see below).

As to the penalty provisions for earlier returns, see: **Late returns: 2009–10 and earlier years** below.

For 2010–11 returns, the penalty percentages where information is withheld are those which applied when the regime in *FA 2009, Sch 55* was originally introduced (ie prior to the introduction of the offshore income penalty regime from 6 April 2011 – see below). The penalty percentages are the same as shown in Category 1 above.

(2) *Offshore income etc* – The penalty regime for late returns was amended (by *FA 2010, s 35, Sch 10*) in relation to offshore income etc. The amendments were introduced by Treasury order (*SI 2011/975*) with effect from 6 April 2011. The provisions apply to returns etc for 2011–12 onwards.

(3) *Classification of territories* – The categories are classified in accordance with the penalty regime for errors (in *FA 2007, Sch 24, para 21A*). Category 1 and Category 3 territories are designated by Treasury order (*SI 2011/976*). A Category 2 territory is one that is neither a Category 1 nor a Category 3 territory. A list of Category 1 and Category 3 territories is available on HMRC's website: www.hmrc.gov.uk/news/territories-category.htm. Any Treasury order classifying a territory for that purpose shall have effect for failure to make a return only where the obligation to file arises on or after the date on which the classification in question entered into force (*FA 2009, Sch 55, para 6A(7)*).

(4) *Category 1 information* – This is information involving:

   (a) A domestic matter; or

   (b) An offshore matter, where the territory is in *Category 1* or it is information which would enable or assist HMRC to assess a tax other than income tax or CGT.

(5) *Category 2 information* – This is information involving an offshore matter, in a *Category 2* territory, which would enable or assist HMRC to assess an income tax or CGT liability.

Self assessment penalty provisions

(6) *Category 3 information* – This is information involving an offshore matter, in a *Category 3* territory, which would enable or assist HMRC to assess an income tax or CGT liability.

(7) *Penalty aggregation* – A taxpayer may become liable to more than one category of penalty in respect of the same return etc *(FA 2009, Sch 55, para 1(3))*. However, where more than one tax-geared penalty arises, the aggregate must not exceed the following *(FA 2009, Sch 55, para 17(3))*:

- Deliberate withholding of Category 3 information – 200%
- Deliberate withholding of Category 2 information – 150%
- All other cases – 100%

(8) *Penalty reductions* – HMRC may reduce a penalty in 'special circumstances' which does not include inability to pay *(FA 2009, Sch 55, para 16)*. In addition, a defence of 'reasonable excuse' may be available *(Sch 55, para 23)*.

Late returns: 2009–10 and earlier years

(TMA 1970, s 93)

(1) *General* – The following penalties apply to the failure to make a tax return (for individuals and trustees) for 2009–10 and earlier years:

- £100 if the return is not delivered by the filing date (see **Self assessment tax return filing dates: Individuals and trustees** above);
- A further penalty of up to £60 per day if the failure continues and HMRC obtain a direction from the tribunal to charge daily penalties;
- A further £100 (where a daily penalty is not imposed) if the failure continues more than 6 months from the filing date.
- A tax-related penalty if the failure continues more than one year from the filing date, of up to the amount of any tax liability which would have been shown on the return.

(2) *Penalty 'cap'* – The above fixed penalties of £100 cannot exceed the tax liability which would be shown in the return *(TMA 1970, s 93(7))*, or the amount of tax outstanding at the due date if the return had been delivered on the filing date *(s 93(9))*, ie any payments on account (under *TMA 1970, s 59A*) or payments otherwise made before the filing date are taken into account, as is any PAYE or other tax deducted at source in respect of that year (EM4562).

(3) *Reasonable excuse* – The above fixed penalties of £100 can be set aside by the tribunal if the taxpayer had a reasonable excuse for not delivering the return throughout the period of default *(TMA 1970, s 93(8))*. Information on what HMRC consider to be a 'reasonable excuse' is available on the HMRC website (see www.hmrc.gov.uk/sa/deadlines-penalties.htm#3).

(4) *Penalty exception* – Following the decision in *Steeden v Carver* [1999] STC (SCD) 283, HMRC will not charge a penalty where a return is delivered on the day after the filing date (see SALF208 and SAM120650).

(5) *Partnerships (TMA 1970, s 93A)* – The following penalties apply to the failure to make a partnership tax return:

1 Personal Taxation

- £100 per 'relevant partner' (ie each person who was a partner at any time during the period covered by the return) if the return is not delivered by the filing date;
- A further penalty of up to £60 per day per relevant partner if the failure continues and HMRC obtain a direction from the tribunal to charge daily penalties;
- A further £100 per relevant partner (where a daily penalty is not imposed) if the failure continues more than 6 months from the filing date.

The fixed £100 penalties are not subject to the potential reduction described in note 2 above. However, there is no tax-related penalty for the late filing of partnership returns, as the partnership itself is not liable to tax.

Failure to notify liability, etc

(FA 2008, s 123, Sch 41)

Category 1 Territory

Behaviour	Unprompted disclosure			Prompted disclosure		
	Maximum penalty	Minimum penalty Case A	Case B	Maximum penalty	Minimum penalty Case A	Case B
Any other case*	30%	0%	10%	30%	10%	20%
Deliberate but not concealed	70%	20%	–	70%	35%	–
Deliberate and concealed	100%	30%	–	100%	50%	–

Category 2 Territory

Behaviour	Unprompted disclosure			Prompted disclosure		
	Maximum penalty	Minimum penalty Case A	Case B	Maximum penalty	Minimum penalty Case A	Case B
Any other case*	45%	0%	15%	45%	15%	30%
Deliberate but not concealed	105%	30%	–	105%	52.5%	–
Deliberate and concealed	150%	45%	–	150%	75%	–

Category 3 Territory

Behaviour	Unprompted disclosure			Prompted disclosure		
	Maximum penalty	Minimum penalty Case A	Case B	Maximum penalty	Minimum penalty Case A	Case B
Any other case*	60%	0%	20%	60%	20%	40%
Deliberate but not concealed	140%	40%	–	140%	70%	–
Deliberate and concealed	200%	60%	–	200%	100%	–

Self assessment penalty provisions

* *Case A and Case B* – These apply to 'any other case'. Case A applies if HMRC become aware of the failure less than 12 months after the tax first becomes unpaid due to the failure. Otherwise, Case B applies (FA 2008 Sch 41 para 13(3)).

Notes

(1) *General* – The penalties regime for failure to notify (and certain VAT and excise wrongdoing – see note (7) below) generally applies (except in relation to offshore income – see note (2) below) where the obligation to notify arises on or after 1 April 2010. For direct tax purposes, the first tax periods for which the penalties will therefore apply are 2009–10 (income tax and capital gains tax) and accounting periods ending from 31 March 2010 (corporation tax). For indirect tax purposes, the new penalty regime applies where the obligation to notify arises on or after 1 April 2010 (*SI 2009/511; see also CH71120*).

The maximum penalty levels when the regime in *FA 2008, Sch 41* was originally introduced (ie prior to the introduction of the penalty regime for offshore income from 6 April 2011) are the same as in *Category 1* above, ie:

- Deliberate and concealed act or failure – 100%;
- Deliberate but not concealed – 70%; and
- Any other case – 30%.

The 30% penalty is subject to the following possible reductions for disclosure:

- Unprompted – A minimum of 0% if HMRC become aware of the failure less than 12 months after the tax first becomes unpaid due to the failure; or a minimum of 10% in any other case;
- Prompted – A minimum of 10% if HMRC become aware of the failure less than 12 months after the tax first becomes unpaid due to the failure; or a minimum of 20% in any other case;

(2) *Offshore income etc* – The penalty regime for failure to notify etc was amended (by *FA 2010, s 35, Sch 10*) in relation to offshore income etc. The amendments were introduced by Treasury order (*SI 2011/975*) with effect from 6 April 2011.

(3) *Classification of territories* – The above categories are classified in accordance with the penalty regime for errors (*FA 2007, Sch 24, para 21A*). *Category 1* and *Category 3* territories are designated by Treasury order (*SI 2011/976*). A Category 2 territory is one that is neither a *Category 1* nor a *Category 3* territory. A list of *Category 1* and *Category 3* territories is available on HMRC's website: www.hmrc.gov.uk/news/territories-category.htm. Any Treasury order classifying a territory for that purpose shall have effect for failure to notify liability only where the date the obligation to notify arises on or after the date on which the classification in question entered into force (FA 2008, Sch 41, para 6A(7)).

(4) *Category 1 failure* – This involves:

   (a) A domestic matter; or

   (b) An offshore matter, where either the territory is in *Category 1*, or the tax at stake is other than income tax or CGT.

(5) *Category 2 failure* – This involves an offshore matter, in a *Category 2* territory, where the tax at stake is income tax or CGT.

1 Personal Taxation

(6) *Category 3 failure* – This involves an offshore matter, in a *Category 3* territory, where the tax at stake is income tax or CGT.

(7) *Other penalties* – Separate penalty provisions apply in respect of the unauthorised issue of an invoice showing VAT *(FA 2008, Sch 41, para 2)*, and certain excise wrongdoings *(FA 2008, Sch 41, paras 2, 3, 4, 6B–6C)*. These are treated as Case B.

(8) *Reductions and exceptions* – HMRC may reduce a penalty in 'special circumstances', which does not include inability to pay, and a defence of 'reasonable excuse' may also be available in some cases *(FA 2008, Sch 41, paras 14, 20)*.

Errors in returns, etc

(FA 2007, s 97, Sch 24)

Category 1 Territory

Behaviour	Unprompted disclosure		Prompted disclosure	
	Maximum penalty	Minimum penalty	Maximum penalty	Minimum penalty
Careless	30%	0%	30%	15%
Deliberate but not concealed	70%	20%	70%	35%
Deliberate and concealed	100%	30%	100%	50%

Category 2 Territory

Behaviour	Unprompted disclosure		Prompted disclosure	
	Maximum penalty	Minimum penalty	Maximum penalty	Minimum penalty
Careless	45%	0%	45%	22.5%
Deliberate but not concealed	105%	30%	105%	52.5%
Deliberate and concealed	150%	45%	150%	75%

Category 3 Territory

Behaviour	Unprompted disclosure		Prompted disclosure	
	Maximum penalty	Minimum penalty	Maximum penalty	Minimum penalty
Careless	60%	0%	60%	30%
Deliberate but not concealed	140%	40%	140%	70%
Deliberate and concealed	200%	60%	200%	100%

Notes

(1) *General* – The penalties regime for errors generally applies (except in relation to offshore income – see note (4) below) to returns for tax periods commencing from 1 April 2008, and for which the filing date is on or after 1 April 2009 *(SI 2008/568;* see also CH81012).

The levels of penalty applicable when the regime was originally introduced (ie for periods prior to the introduction of the penalty regime in respect of offshore income from 6 April 2011) are the same as in *Category 1* above.

(2) *Disclosure* – The maximum penalties above are subject to potential reduction, depending on whether the disclosure of the inaccuracy is 'prompted' or 'unprompted', and reflecting the quality of the disclosure.

(3) *Other penalties* – A penalty can also apply to an error in a taxpayer's document which is attributable to another person (*FA 2007, Sch 24, para 1A*). Penalties range from 30% to 100% for unprompted disclosure, and 50% to 100% for prompted disclosure.

In addition, a penalty can apply if the taxpayer fails to notify HMRC of the under assessment of a relevant tax liability within 30 days from the date of the assessment (*FA 2007, Sch 24, para 2*). Penalties range from 0% to 30% for unprompted disclosure, and 15% to 30% for prompted disclosure.

(4) *Offshore income etc* – The penalty regime for errors was amended (by *FA 2010, s 35, Sch 10*) in relation to offshore income etc. The amendments were introduced by Treasury order (*SI 2011/975*) with effect from 6 April 2011.

(5) *Classification of territories* – *Category 1* and *Category 3* territories are designated by Treasury order (The Penalties, Offshore Income etc (Designation of Territories) Order 2011, *SI 2011/976*). A *Category 2* territory is one that is neither a *Category 1* nor a *Category 3* territory (*FA 2007, Sch 24, para 21A*). A list of *Category 1* and *Category 3* territories is available on HMRC's website: www.hmrc.gov.uk/news/territories-category.htm

(6) *Category 1 inaccuracy* – This involves:
  (a) A domestic matter; or
  (b) An offshore matter, where either the territory is in *Category 1*, or the tax at stake is other than income tax or CGT.

(7) *Category 2 inaccuracy* – This involves an offshore matter, in a *Category 2* territory, where the tax at stake is income tax or CGT.

(8) *Category 3 inaccuracy* – This involves an offshore matter, in a *Category 3* territory, where the tax at stake is income tax or CGT.

(9) *Special reductions and suspensions* – HMRC may reduce a penalty in 'special circumstances', which does not include inability to pay, and penalties may be suspended at HMRC's discretion in appropriate cases (*FA 2007, Sch 24, paras 11, 14*).

FAILURE TO KEEP OR RETAIN TAX RECORDS

(*TMA 1970, s 12B, FA 2008, s 115, Sch 37*)

(1) The maximum penalty for failing to keep and preserve records (in accordance with *TMA 1970, s 12B*) is £3,000 per tax year (or accounting period) (*s 12B(5)*).

(2) The record keeping requirements introduced in *Finance Act 2008* apply for direct tax and VAT purposes from 1 April 2009 (*SI 2009/402*) and for other taxes and duties generally from 1 April 2010 (*SI 2010/815*).

PAYMENTS ON ACCOUNT

(*TMA 1970, s 59A(6)*)

The maximum penalty for fraudulent or negligent claims by taxpayers to reduce payments on account is the difference between the correct amount payable on account and the amount of any payment on account made by him.

1 Personal Taxation

INFORMATION AND INSPECTION POWERS

(*FA 2008, s 113, Sch 36*)

Failure to comply with an information notice or obstruction	
(*FA 2008, Sch 36, paras 39, 40, 50*)	
• Initial penalty	£300
• Continued failure	Up to £60 per day on which failure or obstruction continues
• Continued failure where significant tax is at risk	Penalty may be decided by the Upper Tribunal (See Note 3)
Inaccurate information and documents	Up to £3,000 for each inaccuracy
(*FA 2008, Sch 36, para 40A*)	

Notes

(1) The above penalty regime applies with effect for information notices issued or inspections carried out from 1 April 2009 for direct tax (and VAT) purposes (*SI 2009/404, art 2*), and for other taxes and duties generally from 1 April 2010 (*FA 2009, s 96, Sch 48; SI 2009/3054*).

(2) Penalties for the above offences do not arise if there is a 'reasonable excuse' for the failure or obstruction (*FA 2008, Sch 36, para 45*).

(3) Information notices and inspections – In relation to a failure to comply with an information notice, or a deliberate obstruction during an inspection:

    (a) A penalty for obstruction is only due in relation to an inspection which has been approved by the tribunal.

    (b) If the failure or obstruction continues after an initial penalty is charged (under *FA 2008, Sch 36, para 39*), an additional tax-related penalty can be imposed if an HMRC officer has reason to believe that the failure or obstruction may result in a significant loss of tax. However, HMRC must first apply to the Upper Tribunal for the imposition of the additional penalty (see *FA 2008, Sch 36, para 50*).

Interest payable on overdue income tax, national insurance contributions and capital gains tax etc

Period from	Rate %
29 September 2009	3.0
24 March 2009 to 28 September 2009	2.5
27 January 2009 to 23 March 2009	3.5
6 January 2009 to 26 January 2009	4.5
6 December 2008 to 5 January 2009	5.5
6 November 2008 to 5 December 2008	6.5
6 January 2008 to 5 November 2008	7.5
6 August 2007 to 5 January 2008	8.5
6 September 2006 to 5 August 2007	7.5

Information and inspection powers

Period from	Rate %
6 September 2005 to 5 September 2006	6.5
6 September 2004 to 5 September 2005	7.5
6 December 2003 to 5 September 2004	6.5
6 August 2003 to 5 December 2003	5.5
6 November 2001 to 5 August 2003	6.5
6 May 2001 to 5 November 2001	7.5
6 February 2000 to 5 May 2001	8.5

Note

The interest regime in *FA 2009, ss 101–103* ('Late payment interest on sums to be paid by HMRC', 'Repayment interest on sums to be paid by HMRC' and 'Rates of interest') applies with effect from 31 October 2011, for the purposes of self-assessment payments and repayments (*SI 2011/701*).

Rates of interest on repayments of income tax, national insurance contributions and capital gains tax etc*

Period from	Rate %
29 September 2009	0.50
27 January 2009 to 28 September 2009	0.00
6 January 2009 to 26 January 2009	0.75
6 December 2008 to 5 January 2009	1.50
6 November 2008 to 5 December 2008	2.25
6 January 2008 to 5 November 2008	3.00
6 August 2007 to 5 January 2008	4.00
6 September 2006 to 5 August 2007	3.00
6 September 2005 to 5 September 2006	2.25
6 September 2004 to 5 September 2005	3.00
6 December 2003 to 5 September 2004	2.25
6 August 2003 to 5 December 2003	1.50
6 November 2001 to 5 August 2003	2.25
6 May 2001 to 5 November 2001	3.00
6 February 2000 to 5 May 2001	4.00

* See note to table '**Interest payable on overdue income tax, national insurance contributions and capital gains tax etc**' above.

2

Expenses and benefits

COMPANY CAR BENEFIT CHARGES

Table of appropriate percentages to 5 April 2012

(*ITEPA 2003, s 139*)

CO_2 emissions g/km	2011–12	2010–11	2008–09 to 2009–10	2005–06 to 2007–08
75	5%	5%	N/A	N/A
120	10%	10%	10%	15%
125	15%	15%	15%	15%
130	16%	15%	15%	15%
135	17%	16%	15%	15%
140	18%	17%	16%	16%
145	19%	18%	17%	17%
150	20%	19%	18%	18%
155	21%	20%	19%	19%
160	22%	21%	20%	20%
165	23%	22%	21%	21%
170	24%	23%	22%	22%
175	25%	24%	23%	23%
180	26%	25%	24%	24%
185	27%	26%	25%	25%
190	28%	27%	26%	26%
195	29%	28%	27%	27%
200	30%	29%	28%	28%
205	31%	30%	29%	29%
210	32%	31%	30%	30%
215	33%	32%	31%	31%
220	34%	33%	32%	32%
225	35%	34%	33%	33%
230	35%	35%	34%	34%
235	35%	35%	35%	35%
240	35%	35%	35%	35%
245	35%	35%	35%	35%
250	35%	35%	35%	35%
255	35%	35%	35%	

Company car benefit charges

Notes

(1) The income tax charge is based on percentage of car's list price graduated according to the level of CO_2 emissions measured in grams per kilometre (g/km) and rounded down to the nearest 5g/km.

(2) For ultra-low emissions vehicle percentages in 2010–11 and later years, see **Ultra-low emission cars** below.

(3) From 6 April 2012 the 10% band will apply to cars with emissions not exceeding 99 g/km.

COMPANY CAR BENEFIT CHARGES: 2012–13 TO 2013–14

(ITEPA 2003, s 139; FA 2010, ss 58, 59; FA 2011, s 51)

Table of appropriate percentages from 6 April 2012

CO_2 emissions (g/km) not exceeding	Appropriate percentage 2013–14	Appropriate percentage 2012–13
0	0	0
75	5	5
94	10	10
99	11	10
100	12	11
105	13	12
110	14	13
115	15	14
120	16	15
125	17	16
130	18	17
135	19	18
140	20	19
145	21	20
150	22	21
155	23	22
160	24	23
165	25	24
170	26	25
175	27	26
180	28	27
185	29	28
190	30	29
195	31	30
200	32	31
205	33	32
210	34	33
215	35	34
220 and above	35	35

2 *Expenses and benefits*

Notes

(1) Emissions figure should be rounded down to the nearest multiple of five, except that rounding does not apply to cars with emissions below 100g/km.

(2) All diesel cars are subject to the 3% supplement up to a maximum of 35% (see **Diesel cars** below).

Table of appropriate percentages from 6 April 2014

CO_2 emissions (g/km)	Appropriate percentage 2016–17 Petrol and Diesel	Appropriate percentage 2015–16 Petrol	Appropriate percentage 2015–16 Diesel	Appropriate percentage 2014–15 Petrol	Appropriate percentage 2014–15 Diesel
0	15	13	16	0	0
1–75	15	13	16	5	8
76–94	15	13	16	11	14
95–99	16	14	17	12	15
100–104	17	15	18	13	16
105–109	18	16	19	14	17
110–114	19	17	20	15	18
115–119	20	18	21	16	19
120–124	21	19	22	17	20
125–129	22	20	23	18	21
130–134	23	21	24	19	22
135–139	24	22	25	20	23
140–144	25	23	26	21	24
145–149	26	24	27	22	25
150–154	27	25	28	23	26
155–159	28	26	29	24	27
160–164	29	27	30	25	28
165–169	30	28	31	26	29
170–174	31	29	32	27	30
175–179	32	30	33	28	31
180–184	33	31	34	29	32
185–189	34	32	35	30	33
190–194	35	33	36	31	34
195–199	36	34	37	32	35
200–204	37	35	37	33	35
205–209	37	36	37	34	35
210 and above	37	37	37	35	35

Notes

(1) The appropriate percentage for company cars emitting more CO_2 than 75g/km is increased by one percentage point to a maximum of 35% in 2014–15 (Budget, 21 March 2012; *FB 2012, cl 17*).

(2) Future Finance Bills will provide that the appropriate percentage for zero emission and all low carbon cars emitting less CO_2 than 95g/km will be 13% in 2015–16, and that this will increase by two percentage points in 2016–17 (Budget, 21 March 2012).

Company car benefit charges

Diesel cars

(ITEPA 2003, s 141)

There is a 3% supplement on diesel cars to a maximum of 35%, subject to the following:

- before 5 April 2006, no supplement applies to diesel cars first registered before 1 January 2006 that met the Euro IV emissions standard;
- from 6 April 2006, the supplement applies to all diesel cars first registered from 1 January 2006 (*EIM24810*);
- from 6 April 2011, the diesel supplement applies to all diesel cars (nb as to diesel supplements generally, see *EIM24855*).
- future *Finance Bill* will provide that the 3% supplement for diesel cars will be phased out in 2016–17 (Budget, 21 March 2012).

Qualifying low emissions cars (QUALECs)

(ITEPA 2003 s 139(3A); FA 2010 s 59)

(1) From 6 April 2008 to 5 April 2012 a lower tax charge applies if the car is a QUALEC.

(2) A car is a QUALEC if its CO_2 emissions figure does not exceed the qualifying limit for the year (120g/km from 2008–09).

(3) Where the car qualifies as a QUALEC, the appropriate percentage is 10% (for petrol cars, but with a 3% supplement for diesels). See below as to ultra-low emission cars.

Ultra-low emission cars

(ITEPA 2003, s 139; FA 2010 s 59)

From 6 April 2010, a reduced appropriate percentage of 5% applies, for five years, for company cars with an approved CO_2 emissions figure not exceeding 75g/km (*ITEPA 2003, s 139(1B)*).

Alternative fuel cars (from 6 April 2011)

(ITEPA 2003, ss 137, 140; SI 2001/1123 as amended; EIM24730)

Type of car	Discounted charge
Zero-emission cars (including Electric only)	Appropriate percentage of list price (no adjustment)
Diesel cars (all Euro standards)	Appropriate percentage of list price plus 3% supplement
All other	Appropriate percentage of list price (no adjustment)

Notes

(1) A special percentage of 0% applies to cars which cannot produce CO_2 emissions under any circumstances when driven, for tax years 2010–11 to 2014–15 inclusive

2 Expenses and benefits

(*ITEPA 2003, s 140(3A)*). Although current legislation provides that this will increase to 9% from 2015–16 onwards, future *Finance Bill*s will provide that this will increase to 13% (for petrol) and 16% (for diesel) in 2015–16 and then be consolidated at 15% (for petrol and diesel) in 2016–17 (Budget, 21 March 2012).

(2) Simplified arrangements for alternative fuels apply from 2011–12 (*SI 2010/695*). The 3% diesel supplement will apply to all diesel powered cars until it is phased out in 2016–17, and alternative fuel reductions generally cease to be available (although see note 1 above regarding cars which cannot produce CO_2 emissions, such as electric cars (see *EIM24730*).

Cars registered with no CO_2 emission figures

(ITEPA 2003, ss 140–142; see also EIM24950, EIM24975))

Cylinder capacity of car	Registered on or after 1 January 1998	Registered before 1 January 1998
1,400 cc or less	15%	15%
Over 1,400cc to 2,000cc	25%	22%
Over 2,000 cc	35%	32%

Note

A 3% addition applies to diesel cars to a maximum of 35%.

Fuel benefit charges

(ITEPA 2003, ss 149–153)

Car fuel benefit multiplier

Tax year	£	Tax year	£
2012–13	20,200	2008–09	16,900
2011–12	18,800	2007–08	14,400
2010–11	18,000	2006–07	14,400
2009–10	16,900	2005–06	14,400

Notes

(1) The multiplier of £20,200 which applies for 2012–13 will increase by 2% above RPI in 2013–14 (Budget, 21 March 2012).

(2) Fuel benefit is nil, or is reduced, in the following circumstances:
- The benefit is nil if the employee is required to make good the full cost of all fuel provided for private use and actually does so;
- The same applies if fuel is made available only for business travel (*ITEPA 2003, s 151*);

Company car benefit charges

- The benefit is proportionately reduced if the company car is only available for part of the year, where the benefit ceases part way through a tax year (and is not reinstated in that year), or where the benefit of the company car is shared *(ITEPA 2003, ss 153–154)*.

(3) The benefit charge for fuel provided for private motoring is calculated by applying the appropriate percentage to the relevant multiplier in the table above. The 'appropriate percentage' is broadly that used to calculate the car benefit *(ITEPA 2003, s 150)*. The following tables show the resulting cash equivalent of the car fuel benefit.

CO_2 emission grams per kilometre	Petrol 2011–12 £	Petrol 2010–11 £	Petrol 2009–10 £	Diesel 2011–12 £	Diesel 2010–11 £	Diesel 2009–10 £
120	1,880	1,800	1,690	2,444	2,340	2,197
125	2,820	2,700	2,535	3,384	3,240	3,042
130	3,008	2,700	2,535	3,572	3,240	3,042
135	3,196	2,880	2,535	3,760	3,420	3,042
140	3,384	3,060	2,704	3,948	3,600	3,211
145	3,572	3,240	2,873	4,136	3,780	3,380
150	3,760	3,420	3,042	4,324	3,960	3,549
155	3,948	3,600	3,211	4,512	4,140	3,718
160	4,136	3,780	3,380	4,700	4,320	3,887
165	4,324	3,960	3,549	4,888	4,500	4,056
170	4,512	4,140	3,718	5,076	4,680	4,225
175	4,700	4,320	3,887	5,264	4,860	4,394
180	4,888	4,500	4,056	5,452	5,040	4,563
185	5,076	4,680	4,225	5,640	5,220	4,732
190	5,264	4,860	4,394	5,828	5,400	4,901
195	5,452	5,040	4,563	6,016	5,580	5,070
200	5,640	5,220	4,732	6,204	5,760	5,239
205	5,828	5,400	4,901	6,392	5,940	5,408
210	6,016	5,580	5,070	6,580	6,120	5,577
215	6,204	5,760	5,239	6,580	6,300	5,746
220	6,392	5,940	5,408	6,580	6,300	5,915
225	6,580	6,120	5,577	6,580	6,300	5,915
230	6,580	6,300	5,746	6,580	6,300	5,915
235	6,580	6,300	5,915	6,580	6,300	5,915

CO_2 emissions (g/km) not exceeding	Petrol 2012–13 £	Diesel 2012–13 £
0	0	0
75	1,010	1,616
99	2,020	2,626

continued

2 Expenses and benefits

CO₂ emissions (g/km) not exceeding	Petrol 2012–13 £	Diesel 2012–13 £
100	2,222	2,828
105	2,424	3,030
110	2,626	3,232
115	2,828	3,434
120	3,030	3,636
125	3,232	3,838
130	3,434	4,040
135	3,636	4,242
140	3,838	4,444
145	4,040	4,646
150	4,242	4,848
155	4,444	5,050
160	4,646	5,252
165	4,848	5,454
170	5,050	5,656
175	5,252	5,858
180	5,454	6,060
185	5,656	6,262
190	5,858	6,464
195	6,060	6,666
200	6,262	6,868
205	6,464	7,070
210	6,666	7,070
215	6,868	7,070
220 and above	7,070	7,070

Mileage allowances

Advisory fuel rates for company cars
(*www.hmrc.gov.uk/cars/advisory-fuel-current.htm*)

Engine size	Cost per Mile		
	Petrol	Diesel	LPG
From 1 March 2012			
Up to 1,400 cc	15p		10p
1,401–2,000 cc	18p		12p
Over 2,000 cc	26p		18p

Company car benefit charges

Engine size	Cost per Mile		
	Petrol	Diesel	LPG
Up to 1,600 cc		13p	
1,601 cc		15p	
Over 2,000 cc		19p	
From 1 December 2011			
Up to 1,400 cc	15p		10p
1,401–2,000 cc	18p		12p
Over 2,000 cc	26p		18p
Up to 1,600 cc		12p	
1,601 cc		15p	
Over 2,000 cc		18p	
From 1 September 2011			
Up to 1,400 cc	15p		11p
1,401–2,000 cc	18p		12p
Over 2,000 cc	26p		18p
Up to 1,600 cc		12p	
1,601 cc		15p	
Over 2,000 cc		18p	
From 1 June 2011			
Up to 1,400 cc	15p		11p
1,401–2,000 cc	18p		13p
Over 2,000 cc	23p		18p
Up to 1,600 cc		12p	
1,601 cc		15p	
Over 2,000 cc		18p	
From 1 March 2011			
1,400 cc or less	14p	13p	10p
1,401 cc to 2,000 cc	16p	13p	12p
Over 2,000 cc	23p	16p	17p
From 1 December 2010			
1,400 cc or less	13p	12p	9p
1,401 cc to 2,000 cc	15p	12p	10p
Over 2,000 cc	21p	15p	15p
From 1 June 2010			
1,400 cc or less	12p	11p	8p
1,401 cc to 2,000 cc	15p	11p	10p
Over 2,000 cc	21p	16p	14p
From 1 December 2009			
1,400 cc or less	11p	11p	7p
1,401 cc to 2,000 cc	14p	11p	8p
Over 2,000 cc	20p	14p	12p
From 1 July 2009			
1,400 cc or less	10p	10p	7p
1,401 cc to 2,000 cc	12p	10p	8p
Over 2,000 cc	18p	13p	12p

continued

2 Expenses and benefits

Engine size	Cost per Mile		
	Petrol	**Diesel**	**LPG**
From 1 January 2009			
1,400 cc or less	10p	11p	7p
1,401 cc to 2,000 cc	12p	11p	9p
Over 2,000 cc	17p	14p	12p
From 1 July 2008			
1,400 cc or less	12p	13p	7p
1,401 cc to 2,000 cc	15p	13p	9p
Over 2,000 cc	21p	17p	13p
From 1 January 2008			
1,400 cc or less	11p	11p	7p
1,401 cc to 2,000 cc	13p	11p	8p
Over 2,000 cc	19p	14p	11p
From 1 August 2007			
1,400 cc or less	10p	10p	6p
1,401 cc to 2,000 cc	13p	10p	8p
Over 2,000 cc	18p	13p	10p
From 1 February 2007			
1,400 cc or less	9p	9p	6p
1,401 cc to 2,000 cc	11p	9p	7p
Over 2,000 cc	16p	12p	10p
From 1 July 2006			
1,400 cc or less	11p	10p	7p
1,401 cc to 2,000 cc	13p	10p	8p
Over 2,000 cc	18p	14p	11p
From 1 July 2005			
1,400 cc or less	10p	9p	7p
1,401 cc to 2,000 cc	12p	9p	8p
Over 2,000 cc	16p	13p	10p
From January 2002 (introduction of rates)			
1,400 cc or less	10p	9p	6p* / 7p**
1,401 cc to 2,000 cc	12p	9p	7p* / 8p**
Over 2,000 cc	14p	12p	9p* / 10p**

* Period from January 2002 to 5 April 2004
** Period from 6 April 2004 to 30 June 2005

Note

Petrol hybrid cars are treated as petrol cars for this purpose.

Company car benefit charges

Approved mileage allowance payments (AMAPs) rates for private vehicles
(*ITEPA 2003, ss 229–232, 235, 236*)

	Rate per business mile			
	From 2011–12		2002–3 to 2010–11	
	First 10,000 miles	Over 10,000 miles	First 10,000 miles	Over 10,000 miles
Cars	45p	25p	40p	25p
Allowance for each passenger making the same trip	5p	5p	5p	5p
Motorcycles	24p	24p	24p	24p
Bicycles	20p	20p	20p	20p

Notes

(1) Where the employer pays less than the authorised rate, the employee may claim tax relief (Mileage Allowance Relief) on the difference.

(2) The rate applying to passengers was extended to volunteers with effect from 6 April 2011.

Vans

(*ITEPA 2003, ss 154–164*)

Tax Year	Van's age at end of tax year	
	Under 4 years	4 years or more
2012–13	£3,000	£3,000
2011–12	£3,000	£3,000
2010–11	£3,000	£3,000
2009–10	£3,000	£3,000
2008–09	£3,000	£3,000
2007–08	£3,000	£3,000
2006–07	£500	£350
2005–06	£500	£350

Notes

(1) For the tax years 2010–11 to 2014–15 inclusive, the cash equivalent will be nil for vans which cannot produce CO_2 emissions under any circumstances when driven (*ITEPA 2003, s 155(2)*). The cash equivalent will revert to £3,000 for the tax year 2015–16 onwards.

(2) No van benefit charge arises if the restricted private use condition is satisfied (see *ITEPA 2003, s 155(4)*).

2   *Expenses and benefits*

Fuel for company vans

(*ITEPA 2003, ss 160–164*)

Tax Year	Fuel benefit charge £
2012–13	550
2011–12	550
2010–11	550
2009–10	500
2008–09	500
2007–08	500
2006–07 and prior years	no taxable benefit

Notes

(1) The figure of £550 was introduced with effect from 2010–11 (*SI 2010/406*). It remains unchanged for 2012–13 but will be increased by RPI in 2013–14 (Budget, 21 March 2012).

(2) From 2010–11, if the van cannot produce CO_2 emissions under any circumstances when driven, there is no chargeable benefit (*ITEPA 2003, s 160(1)(c)*).

Buses

(*ITEPA 2003, s 242, 243*)

(1) **Works buses** – No income tax charge arises on the provision for employees of a works transport service, if the following conditions are satisfied:
   (a) the service is available generally to employees of the employer (or each employer) concerned;
   (b) the main use of the service is for qualifying journeys by those employees; and
   (c) the service–
       (i) is used only by the employees for whom it is provided or their children, or
       (ii) is substantially used only by those employees or children.

(2) **Public buses** – No charge to tax arises in respect of support provided for public bus services, if the following conditions are satisfied:
   (a) the service is available to employees generally;
   (b) it is used for qualifying journeys by employees of one or more employers; and
   (c) either:
       (i) it is a local bus service; or
       (ii) the bus must be provided to other passengers on terms that are as favourable as the terms on which the bus is provided to employees.

TRAVEL AND SUBSISTENCE

Daily subsistence rate

(See HMRC's Employment Income Manual, at *EIM05231*)

Description	Rate (maximum) £	Detail
Breakfast	5	Irregular early starters
One meal (5 hour)	5	Away for at least 5 hours
Two meals (10 hour)	10	Away for at least 10 hours
Late evening meal	15	Irregular late finishers

Incidental overnight expenses and benefits

(*ITEPA 2003, ss 240, 241*)

From	Permitted amount per night	
	In UK £	Overseas £
6 April 1995	5	10

Note

The allowance applies to employees' minor personal expenditure. The above figures represent the maximum daily amounts whilst on business-related activities. If exceeded the whole amount provided is taxable.

MOBILE PHONES

(*ITEPA 2003, s 319; see also EIM21779*)

(1) No chargeable benefit arises (from 2006–07 onwards) on employer-provided mobile phones. The exemption is restricted to one mobile phone per employee. There is no exemption for mobile phones provided for family members.

(2) There is no tax charge under *ITEPA 2003, s 62* (general earnings) or *ITEPA 2003, Pt 3, Ch 4* (vouchers and credit tokens) on the provision of a mobile phone.

(3) For these purposes 'mobile phone' used to be interpreted narrowly and excluded personal digital assistants, iPhones and similar instruments. However, HMRC now accept that smartphones satisfy the conditions to qualify as 'mobile phones' and that many modern consumer PDAs are now also likely to be smartphones, though this does not apply to devices that are solely PDAs. Where an employer has wrongly accounted for Class 1A NICs or an employee has wrongly paid tax on a benefit in kind, repayment claims can be made within the normal time limits (HMRC Brief 02/12, 20 February 2012).

CHILDCARE VOUCHERS

(ITEPA 2003, ss 270A, 318A)

Year	Weekly Limit £
2012–13	55
2011–12	55
2010–11	55
2009–10	55
2008–09	55
2007–08	55
2006–07	55

Note

From April 2011 new income tax limits of £28 per week for higher rate taxpayers and £22 per week for additional rate taxpayers apply.

RELOCATION EXPENSES

(ITEPA 2003, s 271–289)

(1) Exemption for qualifying removal expenses and benefits up to a maximum of £8,000 on a change of residence.

(2) The relief from an employment income charge applies to relocation expenses in relation to payments made or expenses provided in connection with the engagement of a new employee or the change of duties or place of work of an existing employee.

TERMINATION PAYMENTS

(ITEPA 2003, Pt. 6, Ch. 3)

Tax year	Threshold
From 1998–99 onwards	£30,000

Notes

(1) A payment or benefit given in respect of the termination of an office or employment by the death of the holder is excepted from a tax charge under the above termination payment provisions.

(2) The termination payment provisions do not apply if the payment or benefit is otherwise chargeable to income tax, such as payments chargeable under *ITEPA 2003, s 394* if a non-approved or employer-financed retirement benefits scheme exists.

SCHOLARSHIPS

(ITEPA 2003, s 211–215; SP 4/86)

Period	Specified amount
From 1 September 2007	£15,480
From 1 September 2005–31 August 2007	£15,000
From 6 April 1992–31 August 2005	£7,000

ACTUAL OFFICIAL RATE OF INTEREST – EMPLOYMENT RELATED LOANS

(ITEPA 2003, s 181)

Period	Rate %
From 6 April 2010	4.00
1 March 2009–5 April 2010	4.75
6 April 2007–28 February 2009	6.25
6 January 2002–5 April 2007	5.00

AVERAGE OFFICIAL RATES OF INTEREST – EMPLOYMENT RELATED LOANS

(ITEPA 2003, s 182)

Year	Average official rate %
2011–12	4.00
2010–11	4.00
2009–10	4.75
2008–09	6.10
2007–08	6.25
2006–07	5.00
2005–06	5.00

Note

The average official rates of interest are used if the loan was outstanding throughout the year and the normal averaging method of calculation is being used.

FLAT RATE EXPENSES

(ITEPA 2003, s 367; EIM32712)

Occupation			Deduction from 2008–09 onwards	Deduction from 2004–05 to 2007–08
			£	£
Agriculture		All workers	100	70
Airlines		Uniformed flight deck crew	850	850
Aluminium	A	Continual casting operators, process operators, de-dimplers, driers, drill punchers, dross unloaders, firemen, furnace operators and their helpers, leaders, mouldmen, pourers, remelt department labourers, roll flatteners	140	130
	B	Cable hands, case makers, labourers, mates, truck drivers and measurers, storekeepers	80	60
	C	Apprentices	60	45
	D	All other workers	120	100
Banks and Building societies		Uniformed employees	60	45
Brass and copper		All workers	120	100
Building	A	Joiners and carpenters	140	105
	B	Cement works and roofing (asphalt) labourers	80	55
	C	Labourers and navvies	60	45
	D	All other workers	120	85
Building materials	A	Stone-masons	120	85
	B	Tilemakers and labourers	60	45
	C	All other workers	80	55
Clothing	A	Lacemakers, hosiery bleachers, dyers, scourers and knitters, knitwear bleachers and dyers	60	45
	B	All other workers	60	45

Flat rate expenses

Occupation			Deduction from 2008–09 onwards £	Deduction from 2004–05 to 2007–08 £
Constructional engineering	A	Blacksmiths and their strikers, burners, caulkers, chippers, drillers, erectors, fitters, holders up, markers off, platers, riggers, riveters, rivet heaters, scaffolders, sheeters, template workers, turners, welders	140	115
	B	Banksmen labourers, shop-helpers, slewers, straighteners	80	60
	C	Apprentices and storekeepers	60	45
	D	All other workers	100	75
Electrical and electricity supply	A	Those workers incurring laundry costs only (generally CEGB employees)	60	45
	B	All other workers	120	90
Trades ancillary to Engineering	A	Pattern makers	140	120
	B	Labourers, supervisory and unskilled workers	80	60
	C	Apprentices and storekeepers	60	45
	D	Motor mechanics in garage repair shop	120	100
	E	All other workers	120	100
Fire service		Uniformed firefighters and fire officers	80	60
Food		All workers	60	45
Forestry		All workers	100	70
Glass		All workers	80	60
Healthcare	A	Ambulance staff on active service (ie excluding staff who take telephone calls or provide clerical support)	140	110
	B	Nurses and midwives, chiropodists, dental nurses, occupational speech physios and therapists, phlebotomists, radiographers	100	70
	C	Plaster room orderlies, hospital porters, ward clerks, sterile supply workers, hospital domestics, hospital catering staff	100	60
	D	Laboratory staff, pharmacists, pharmacy assistants	60	45

continued

2 *Expenses and benefits*

Occupation			Deduction from 2008–09 onwards	Deduction from 2004–05 to 2007–08
			£	£
Healthcare – *contd*	E	Uniformed ancillary staff – maintenance workers, grounds staff, drivers, parking attendants and security guards, receptionists and other uniformed staff	60	45
Heating	A	Pipe fitters and plumbers	120	100
	B	Coverers, laggers, domestic glaziers, heating engineers and their mates	120	90
	C	All gas workers, all other workers	100	70
Iron Mining	A	Fillers, miners and underground workers	120	100
	B	All other workers	100	75
Iron and steel	A	Day labourers, general labourers, stockmen, time-keepers, warehouse staff and weighmen	80	60
	B	Apprentices	60	45
	C	All other workers	140	120
Leather	A	Curriers (wet workers), fellmongering workers, tanning operatives (wet)	80	55
	B	All other workers	60	45
Particular engineering	A	Pattern makers	140	120
	B	All chainmakers; cleaners, galvanisers, tinners and wire drawers in the wire drawing industry; tool-makers in the lock making industry	120	100
	C	Apprentices and storekeepers	60	45
	D	All other workers	80	60
Police force		Police officers (ranks up to and including Chief Inspector)	140	110 (2007–08) 55 (2004–05 to 2006–07)
Precious metals		All workers	100	70
Printing	A	Letterpress Section – Electrical engineers (rotary presses), electrotypers, ink and roller makers, machine minders (rotary), maintenance engineers (rotary)	140	105

Flat rate expenses

Occupation			Deduction from 2008–09 onwards	Deduction from 2004–05 to 2007–08
			£	£
Printing – *contd*	B	Bench hands (P & B), compositors (LP), readers (LP), T & E Section wireroom operators, warehousemen (PBM)	60	45
	C	All other workers	100	70
Prisons		Uniformed prison officers	80	55
Public service	A	Dock and inland waterways:		
		– Dockers, dredger drivers, hopper steerers	80	55
		– All other workers	60	45
	B	Public transport:		
		– Garage hands (including cleaners and mechanics)	80	55
		– Conductor and drivers	60	45
Quarrying		All workers	100	70
Railways	A	(See the appropriate category for craftsmen, eg engineers, vehicle builders etc.)	100	70
	B	All other workers	100	70
Seamen	A	Carpenters on passenger liners	165	165
	B	Carpenters on cargo vessels, tankers, coasters and ferries	140	130
Shipyards	A	Blacksmiths and their strikers, boilermakers, burners, carpenters, caulkers, drillers, furnacemen (platers), holders up, fitters, platers, plumbers, riveters, sheet iron workers, shipwrights, tubers, welders	140	115
	B	Labourers	80	60
	C	Apprentices and storekeepers	60	45
	D	All other workers	100	75
Textiles and textile printing	A	Carders, carding engineers, overlookers and technicians in spinning mills	120	85
	B	All other workers	80	60

continued

2 Expenses and benefits

Occupation			Deduction from 2008–09 onwards	Deduction from 2004–05 to 2007–08
			£	£
Vehicles	A	Builders, railway wagon etc. repairers and railway wagon lifters	140	105
	B	Railway vehicle painters and letterers, railway wagon etc. builders' and repairers' assistants	80	60
	C	All other workers	60	45
Wood and furniture	A	Carpenters, cabinet makers, joiners, wood carvers and woodcutting machinists	140	115
	B	Artificial limb makers (other than in wood), organ builders and packaging case makers	120	90
	C	Coopers not providing own tools, labourers, polishers and upholsterers	60	45
	D	All other workers	100	75

Notes

(1) For most classes of industry a tax deduction is given for certain amounts 'representing the average annual expenses incurred by employees of the class to which the employee belongs in respect of the repair and maintenance of work equipment'. The term 'flat rate expense allowance' is often used for this purpose.

(2) 'Workers' and 'all other workers' are references to manual workers or to workers who have to pay for the upkeep of tools and special clothing.

(3) 'Firemen' means persons engaged to light and maintain furnaces.

(4) 'Constructional engineering' means engineering undertaken on a construction site, including buildings, shipyards, bridges, roads and other similar operations.

(5) 'Particular engineering' means engineering undertaken on a commercial basis in a factory or workshop for the purposes of producing components such as wire, springs, nails and locks.

(6) For industries not listed in the table, a standard amount of £60 can be claimed for the laundry costs of uniforms or protective clothing (www.hmrc.gov.uk/incometax/relief-tools.htm#2).

3

PAYE, student loans and CIS

PAYE AND STUDENT LOANS

PAYE thresholds

(SI 2003/2682, reg 9)

| | 2012–13 | 2011–12 | 2010–11 | 2009–10 | 2008–09 | 2007–08 | 2006–07 |
	£	£	£	£	£	£	£
Weekly	156	144	125	125	116	100	97
Monthly	675	623	540	540	503	435	420
Annual	8,105	7,475	6,475	6,475	6,035	5,225	5,035

PAYE codes

(SI 2003/2682, reg 7)

PAYE code	Application
L	Tax code for those eligible for the basic personal allowance. Also used for 'emergency' tax codes
P	Tax code for individuals aged 65–74 and eligible for the full personal allowance
Y	Tax code for individuals aged 75 or over and eligible for the full personal allowance
T	Tax code used where HMRC are reviewing other items in tax code (eg the income-related reduction in the personal allowance) Also used if allowances have been used up or reduced to nil ('0T')
K	Tax code used where total coding 'deductions' (eg other income) exceed allowances
BR	Used when all income is taxable at the basic rate
D0	Used when all income is taxable at the higher rate (eg due to a second job or pension)
D1	Used if earnings in one employment exceed £150,000, all earnings from a second employment will be taxed at the additional rate (from 2011–12)
NT	Used when no tax is to be deducted from the income or pension

3   PAYE, student loans and CIS

PAYE code	Application
OT	Used as default PAYE tax code to deduct tax at the basic, higher and additional rates in certain circumstances (eg for new employees without form P45 and with no P46 completed, and for pension income of a person still in receipt of employment income) (from 2011–12)

Notes

(1)   PAYE codes are used by employers or pension providers to calculate the amount of tax, if any, to be deducted from an individual's pay or pension.

(2)   For further information on tax codes generally, see: www.hmrc.gov.uk/incometax/tax-codes-basics.htm.

Returns

(SI 2003/2682, regs 67, 73, 74, 85, 90)

Forms	Due Date
P14, P35, P38A *(SI 2003/2682, regs 73, 74)*	19 May following the end of the tax year
P60 (to employee) *(SI 2003/2682, reg 67)*	31 May following the end of the tax year
P9D, P11D, P11D(b) *(SI 2003/2682, reg 85; SI 2001/1004, reg 80)*	6 July following the end of the tax year
P46 (Car) *(SI 2003/2682, reg 90)*	28 days following the end of the relevant tax quarter. The tax quarters are: • 5 July • 5 October • 5 January • 5 April

Late PAYE returns: Current regime

(1)   **PAYE returns** – The penalties for late filing of forms P35 and P14 as follows *(TMA 1970, s 98A)*:

   (a)   *Up to 12 months late* – £100 for each 50 employees (or part thereof) for each month the failure continues;

   (b)   *Over 12 months late* – penalty up to the amount of PAYE etc due and unpaid at 19 April following year end.

(2)   **Benefits and expenses** – The penalties for late filing of forms P11D and P9D are as follows *(TMA 1970, s 98(1)(b))*

   (a)   Initial penalty of up to £300 per form;

   (b)   Continuing penalty of up to £60 for each day on which the penalty continues after imposition of initial penalty.

(3)   **Returns of Class 1A NIC** – Separate penalty provisions apply to the late filing of form P11D(b), which are similar to the above penalties for the late filing of PAYE returns *(SI 2001/1004, reg 81(2))*.

Penalties for late PAYE returns: New regime (from a date to be appointed)

(FA 2009, s 106, Sch 55)

(1) **General** – A new penalty regime for the failure to make or deliver PAYE returns (and certain other returns, etc) by the filing deadline was introduced in *FA 2009, s 106, Sch 55*. The new regime is to be brought into force from a date still to be appointed by Treasury order.

HMRC will consult during 2012 on new models for late payment and late filing penalties as part of their Real Time Information (RTI) project for PAYE (for details of RTI see further below).

(2) **Penalties** (See **Personal Taxation: Late returns: 2010–11 and later tax years**) – for a table of penalties, which will apply under the new regime, after the appointed day, to annual returns of payments and net tax deducted for PAYE regulation purposes, together with amended returns after the year end (*FA 2009, Sch 55, para 1(5)*).

Penalties for incorrect returns

(FA 2007, s 97, Sch 24, para 1)

Behaviour	Unprompted disclosure Maximum penalty	Unprompted disclosure Minimum penalty	Prompted disclosure Maximum penalty	Prompted disclosure Minimum penalty
Careless	30%	0%	30%	15%
Deliberate but not concealed	70%	20%	70%	35%
Deliberate and concealed	100%	30%	100%	50%

Notes

(1) The above penalty regime applies to inaccuracies in returns due to be filed from 1 April 2009 where the tax period begins from 1 April 2008.

(2) For earlier tax years, the maximum penalty for incorrect PAYE returns is 100% of the difference between the amount payable under the return and the amount payable had the return been correct. For incorrect forms P9D and P11D, the maximum penalty is up to £3,000 per incorrect form (*TMA 1970, ss 98, 98A*).

(3) See the HMRC website at www.hmrc.gov.uk/about/new-penalties/penalty-pres-agent.pdf for further information on penalties.

Late payments of PAYE

(FA 2009, s 107, Sch 56)

Default penalties

Number of times payments late in the tax year	Penalty %	Amount to which penalty percentages apply
1	No penalty (as long as the payment is less than 6 months late – see below)	Total amount that is late in the tax year (ignoring the first late payment in that tax year)

continued

3 PAYE, student loans and CIS

Number of times payments late in the tax year	Penalty %	Amount to which penalty percentages apply
2–4	1%	
5–7	2%	
8–10	3%	
11 or more	4%	

Notes

(1) *Further penalties*

Where monthly or quarterly payments remain unpaid after 6 months, a penalty of 5% may be imposed.

A further penalty of 5% may be imposed where payments remain outstanding after 12 months.

Such penalties may be charged in addition to the default penalties outlined above, and apply even where only one payment in the tax year is late.

(2) *Commencement* – The penalty regime for failure to pay PAYE and NIC on time commenced on 6 April 2010 (*SI 2010/466, art 3*). It applies to late payments relating to the tax year 2010–11 onwards, including student loan and construction industry scheme deductions (see **Late CIS payments** below), and annual payments of employers' Class 1A and 1B NIC (see CH152100). The late payment penalty regime applies to all employers and contractors, regardless of the number of employees or subcontractors.

(3) *Small employers* – A small employer who makes quarterly payments can only have a maximum of four failures in a tax year, so the maximum initial default penalty rate is 1% (CH152550). However, further penalties may still arise (see note (1)).

(4) *Appeals, reductions, etc* – The imposition and/or amount of penalty are subject to an appeal procedure. HMRC may also reduce a penalty due to 'special circumstances' at its discretion. Penalties are suspended if the contractor has an agreement for deferred payment in place (ie a 'time to pay' arrangement) with HMRC, which is not broken. Liability to a penalty does not arise if there is a 'reasonable excuse' for the failure (*FA 2009, Sch 56, paras 9, 10, 13, 16*).

PAYE electronic communications – penalties: relevant annual returns

(*SI 2003/2682, regs 210A, 210AA*)

Number of employees for whom particulars should have been included	2010–11 and subsequent years	2009–10	2004–5 to 2008–09
1–5	£100	£0	£0
6–49	£300	£100	£0

PAYE and student loans

Number of employees for whom particulars should have been included	2010–11 and subsequent years	2009–10	2004–5 to 2008–09
50–249	£600	£600	£600 (nil for 2004–05)
250–399	£900	£900	£900
400–499	£1,200	£1,200	£1,200
500–599	£1,500	£1,500	£1,500
600–699	£1,800	£1,800	£1,800
700–799	£2,100	£2,100	£2,100
800–899	£2,400	£2,400	£2,400
900–999	£2,700	£2,700	£2,700
1,000 or more	£3,000	£3,000	£3,000

Note

The above penalties apply to failures to comply with *SI 2003/2682, reg 205* (ie in relation to the mandatory use of electronic communications), in respect of a failure to deliver 'specified information' (from 2011–12; previously 'relevant annuals returns'), ie forms P35 and P14 (*SI 2003/2682, regs 206A, 207*).

PAYE electronic communications – penalties: specified information

(*SI 2003/2682, reg 210B*)

Penalty	Number of items of specified information the employer has failed to deliver in the tax quarter		
	Tax year ending 5 April 2014 and subsequent years	Tax years ending 5 April 2012 and 2013	Tax year ending 5 April 2011
£0	n/a	1–2	1–5
£100	1–49	3–49	6–49
£300	50–149	50–149	50–149
£600	150–299	150–299	150–299
£900	300–399	300–399	300–399
£1,200	400–499	400–499	400–499
£1,500	500–599	500–599	500–599
£1,800	600–699	600–699	600–699
£2,100	700–799	700–799	700–799
£2,400	800–899	800–899	800–899
£2,700	900–999	900–999	900–999
£3,000	1,000 or more	1,000 or more	1,000 or more

Notes

(1) The above penalties apply to failures by employers to deliver specified information.

(2) 'Specified information' means form P45 (Parts 1 or 3), form P46 or form P46(Pen) (*SI 2003/2682, reg 207*).

3 PAYE, student loans and CIS

PAYE surcharges (to 5 April 2010)

Default number	Specified percentage for each default in a surcharge period %
1	0.00
2	0.00
3	0.17
4	0.17
5	0.17
6	0.33
7	0.33
8	0.33
9	0.58
10	0.58
11	0.58
12 and over	0.83

Notes

(1) The default surcharge provisions (*SI 2003/2682, reg 203*) were repealed with effect from 6 April 2010.

(2) However, the provisions continue to have effect in relation to surcharges arising in respect of late payments of tax where the tax was chargeable in respect of a tax period ending on or before 5th April 2010 (*SI 2010/466, art 4(3)*).

PAYE and Class 1 NIC etc – monthly accounting periods

(*SI 2003/2682, reg 69*)

Tax Period	Tax Month	Payment due (Electronic)	Payment due (Other)
6 Apr–5 May	1	22 May	19 May
6 May–5 Jun	2	22 June	19 June
6 Jun–5 Jul	3	22 July	19 July
6 Jul–5 Aug	4	22 August	19 August
6 Aug–5 Sep	5	22 September	19 September
6 Sept–5 Oct	6	22 October	19 October
6 Oct–5 Nov	7	22 November	19 November
6 Nov–5 Dec	8	22 December	19 December
6 Dec–5 Jan	9	22 January	19 January
6 Jan–5 Feb	10	22 February	19 February
6 Feb–5 Mar	11	22 March	19 March
6 Mar–5 Apr	12	22 April	19 April

Notes

(1) Electronic payments must be cleared through HMRC's bank account within 17 days after the end of the tax period. This is generally the 22nd of the following month, as indicated above. However, if the 22nd falls on a weekend or a bank holiday, the payment must reach HMRC on the previous working day.

(2) Non-electronic payments are due 14 days following the end of the tax period. Thus employers who pay by post must ensure that payment reaches HMRC no later than 19th of the month. For interest purposes HMRC treat payments as being received on the day that the cheque is received (see www.hmrc.gov.uk/paye/file-or-pay/payments/deadlines.htm).

PAYE and Class 1 NIC etc – quarterly accounting periods

(SI 2003/2682, reg 70)

Tax Period	Tax Month	Payment due (Electronic)	Payment due (Other)
6 Apr–5 Jul	1–3	22 July	19 July
6 Jul–5 Oct	4–6	22 October	19 October
6 Oct–5 Jan	7–9	22 January	19 January
6 Jan–5 Apr	10–12	22 April	19 April

Note

Employers who have reasonable grounds for believing that the 'average monthly amount' will be less than £1,500 can generally choose to make quarterly payments.

Interest on PAYE paid late

(SI 2003/2682, regs 82, 83)

(1) Where an employer has not paid to HMRC the net tax payable under PAYE within 14 days of the end of the tax year (or 17 days, if the payment is made electronically), the unpaid tax carries interest at the prescribed rate from the reckonable date until the date of payment.

(2) Interest payable on PAYE paid late is in addition to and separate from any penalties for late payment of PAYE.

(3) Certain repayments of tax to the employer after the end of the tax year to which it relates also attract interest.

Student Loans

(SI 2009/470, reg 29; SI 2011/784, reg 6)

Year	Percentage	Threshold Annual	Monthly	Weekly
2012–13	9%	£15,795	£1,316.25	£303.75
2011–12	9%	£15,000	£1,250.00	£288.46
2010–11	9%	£15,000	£1,250.00	£288.46
2009–10	9%	£15,000	£1,250.00	£288.46
2008–09	9%	£15,000	£1,250.00	£288.46
2007–08	9%	£15,000	£1,250.00	£288.46
2006–07	9%	£15,000	£1,250.00	£288.46

Notes

(1) HMRC is responsible for collecting student loan repayments by new borrowers after August 1998.

(2) The 'threshold' (see above) is the amount of earnings above which the student loan repayments become due. The amount of repayment is calculated as a percentage of earnings over that threshold.

(3) The Government has announced that they intend to raise the annual threshold to £21,000 with effect from April 2016.

REAL TIME INFORMATION (RTI)

Proposed changes to PAYE

HMRC plan to implement Real Time Information by October 2013 to support the new Universal Credit being introduced by the Department for Work and Pensions. Under RTI, existing PAYE regulations will remain largely unchanged, but employers will have to use new online procedures to account for the income tax and NICs deducted for each pay period on or before the date their employees are paid. Further information about RTI can be found at www.hmrc.gov.uk/rti/index.htm.

CONSTRUCTION INDUSTRY SCHEME (CIS)

CIS returns

(FA 2004, s 70; SI 2005/2045, reg 4)

- **Filing date** – Contractors are required to submit monthly returns to HMRC, no later than 14 days after the end of every tax month. Returns may be submitted on paper (form CIS300) or electronically.

- **'Nil' returns** – Contractors who have not paid any subcontractors in the previous tax month must nevertheless submit 'nil' returns, unless HMRC have been notified that no further payments will be made, in which case HMRC may cease to require monthly returns for up to six months, or until payments to subcontractors recommence (www.hmrc.gov.uk/cis/returns/returns-records.htm#4).

Late CIS returns (from October 2011)

(FA 2009, s 106; Sch 55, paras 7–13)

Period	Penalty
Up to 2 months late	£100
More than 2 months late	£200
More than 6 months late	Greater of: • 5% of tax liability; and • £300
More than 12 months late Other cases (ie not included below) (also see below for returns relating only to persons registered for gross payment)	Greater of: • 5% of tax liability; and • £300
Information [deliberately]* withheld: Deliberate but not concealed	Greater of: • 70% of tax liability; and • £1,500
Deliberate and concealed	Greater of: • 100% of tax liability; and • £3,000
More than 12 months late – Information [deliberately]* withheld: Return relating only to persons registered for gross payment	
Deliberate but not concealed	£1,500
Deliberate and concealed	£3,000

* 'Deliberately' inserted (by *F(No 3)A 2010, s 26, Sch 10 paras 1, 5, 6* with effect from 6 October 2011 (SI 2011/2391).

Notes

(1) **Commencement** – The penalty regime for failing to make CIS returns under *FA 2009, Sch 55* takes effect from October 2011. The first return to attract a penalty under *Sch 55* will be the return due for the month ended 5 November 2011 (see CH61120).

(2) **Contractors new to CIS** – For contractors who have not submitted any previous returns and are filing their first returns late, an upper limit of £3,000 applies to the total 'fixed' penalties (ie. £100 and £200) arising. The £3,000 upper limit does not replace any 'tax geared' penalties, but the £300 minimum penalties that would otherwise be charged where the tax geared penalty is less than £300 is removed (*FA 2009, Sch 55, para 13*).

Late CIS returns (to October 2011)

(TMA 1970, s 98A)

The penalties for late filing of monthly CIS returns were as follows:

3 PAYE, student loans and CIS

- *Up to 12 months late* – £100 for each 50 employees (or part thereof) for each month the failure continues; and
- *Over 12 months late* – Up to £3,000.

Notes

(1) **New regime** – A new penalty regime for the late filing of CIS returns applies from October 2011 (see above).

(2) **Calculation of penalties** – In some cases, penalties based on the new rules may be lower than those charged under the above regime. As a transitional measure, contractors who were charged penalties for filing a monthly CIS return late before October 2011 could ask HMRC to calculate penalties under the new penalty regime and reduce their penalties accordingly if this calculation resulted in a lower amount (see www.hmrc.gov.uk/cis/penalties-late-returns.htm).

CIS payments

(*FA 2004, s 62; SI 2005/2045, regs 7, 8*)

- **Payment dates** – Contractors are normally required to make monthly payments to HMRC of deductions from contract payments, within 17 days after the end of the tax period if made electronically, or otherwise within 14 days after the end of the tax period.
- **Quarterly payments** – A contractor who has reasonable grounds for believing that the 'average monthly amount' will be less than £1,500 can choose to pay tax on a quarterly basis (ie for quarters ending 5 July, 5 October, 5 January and 5 April).

Late CIS payments

(*FA 2009, s 107, Sch 56, paras 6–8*)

- **Penalties** – A penalty regime applies to the failure to make CIS payments on time. For a table of penalties, see **Late payments of PAYE**.
- **Scope** – The potential penalties for a tax year comprise 'default' penalties for unpaid CIS deductions at the penalty date, and two further penalties for CIS deductions which are more than 6 and 12 months late. Penalties apply for the failure to pay all or part of the amounts due. HMRC guidance and worked examples regarding the late payment regime for CIS purposes are contained in HMRC's Compliance Handbook (CH153000 onwards).
- **Commencement** – The penalty regime for failure to make CIS payments on time in *FA 2009, Sch 56* applies with effect from 6 April 2010 (*SI 2010/466, art 3*).
- **Appeals, reductions, etc** – The imposition and/or amount of penalty are subject to an appeal procedure. HMRC may also reduce a penalty due to 'special circumstances' which does not include ability to pay. Penalties are suspended if the contractor has an agreement for deferred payment in place (ie a 'time to pay' arrangement) with HMRC, which is not broken. Liability to a penalty does not arise if there is a 'reasonable excuse' for the failure (*FA 2009, Sch 56, paras 9, 10, 13, 16*).

4

Shares and Share options

On 6 March 2012 the Office of Tax Simplification published its 'Review of tax advantaged employee share schemes: Final report' (www.hm-treasury.gov.uk/ots_essreview.htm). The Government has announced that it will consider the recommendations of the OTS and will consult on how to take these proposals forward in the *Finance Bill 2013*. Furthermore, HM Treasury will conduct an internal review to examine the role of employee ownership in supporting growth and examine options to remove barriers, including tax barriers, to its wider take-up (Budget, 21 March 2012).

APPROVED SHARE INCENTIVE PLANS (SIPs)

(ITEPA 2003, Pt 7, Ch 6, Sch 2; ITTOIA 2005, ss 392–396, 405–408, 770; SI 2001/1004, reg 22(8), Sch 3, Pt 9, para 7)

Type of share	When shares acquired	Shares taken from plan during the first 3 years	Shares taken from plan during years 3–5	Shares taken from plan after 5 years
Free shares and Matching shares	No income tax or NICs to pay on the value of the shares (*ITEPA 2003, s 490*)	Income tax payable on the market value of the shares when taken out of the plan (*ITEPA 2003, s 505(2)*)	Income tax payable on the lower of the market value of the shares: • When awarded, or • When taken out of plan (*ITEPA 2003, s 505(3)*)	No income tax or NICs to pay

continued

4 Shares and Share options

Type of share	When shares acquired	Shares taken from plan during the first 3 years	Shares taken from plan during years 3–5	Shares taken from plan after 5 years
Partnership shares	No income tax or NICs to pay on the money used to buy the shares (*ITEPA 2003, s 492*)	Income tax payable on the market value of the shares when taken out of the plan (*ITEPA 2003, s 506(2)*)	Income tax payable on the lower of: • the pay used to buy the shares, or • the market value of the shares when taken out of the plan (*ITEPA 2003, s 506(3)*)	No income tax or NICs
Dividend shares	No income tax or NICs on dividends used to buy dividend shares (*ITEPA 2003, ss 490(1)(b), 493, 496; ITTOIA 2005, s 770(2)*)	Dividends used to buy shares are taxed as a dividend in the year the shares are taken out of the plan (*ITTOIA 2005, ss 394(2), 407(2)*)	No income tax or NICs	No income tax or NICs

Notes

(1) A SIP is an HMRC approved plan which offers tax and National Insurance advantages. The SIP must satisfy various conditions, and the company should send details of its SIP to HMRC for formal approval prior to starting the plan (*ITEPA 2003, Sch 2, Pt 10*).

(2) The purpose of a SIP must be "to provide benefits to employees in the nature of shares in a company which give them a continuing stake in that company". The SIP cannot be restricted to particular groups or individuals. However, companies can exclude employees who have not worked for the company for a minimum period of time. Individual companies can set their own minimum limit, but it cannot be longer than 18 months (*ITEPA 2003, Sch 2, paras 7, 8, 16*).

(3) There is generally no National Insurance liability when an employee acquires shares from a SIP. However, a Class 1 NIC liability (and a income tax charge) may arise if the employee leaves the company, or takes shares out of the plan, within five years of joining it (see National Insurance Manual, NIM06806-06807).

ENTERPRISE MANAGEMENT INCENTIVES (EMI)

(ITEPA 2003, Pt 7, Ch 9, Sch 5)

Taxation

(ITEPA 2003, Pt 7 Ch 9)

The tax and National Insurance contributions implications of EMI options include the following:

- *Grant of EMI option* – No income tax or National Insurance contributions charges arise on the grant of a qualifying EMI option.
- *Exercise of EMI option* – If the option is exercised within ten years of the date of grant and there has been no disqualifying event, no charge to income tax or National Insurance contributions charges arise provided that the employee buys the shares at a price at least equal to market value on the day the option was granted. If the option is a replacement option, it must be exercised within ten years of grant of the original option in order to qualify for tax relief *(ITEPA 2003, ss 529–530)*.

  An income tax charge may arise on the exercise of a qualifying EMI option in the following circumstances, and a National Insurance contributions liability may also arise if the shares are 'readily convertible assets' (as defined in *ITEPA 2003, s 702*; see *NIM06835*):

  - the option was granted at a discount to market value (ie the option price is less than the market value at the date of grant) *(ITEPA 2003, s 531)*; or
  - the option is exercised more than 40 days after a disqualifying event *(ITEPA 2003, s 532)*.

- *Capital Gains Tax* (CGT) – A sale of qualifying EMI shares is potentially subject to CGT.
- *National Insurance Contributions* – As to the circumstances in which a liability arises (under *SSCBA 1992, s 4(4)*) in respect of EMI shares or options, see *NIM06810*.

General requirements

(ITEPA 2003, Sch 5, Pt 2)

- *Purpose* – The EMI option must be granted for qualifying purposes (see *Sch 5, para 4*);
- *Maximum employee entitlement* – An employee may be granted qualifying options over shares with a total value of £120,000 *(Sch 5, paras 5–6)*; the Government has announced that it will increase this limit by Treasury Order to £250,000, to commence at the earliest opportunity following EU State aid approval (Budget, 21 March 2012);
- *Maximum company limit* – The total value of shares under EMI options granted by the company must not exceed £3 million *(Sch 5, para 7)*.

Qualifying companies

(ITEPA 2003, Sch 5, Pt 3)

- *Independence and qualifying subsidiaries* – The company must satisfy certain requirements (in *Sch 5, paras 8–11B*) as appropriate;

4 Shares and Share options

- *Gross assets* – The value of the company's gross assets must not exceed £30 million at the date the EMI option is granted (if the company is a member of a group of companies, the limits are applied to the gross assets of the group as a whole) (*Sch 5, para 12*);
- *Number of employees* – The company must have fewer than 250 'full-time equivalent employees' at the date on which a qualifying EMI option is granted (this requirement applies to employees of a parent company and all its qualifying subsidiaries) (*Sch 5, para 12A*);
- *Trading activities* – A qualifying trade must be carried on (*Sch 5, paras 13–23*).

Eligible employees

(*ITEPA 2003, Sch 5, Pt 4*)

- *Employment* – The individual must be an employee of the company whose shares are the subject of the options (or for a group, employees of a qualifying subsidiary (*Sch 5, para 25*);
- *Working time* – The employee must be required to spend on average at least 25 hours per week or, if less, 75% of working time on the business of the company whose shares are subject to the EMI option or a qualifying subsidiary (*Sch 5, para 26–27*).
- *No material interest* – The employee must not have a material interest in the company whose shares are under option, or (if that company is a parent company) in any group company. A 'material interest' is either beneficial ownership of, or the ability to control directly or indirectly, more than 30% of the ordinary share capital of the company, or where the company is a close company, possession of or entitlement to acquire rights that would give more than 30% of the assets available for distribution on a winding up (*Sch 5, paras 28–33*).

Requirements relating to options

(*ITEPA 2003, Sch 5, Pt 5*)

- *Type of shares* – The option must be a right to acquire shares that are part of the ordinary share capital of the company, are fully paid up and are not redeemable (*Sch 5, para 35*).
- *Exercise of option* – It must be possible for the option to be exercised within ten years from the date of grant (*Sch 5, para 36*).
- *Terms of option to be agreed in writing* – The option must be a written agreement between the person granting the option and the employee, which contains the information specified in *Sch 5, para 37*.
- *Options not transferable* – The option terms must prohibit the option holder from transferring their rights under it. If the option terms allow for its exercise after the option holder's death, the option cannot be exercised more than one year after the date of death (*Sch 5, para 38*).

Notes

(1) EMIs are tax advantaged share options. They are designed to help small, higher risk companies recruit and retain employees. Guidance on the EMI scheme conditions is included in HMRC's Employee Share Schemes User Manual (www.hmrc.gov.uk/manuals/essum/ESSUM50000.htm).

(2) Notice of the option must be given within 92 days after its grant (*ITEPA 2003, Sch 5, para 44*). HMRC provide a form (EMI 1) to notify grants of EMI options, which is available via HMRC's website (www.hmrc.gov.uk/shareschemes/emi/emi-10-09.pdf).

(3) Employers operating an EMI scheme must submit an annual return to HMRC before 7 July in the following tax year (*ITEPA 2003, Sch 5, para 52*). HMRC provide an annual return form (EMI 40), which is available via HMRC's website (www.hmrc.gov.uk/shareschemes/emi40-2012.pdf).

(4) The Government will make reforms in the *Finance Bill 2013*, subject to EU State aid approval:

- so that gains made on shares acquired through exercising EMI options on or after 6 April 2012 will be eligible for capital gains tax entrepreneurs' relief; and

- the Government will consult on ways to extend access to EMI for academics who are employed by qualifying companies (Budget, 21 March 2012).

COMPANY SHARE OPTION PLANS (CSOPS)

(*ITEPA 2003, Pt 7, Ch 8, Sch 4*)

Taxation

(*ITEPA 2003, ss 524, 526*)

Grant of option – A tax charge can arise if an option is granted at a discount (ie the consideration (if any) for the grant of the option and the amount payable on exercise is less than the market value of the relevant shares) (*s 526*).

Exercise of option – No income tax charge arises if the following conditions are satisfied (s 524):

- The option is exercised in accordance with the provisions of the scheme at a time when the scheme is approved; and

- The avoidance of tax or National Insurance Contributions is not the main purpose (or one of the main purposes) of any arrangement under which the option was granted or exercised; and

- One of the following conditions is met:
  - The option is exercised on after the third anniversary of the date of grant and not later than the tenth anniversary of that date; or
  - The option is exercised before the third anniversary of the date of grant and is so exercised by virtue of a 'good leaver' provision included in the scheme (*s 524(2A)*; see *ESSUM48200*).

For options granted before 9 April 2003, the option must be exercised not less than three years or more than ten years after the date of grant (without exception) and not less than three years after a previous exempt exercise of another option under the same or another approved company share option scheme.

4 Shares and Share options

Capital Gains Tax – A disposal of shares is a chargeable occasion for capital gains tax purposes.

National Insurance Contributions – HMRC guidance on CSOPs for National Insurance Contributions purposes is contained in the National Insurance Manual at NIM06809.

Scheme requirements

(ITEPA 2003, Sch 4)

The requirements for CSOP schemes to be approved by HMRC include the following:

- *General* – The scheme must meet the purpose of providing benefits in the form of share options to employees and directors, and must not include features that are neither essential nor reasonably incidental to that purpose.

  No participant can be granted approved options with a market value of more than £30,000 (calculated at the date of grant) *(Sch 4, Pt 2)*.

- *Eligible employees* – The scheme rules must provide that the individual is a full-time director or a 'qualifying employee' of the scheme organiser (or constituent company in a group scheme). Participation in the scheme is not open to individuals if they and/or their associates have (or have had in the previous 12 months) a material interest in a close company whose shares are being used in the scheme, or in certain other companies. 'Material interest' is defined in the legislation, but broadly means more than 25% of the ordinary share capital of the company, or more than 25% of the assets which would be available for distribution among the participators *(Sch 4, Pt 3)*.

- *Scheme shares* – The CSOP scheme must satisfy various requirements relating to shares that may be subject to share options. For example, eligible shares must be fully paid up and not redeemable. Options cannot be granted over shares in a company which is under the control of a listed company with effect from 24 September 2010, subject to transitional provisions *(Sch 4, Pt 4)*.

- *Share options* – The scheme must meet certain requirements relating to the share options, may make provisions in relation to the acquisition cost of the shares subject to the option and the non-transferability of those options, and provisions as to when they may be exercised in specified circumstances (eg following the participant's death) *(Sch 4, Pt 5)*.

- *Exchange of options* – The scheme rules may allow for an exchange of options on a company reorganisation, if certain conditions are satisfied *(Sch 4, Pt 6)*.

Notes

(1) A CSOP scheme is a share option plan arranged by a company, which provides for share options to be granted to employees and directors. The company can only grant options if HMRC has approved the scheme *(ITEPA 2003, Sch 4 Pt 7)*.

(2) HMRC have produced an informal checklist in respect of CSOP scheme requirements to be satisfied, for approval or review purposes (www.hmrc.gov.uk/manuals/essum/essum47903.htm).

SAVE AS YOU EARN (SAYE) SCHEMES

(ITEPA 2003, Pt 7, Ch 7, Sch 3)

Taxation

(ITEPA 2003, Pt 7, Ch 7)

Grant of option – No income tax charge arises on the grant of an approved SAYE share option. If options are accidentally granted at a discount to the market value of the shares on the agreed valuation date in excess of the permitted 20%, such options should be treated as not having been granted in accordance with the provisions of an approved SAYE share option scheme and so will attract no tax advantages (*ESSUM39350*).

Exercise of option – No income tax charge arises on the exercise of the share option if the following conditions are satisfied (*s 519*):

- The option is exercised in accordance with the provisions of the SAYE scheme at a time when the scheme is approved; and

- The avoidance of tax or National Insurance Contributions is not the main purpose (or one of the main purposes) of any arrangement under which the option was granted or exercised; and

- One of the following conditions is met:
    - The option is exercised on or after the third anniversary of the date on which it was granted; or
    - The option is exercised before the third anniversary of the date of grant in certain defined circumstances such as injury, disability or redundancy.

Interest and bonuses – No income tax liability arises on interest and any bonus payable under a certified SAYE savings arrangement (*ITTOIA 2005, ss 702–703*).

Capital Gains Tax – A disposal of shares is a chargeable occasion for capital gains tax purposes.

National Insurance Contributions – No liability arises when the proceeds of the savings are used to buy shares. As to the National Insurance Contributions position generally, see *NIM06808*.

Scheme requirements

(ITEPA 2003, Sch 3)

General – The scheme must meet the purpose of providing benefits in the form of share options to employees and directors, and must not include features that are neither essential nor reasonably incidental to that purpose. The scheme must provide that every individual who meets certain eligibility criteria may participate (eg an employee (whether full-time or part-time) or full-time director of the scheme organiser or (in the case of a group) of a constituent company, who has been an employee or director at all times during a qualifying period (specified in the scheme rules) not exceeding five years). Participation in the scheme must be on similar terms (*Sch 3, Pt 2*).

4 Shares and Share options

Eligible employees – The scheme rules must provide that the individual is a current director or employee of the scheme organiser (or constituent company in a group scheme). Participation in the scheme is not open to individuals if they and/or their associates have (or have had in the previous 12 months) a material interest in a close company whose shares are being used in the scheme, or in certain other companies. 'Material interest' is defined in the legislation, but broadly means more than 25% of the ordinary share capital of the company, or more than 25% of the assets which would be available for distribution among the participators (*Sch 3, Pt 3*).

Scheme shares – SAYE option scheme shares must form part of the ordinary share capital of the scheme organiser or certain other companies, and must satisfy various other eligibility requirements (eg the shares must be fully paid up and not redeemable), and must not be subject to any restrictions other than those attaching to all shares of the same class, or which are permitted by the approved SAYE option schemes legislation (*Sch 3, Pt 4*).

Linked savings arrangements – The scheme must provide for shares acquired by exercising SAYE scheme options to be bought with funds up to the amount of repayments and interest under a certified SAYE savings arrangement approved by HMRC. Individuals may contract to make monthly contributions over a three or five year period, and may choose to leave the contributions in their accounts for an additional two years (*ESSUM34170–34180*). The scheme must also provide for an individual's contributions to the approved savings arrangement to be sufficient (as far as possible) to secure repayment of the exercise price of the share options granted under the scheme.

The maximum contribution that may be permitted is £250 per month. The minimum contribution cannot exceed £10 per month (nb the current SAYE Prospectus also imposes a minimum monthly contribution under a savings contract of £5 per month (see *ESSUM34510*) (*Sch 3, Pt 5*).

Share options that may be granted under the scheme – The SAYE scheme must satisfy various requirements, including in relation to the exercise price of the option shares, the non-transferability of share options, when the options can be exercised and the 'specified age' of the individual for the purposes of the scheme (*Sch 3, Pt 6*).

Exchange of share options – The scheme rules may allow for an exchange of options on a company reorganisation, if certain conditions are satisfied (*Sch 3, Pt 7*).

Notes

(1) A SAYE scheme allows a company to grant eligible employees and directors an option to purchase the company's shares in the future at a price determined at the time of invitation.

(2) SAYE option schemes are subject to approval by HMRC (*Sch 3, Pt 8*). HMRC have produced a specimen set of scheme rules and other specimen documentation relating to SAYE schemes in the Employee Share Schemes User Manual (*ESSUM38810–38814*). A model SAYE Prospectus is also available from HMRC's website (www.hmrc.gov.uk/shareschemes/model-saye-prospectus.pdf).

SAYE BONUS RATES

(ITEPA 2003, Sch 3, Pt 5)

Contract started on or after	3 year contract Monthly payment multiple	5 year contract Monthly payment multiple	7 year contract Monthly payment multiple
23 September 2011	0.0	0.0	1.6
12 August 2011	0.0	0.9	3.5
27 February 2011	0.1	1.7	4.8
12 September 2010	0.0	0.9	3.2
14 May 2010	0.0	1.8	4.9
29 May 2009	0.3	2.2	5.2
17 February 2009	0.6	2.6	5.6
27 December 2008	1.5	4.8	9.3
1 September 2008	2.4	7.0	12.7
4 April 2008	1.6	5.1	9.8
1 September 2007	2.4	7.2	13.3
1 September 2006	1.8	5.5	10.3
1 September 2005	1.4	4.4	8.4
1 September 2004	1.9	6.1	11.5
24 January 2004	1.7	5.4	10.4
1 September 2003	0.9	3.4	7.1
27 April 2003	1.0	3.7	7.6

Notes

(1) The bonus rate applicable to a SAYE share option scheme is set at the time the savings contract is entered into, and is unaffected by any subsequent change to the rate.

(2) Source: HM Revenue and Customs (www.hmrc.gov.uk/shareschemes/historical-bonus-rates.pdf).

SAYE CONTRACTS – INTEREST RATES ON EARLY WITHDRAWAL

(ITEPA 2003, Sch 3)

Contract started on or after	Interest rate	Contract started on or after	Interest rate
12 August 2011	0.0%		
27 February 2011	0.12%	4 April 2008	0.00%
12 September 2010	0.00%	1 September 2007	0.36%
14 May 2010	0.50%	1 September 2006	2.00%
29 May 2009	2.00%	1 September 2005	1.50%
17 February 2009	3.00%	1 September 2004	2.00%
27 December 2008	2.00%	1 September 2003	1.00%
1 September 2008	3.00%	1 October 2001	2.00%

Note

Source: www.hmrc.gov.uk/shareschemes/historical-bonus-rates.pdf.

4   *Shares and Share options*

SAYE CONTRACTS – INTEREST RATES

(*ITEPA 2003, Sch 3*)

Contract started on or after	3 year contract	5 year contract	7 year contract
23 September 2011	0.00%	0.00%	0.58%
12 August 2011	0.00%	0.59%	1.25%
27 February 2011	0.18%	1.10%	1.70%
12 September 2010	0.00%	0.59%	1.15%
14 May 2010	0.00%	1.16%	1.74%
29 May 2009	0.54%	1.42%	1.84%
17 February 2009	1.08%	1.67%	1.98%
27 December 2008	2.67%	3.04%	3.20%
1 September 2008	4.23%	4.36%	4.28%
4 April 2008	2.84%	3.22%	3.36%
1 September 2007	4.23%	4.48%	4.46%
1 September 2006	3.19%	3.46%	3.52%
1 September 2005	2.49%	2.79%	2.91%
1 September 2004	3.37%	3.82%	3.90%
24 January 2004	3.02%	3.40%	3.55%
1 September 2003	1.61%	2.17%	2.48%
27 April 2003	1.74%	2.34%	2.64%

Note

Source: www.hmrc.gov.uk/shareschemes/historical-bonus-rates.pdf.

5

Pensions, Investment income etc

PENSIONS

(FA 2004, Pt 4, Schs 28–36)

Tax relief is available on contributions to registered pension schemes (subject to potential relief restrictions; see below) as follows (FA 2004, s 190):

- up to 100% of relevant UK earnings for a tax year; or
- up to £3,600 per annum if relevant UK earnings are lower than this amount.

Notes

(1) A relevant UK individual is entitled to tax relief in respect of 'relievable pension contributions'. These exclude contributions after the individual has reached age 75, and any contributions by the individual's employer *(FA 2004, s 188(3))*.

(2) Additional contributions may be made in excess of the above limits, but no further tax relief is available.

(3) Normal minimum pension age is 55 from 6 April 2010 (nb early retirement ages apply to certain professions and occupations; see below).

(4) Tax relief for pension contributions is subject to potential restrictions (see below).

(5) Contracting out through a defined contribution scheme is abolished with effect from 6 April 2012. The *Finance Bill 2013* will contain provisions to bring tax legislation into line with Department for Work and Pensions legislation (Budget, 21 March 2012).

RESTRICTIONS ON RELIEF

(FA 2004, ss 218, 228, 215, 227)

Annual and lifetime allowances

(FA 2004, ss 218, 228)

	2012–13 £	2011–12 £	2010–11 £	2009–10 £	2008–09 £	2007–08 £
Annual Allowance	50,000	50,000	255,000	245,000	235,000	225,000
Lifetime Allowance	1,500,000	1,800,000	1,800,000	1,750,000	1,650,000	1,600,000

5   *Pensions, Investment income etc*

Note

Lifetime allowance – The reduction in the standard lifetime allowance for 2012–13 to £1.5 million (*FA 2011, s 67, Sch 18*) is subject to transitional protection from the lifetime allowance charge in appropriate cases (see below).

Annual allowance charge

(*FA 2004, s 227*)

- *Rate of charge* – From 2011–12, the annual allowance charge is levied at the 'appropriate rate' (ie broadly the individual's marginal tax rate). An individual with an annual allowance charge of over £2,000 will in most cases be able to elect for his pension scheme to pay the liability instead, with scheme benefits being actuarially reduced accordingly (*FA 2004, s 237B*).

  For 2010–11, the annual allowance charge was 40% of the amount by which the total pension input amount exceeded the annual allowance.

- *Carry forward of unused annual allowance* – Any unused annual allowance for up to three tax years preceding 'the current tax year' may be added to the annual allowance available for the current tax year, if it arises for a tax year in which the individual was a member of a registered pension scheme (even if the pension input amount for that year was nil). Unused allowances for 2008–09, 2009–10 and 2010–11 can be carried forward to 2011–12. The earliest years' unused allowance is used first. However, for these purposes the annual allowance is treated as being £50,000 for each of 2008–09, 2009–10 and 2010–11 (*FA 2004, s 228A, inserted by FA 2011, Sch 17, para 5*).

Lifetime allowance charge

(*FA 2004, s 215*)

- 25% of the amount by which total pension savings exceed the lifetime allowance, if taken as a pension; or
- 55% of the excess if taken as a lump sum.
- Transitional provisions in *Finance Act 2011* provide protection from the lifetime allowance charge from 6 April 2012 for individuals with pension savings which were based on the expectation that the lifetime allowance would remain at the previous level of £1.8 million, where certain conditions are satisfied (*FA 2011, s 67, Sch 18*).

PERSONAL PENSION CONTRIBUTIONS AND RETIREMENT ANNUITY PREMIUMS TO 2005–06

(*TA 1988, ss 640, 626 (repealed from 6 April 2006)*)

Maximum contributions

Age in years at beginning of year of assessment	Personal pension contributions	Retirement annuity premiums
	%	%
Below 36	17.5	17.5
36 to 45	20.0	17.5
46 to 50	25.0	17.5

Personal pension contributions and retirement annuity premiums to 2005–06

Age in years at beginning of year of assessment	Personal pension contributions	Retirement annuity premiums
	%	%
51 to 55	30.0	20.0
56 to 60	35.0	22.5
61 or more	40.0	27.5

Note

Life assurance – For contracts of life assurance made before 6 April 2001, up to 5% of the individual's net relevant earnings for the year of assessment could be applied to secure a lump sum payable on death before age 75. For contracts of life assurance made from 6 April 2001, up to 10% of the relevant pension contribution could be so applied (*TA 1988, s 640(3) (repealed)*).

Earnings cap

(*TA 1988, s 640A (repealed)*)

Tax year	Maximum pensionable earnings
2005–06	£105,600
2004–05	£102,000
2003–04	£99,000
2002–03	£97,200
2001–02	£95,400
2000–01	£91,800

Note

(1) *Notional earnings cap* – The rules of many pension schemes limited the level of contributions or benefits by reference to the permitted maximum (under *TA 1988, s 590C*), prior to its repeal from 6 April 2006. However, the permitted maximum could continue to apply from that date for a period up to 5 April 2011, due to transitional provisions (*SI 2006/364*). If *s 590C* had not been repealed, the earnings cap for tax years from 2006–07 would be as follows:

2010–11	£123,600
2009–10	£123,600
2008–09	£117,600
2007–08	£112,800
2006–07	£108,600

(2) The tax year 2010–11 was the last for which HMRC published a notional earnings cap figure. If any schemes still need to know what the earnings cap would have been for tax years after 2010–11, they may calculate it themselves by using the method shown in *TA 1988, s 590C*.

5 Pensions, Investment income etc

EARLY RETIREMENT AGES FOR PROFESSIONS OR OCCUPATIONS

(*FA 2004, Sch 36, paras 21, 23; SI 2005/3451, reg 3, Sch 2*)

- Athletes,
- Badminton players,
- Boxers,
- Cricketers,
- Cyclists,
- Dancers,
- Divers (saturation, deep sea and free swimming)
- Footballers,
- Golfers,
- Ice hockey players,
- Jockeys – flat racing,
- Jockeys – national hunt,
- Members of the Reserve Forces,
- Models,
- Motor cycle riders (Motocross or road racing),
- Motor racing drivers,
- Rugby League players,
- Rugby Union players,
- Skiers (downhill),
- Snooker or billiards players,
- Speedway riders,
- Squash players,
- Table tennis players,
- Tennis players (including real tennis)
- Trapeze artists, and
- Wrestlers

Note

The payment of retirement benefits from a registered pension scheme is generally allowed only from the normal minimum pension age of 55 (prior to 6 April 2010 this was 50). Lower pension ages for certain qualifying occupations were generally abolished from 6 April 2006, but the above occupations are prescribed occupations for the purposes of protecting pre-existing rights to take benefits under a personal pension scheme or retirement annuity contract before the age of 50. The age at which the member has the right to take a pension on 5 April 2006 is the individual's protected pension age (*HMRC Registered Pension Schemes Manual, RPSM03106035*).

INDIVIDUAL SAVING ACCOUNTS (ISAs)

(ITTOIA 2005, Pt 6, Ch 3; SI 1998/1870, reg 4)

	2012–13	2011–12	2010–11	2009–10	
	Age 18 and over	Age 18 and over	Age 18 and over	Age under 50	Age 50 or over
Overall limit	£11,280	£10,680	£10,200	£7,200	£10,200
Cash limit	£5,640	£5,340	£5,100	£3,600	£5,100
	Under 18	Under 18			
Junior ISA	£3,600	£3,600	–	–	–

Notes

(1) Whether or not a person aged 16 to 18 already holds a Junior ISA (see Note 3 below), they may invest in an adult cash ISA up to the cash limit, but not a stocks and shares ISA.

(2) It was announced in the 2011 Budget that from 2012–13 the ISA limits will be increased by reference to the Consumer Prices Index (CPI). For 2011–12 the Retail Prices Index (RPI) was used. The limits will be calculated by reference to the CPI for the September before the start of the following tax year and the increased limit will be rounded to £120. The ISA limits will remain unchanged if the CPI is negative. The cash ISA limit will remain at half the stocks and shares ISA limit.

(3) Provisions for the new Junior ISA (JISA) were introduced in *Finance Act 2011 (ITTOIA 2005, s 695A)*. JISAs became available from 1 November 2011 and are available to UK resident children (under 18s) who do not have a Child Trust Fund (CTF) account. From 2013–14 the JISA limit will be increased by reference to the CPI. The limit can be divided between cash and stocks and shares JISA. When the holder reaches the age of 18, a JISA becomes an adult ISA.

ENTERPRISE INVESTMENT SCHEME (EIS)

(ITA 2007, Pt 5)

EIS income tax relief annual limit

(ITA 2007, s 158)

Shares issued	Maximum annual investment	Rate of relief
From 2012–13	£1,000,000	30%
From 2011–12	£500,000	30%
From 2008–09	£500,000	20%
From 2006–07	£400,000	20%
From 2004–05	£200,000	20%

Notes

(1) *Maximum annual investment* – The maximum EIS annual investment limit for individuals is increased to £1,000,000 with effect from 6 April 2012 (Budget 23 March 2011; *ITA 2007, s 158, as amended by FB 2012, Sch 7, para 3*).

5   Pensions, Investment income etc

(2) *Minimum subscription* – A £500 minimum subscription upon which relief is available in a tax year applies until 2011–12, but this is removed with effect from 2012–13 (Budget, 21 March 2012; *ITA 2007, s 157 as amended by FB 2012, Sch 7, para 2*). The restriction does not apply to subscriptions made through an approved investment fund (*ITA 2007, s 157(2), (3)*).

(3) *Carry back of EIS relief (ITA 2007, s 158(4))* – EIS relief is available for the tax year in which the shares are issued.

However, for shares issued from 2009–10, the investor may claim to treat some or all of the shares as issued in the year preceding that in which the shares were issued. There is no limit on the amount which may be carried back, subject to the overriding relief limit for that earlier year

For shares issued up to and including the tax year 2008–09, where the shares are issued before 6 October in the tax year, up to half can be treated as having been issued in the previous tax year, subject to the following limits:

- 2006–07 to 2008–09 – £50,000;
- 1998–99 to 2005–06 – £25,000.

SEED ENTERPRISE INVESTMENT SCHEME (SEIS)

(FB 2012, cl 38, Sch 6)

Income tax

- Income tax relief worth 50% of the amount invested regardless of the investor's marginal rate of tax.
- Maximum annual investment £100,000.

Capital gains tax

- Capital gains tax (CGT) exemption – For gains on shares within the scope of the SEIS.
- CGT 'holiday' – Exemption from CGT on gains realised from disposals of assets in 2012–13, where the gains are reinvested through the SEIS in the same year.

Notes

(1) *General* – The SEIS is a tax-advantaged venture capital scheme similar to EIS. It is designed to incentivise investment in small, early stage companies. A claim for SEIS is broadly available to individuals ('qualifying investors') who subscribe for relevant shares in a 'qualifying company' where certain requirements are satisfied. The SEIS applies to 'smaller' companies, broadly those with 25 or fewer employees and assets of up to £200,000. An upper limit applies to the total amount of investments in the issuing company of £150,000.

(2) *Scope* – SEIS income tax relief applies to shares issued on or after 6 April 2012 and before 6 April 2017 (subject to any extension by Treasury order).

(3) *Income tax relief* – The income tax relief is given upon making a claim as a reduction in the individual's tax liability for the current tax year. Alternatively, a claim can be made to treat the shares as having been issued in the preceding tax year (but not so as to treat them as acquired before 2012–13).

(4) *CGT reinvestment relief* – For the first year of the SEIS, an effective 'CGT holiday' is available. Gains accruing to an investor in 2012–13, which are realised on the disposal of assets in that tax year and reinvested through SEIS in the same year (ie where the individual has made a qualifying SEIS investment for income tax purposes, and has claimed that relief) are treated as not being chargeable gains for CGT purposes upon making a claim, where certain conditions are satisfied. SEIS reinvestment relief is subject to restriction, including where the amount invested under SEIS exceeds the £100,000 maximum on which an individual can obtain income tax relief in any one tax year.

VENTURE CAPITAL TRUSTS (VCT)

(ITA 2007, Pt 6)

VCT relief annual limit

(ITA 2007, ss 262–263)

Shares issued	Maximum annual investment	Rate of relief
From 6 April 2006	£200,000	30%
From 6 April 2004	£200,000	40%
From 6 April 2000	£100,000	20%

Notes

(1) *Income tax relief* – VCT income tax relief is given for the tax year in which the shares are issued by the VCT. The relief available is the lower of 30% (from 6 April 2006) on amounts up to the above maximum, and the amount which reduces the individual's income tax liability to nil.

(2) *Dividend exemption* – Individual investors are exempt from income tax on dividends in respect of ordinary VCT shares acquired with the above maximum amounts, provided that the shares were acquired for genuine commercial reasons and not for a tax avoidance purpose *(ITTOIA 2005, Pt 6, Ch 5)*.

(3) *CGT exemption* – Disposals of VCT shares by individual investors are exempt from CGT (and losses are not allowable) where the shares were acquired within the above permitted maximum amounts, and if certain other conditions are satisfied *(TCGA 1992, ss 151A, 151B)*.

LEASE PREMIUMS

Short leases

(ITTOIA 2005, s 277; CTA 2009, s 217)

$$P \times \frac{(50 - Y)}{50}$$

Where–

P is the premium, and

Y is the number of complete periods of 12 months (other than the first) comprised in the effective duration of the lease.

5   *Pensions, Investment income etc*

Notes

(1)   A short lease is broadly a lease with 50 years or less to run.

(2)   The amount calculated using the above formula is treated as a property business receipt for the tax year or accounting period in which the lease is granted.

(3)   The amount of the premium for the grant of a short lease which is brought into account as a property business receipt is deducted from the consideration taken into account for capital gains purposes, in accordance with *TCGA 1992, Sch 8, paras 5, 7*.

(4)   The percentage of short lease premium charged as a property business receipt and taken into account for capital gains purposes are summarised in the table below (see *PIM1205*):

Length of lease in years	Percentage of premium taxable as receipt of property business	Percentage of premium chargeable as a capital gain
More than 50	0	100
50	2	98
49	4	96
48	6	94
47	8	92
46	10	90
45	12	88
44	14	86
43	16	84
42	18	82
41	20	80
40	22	78
39	24	76
38	26	74
37	28	72
36	30	70
35	32	68
34	34	66
33	36	64
32	38	62
31	40	60
30	42	58
29	44	56
28	46	54
27	48	52
26	50	50
25	52	48
24	54	46
23	56	44

Relief for premiums paid

Length of lease in years	Percentage of premium taxable as receipt of property business	Percentage of premium chargeable as a capital gain
22	58	42
21	60	40
20	62	38
19	64	36
18	66	34
17	68	32
16	70	30
15	72	28
14	74	26
13	76	24
12	78	22
11	80	20
10	82	18
9	84	16
8	86	14
7	88	12
6	90	10
5	92	8
4	94	6
3	96	4
2	98	2
1 or less	100	0

Leases which are wasting assets

(*TCGA 1992, Sch 8, para 1*)

A short lease is a wasting asset. The allowable expenditure attributable to a short lease therefore reduces over its term. The rate at which the expenditure is written off is fixed in accordance with the table in *TCGA 1992, Sch 8, para 1* (see **Capital Gains Tax**).

RELIEF FOR PREMIUMS PAID

(*ITTOIA 2005, s 61; CTA 2009, s 63*)

(a) Tenant occupies the whole of the land

$$\frac{A}{TRP}$$

Where:

A is the unreduced amount of the taxed receipt; and

TRP is the number of days in the receipt period of the taxed receipt.

(b) Tenant occupies part of the land

$$\frac{F \times A}{TRP}$$

Where:

F is the fraction of the land occupied (calculated on a just and reasonable basis); and

A and TRP have the same meaning as in (a) above.

Notes

(1) In the case of land used in a trade, the income element of a short lease premium is allowable as a deduction from the tenant's business profits for income tax or corporation tax purposes. The above formulae are used to calculate the allowable proportion of the 'taxed receipt' (broadly the amount of the lease taxed on the landlord as a rental business receipt) available as a deduction for the tenant. Relief is also available if the land is sub-let.

(2) The formula in (a) above is relevant if the tenant occupies the whole of the land for trading purposes. The formula in (b) applies if only part of the land is so used.

'SETTLEMENTS' AND CHILDREN

(ITTOIA 2005, s 629)

- The 'settlements' anti-avoidance provisions apply to the income of a relevant child, which would otherwise be income of the settlor. A 'relevant child' is the settlor's minor child (including a stepchild), who is neither married nor in a civil partnership. The child's income is deemed to be that of the parent for income tax purposes.
- However, if the child's settlement income from the parent does not exceed £100, the legislation does not apply in that tax year. This £100 limit for the tax year applies separately to each parent.

COMMUNITY INVESTMENT TAX RELIEF (CITR)

(ITA 2007, Pt 7; CTA 2010, Pt 7)

- CITR applies to investments in accredited Community Development Finance Institutions (CDFIs) made on or after 17 January 2002. Investing individuals (or companies) can claim tax relief of up to 25% of the amount of the investment. To obtain maximum relief under the scheme, the investment must be held for at least five years (or accounting periods).
- The tax relief is spread over the five-year term of the investment, giving tax relief of 5% of the 'invested amount' per year *(ITA 2007, s 335(2); CTA 2010, s 220(3))*
- CITR is given as a reduction in the investor's tax liability, and is limited to the amount of that liability (ie it cannot reduce a liability below zero).
- Relief is claimed for the tax year or accounting period in which the investment falls and the four subsequent tax years or accounting periods *(ITA 2007, s 335(3); CTA 2010, s 220(4))*.

- The 'invested amount' in the case of loans is determined as follows (*ITA 2007, s 337(2); CTA 2010, s 222(2)*):
  - Tax year of investment – the average capital balance for the first year of the five-year period;
  - Next tax year – the average capital balance for the second year of the five-year period;
  - Subsequent years – the average capital balance for the 12–month period beginning with the anniversary of the investment date in the tax year (or accounting period) (or if less, the average capital balance for the six months beginning 18 months after the investment date).
- The conditions to be satisfied in relation to a loan include that the loan must not have been made on terms that allow repayments as follows (*ITA 2007, s 345(3); CTA 2010, s 226(3)*):
  - During the first two years of the five year period – any of the loan capital advanced;
  - During the third year – more than 25% of the loan capital outstanding at the end of those two years;
  - Before the end of the fourth year – more than 50% of that loan capital;
  - Before the end of the period – more than 75% of that loan capital.
- CITR is a notified State aid and has clearance until October 2012. The Budget 2011 announced that re-notification to the European Commission would be undertaken to ensure continuance of the scheme.
- The Government has announced that it will bring forward legislation in the *Finance Bill 2013* which, from April 2013, will relax the CITR on-lending requirements that currently place conditions on the speed with which Community Development Finance Institutions must on-lend the funding they receive, and will introduce new rules to allow investors to carry unused relief forward (Budget, 21 March 2012).

TIME LIMITS – ASSESSMENTS, CLAIMS ETC

Normal time limits (individuals) – Direct taxes

(*TMA 1970, ss 34, 43; FA 2008, s 118, Sch 39*)

Tax year	Claim by
2006–07	5 April 2011
2007–08	5 April 2012
2008–09	5 April 2013
2009–10	5 April 2014
2010–11	5 April 2015
2011–12	5 April 2016
2012–13	5 April 2017

5 Pensions, Investment income etc

Notes

(1) Claims or elections should be made on the tax return or by an amendment to the return. Except where otherwise specified, a relief claim for income tax and capital gains purposes must be made within 4 years after the end of the tax year (or accounting period, for companies). This time limit generally applies for direct tax purposes from 1 April 2010 (but see **Time limits for assessments and claims – Direct taxes** below).

(2) The time limit for claims by individuals prior to April 2010 was generally within 5 years from 31 January following the year of assessment to which it relates (unless otherwise specified).

Time limits for assessments and claims – Direct taxes

(SI 2009/403)

Date claim or HMRC assessment made	Persons within SA – How far claims and HMRC assessments may go back	Persons not within SA – How far HMRC assessments may go back	Persons not within SA – How far claims may go back
1 February 2009–31 January 2010	2003–04	2003–04	2003–04
1 February 2010–31 March 2010	2004–05	2004–05	2004–05
1 April 2010–5 April 2010	2005–06	2005–06	2004–05
6 April 2010–31 January 2011	2006–07	2006–07	2004–05
1 February 2011–5 April 2011	2006–07	2006–07	2005–06
6 April 2011–31 January 2012	2007–08	2007–08	2005–06
1 February 2012–31 March 2012	2007–08	2007–08	2006–07
1 April 2012–5 April 2012	2007–08	2007–08	2007–08
6 April 2012–5 April 2013	2008–09	2008–09	2008–09

Notes

(1) The table shows the time limits for claims and assessments in relation to those who are within the self-assessment regime, and those who are not (*HMRC Compliance Handbook CH51560*).

(2) The 'appointed day' for the introduction of the new time limits for assessments and claims etc is extended to 1 April 2012 in certain circumstances (*SI 2009/403, art 10(2)*). The above transitional provisions relate to individuals, not companies.

6

Taxation of business profits

TAX SIMPLIFICATION FOR SMALL BUSINESSES

Following the Office of Tax Simplification review of small business taxation (see www.hm-treasury.gov.uk/ots.htm), the Government will consult on introducing a voluntary cash accounting basis for unincorporated businesses up to the VAT registration threshold (see Chapter 12), with a view to introducing legislation in the *Finance Bill 2013*. It will also consult on a simplified expenses system for business use of cars, motorcycles and home. The Government will also consult on proposals to introduce a disincorporation relief to assess the potential demand for such a relief as well as the practicalities of how it would work (Budget, 21 March 2012).

The simplified reporting requirement (three line accounts) for the income tax Self Assessment return will continue to be aligned with the VAT registration threshold (Budget, 21 March 2012).

FARMERS, MARKET GARDENERS AND CREATIVE ARTISTS – RELIEF FOR FLUCTUATING PROFITS

(*ITTOIA 2005, Pt 2, Ch 16; BIM73000 et seq; HMRC Help Sheets HS224, HS234*)

General

(1) Special relief is available to individuals and partnerships engaged in farming, market gardening, the intensive rearing in the UK of livestock or fish on a commercial basis for human food production, or individuals who personally create literary or artistic works, to take account of fluctuating profits. The averaging rules do not apply to farming activities carried on by a company.

(2) Profit averaging for creative artists is similar to that applicable for farmers. The relief is available to a taxpayer carrying on a trade or profession on profits wholly or mainly derived from qualifying creative works, ie literary, dramatic, musical or artistic works or designs created by the taxpayer, or one or more of the partners personally where the business is carried on in partnership.

(3) Claims are made in the self assessment return for the later year. An averaging claim must normally be made not later than 12 months after 31 January following the later of the two years to be averaged. However, the time limit may be extended if profits are adjusted for some other reason (*ITTOIA 2005, s 222(6)*; see *BIM73155*).

Full averaging

(4) If relevant profits for two consecutive years of assessment are such that one year's profits do not exceed 70% of the profits of the other year, or if relevant profits for

6 Taxation of business profits

one of the tax years is nil, the effect of a claim is broadly to aggregate the profits for the two years and treat one half of the total as the assessable profit for each year.

(5) An averaging claim requires relevant profits of one of two consecutive tax years to be less than 75% of the profits of the other, or the profits for one of the years to be nil. If the lower profit figure is between 70% and 75% of the higher profit figure, marginal relief may apply.

Marginal relief

(6) If the profits for one year exceed 70% of the profits for the other, but are less than 75% of those profits, marginal relief is available. Marginal relief is calculated as follows (*ITTOIA 2005, s 223(4)*):

Step 1 – Calculate the adjustment, using the following formula:

$$(D \times 3) - (P \times 0.75)$$

where: D is the difference between the relevant profits for the two years; and

P is the higher relevant profits of the two years

Step 2 – Add the adjustment to the relevant profits of the tax year of which those profits are lower.

Step 3 – Deduct the adjustment from the relevant profits of the tax year of which those profits are higher.

(7) A trading loss is treated as a nil profit for averaging purposes.

CAR HIRE COSTS

(*ITTOIA 2005 s 48; CTA 2009, ss 56, 1251(2); BIM47714 et seq*)

(1) For leases commencing on 1 April 2009 (for corporation tax) or 6 April 2009 (for income tax), the amount of deduction which would otherwise be allowable is reduced by 15% if CO_2 emissions exceed 160g/km.

(2) The above restriction does not apply to cars first registered before 1 March 2001, cars with low CO_2 emissions, electrically propelled cars and qualifying hire cars.

(3) Prior to 1 or 6 April 2009, the restricted deduction for hire charges of motor cars with a retail price of more than £12,000 was calculated as follows:

$$\frac{£12{,}000 + \tfrac{1}{2}\,(\text{retail price} - £12{,}000)}{\text{retail price}} \times \text{hire charge}$$

TIME LIMITS FOR CLAIMS AND ELECTIONS

(*TMA 1970, s 43(1)*)

(1) Claims must be made on the tax return or by an amendment to the return. Except where another period is expressly prescribed, a claim for relief in respect of income

Time limits for claims and elections

tax must be within four years after the end of the tax year. Prior to April 2010, the time limit for a claim was five years from 31 January following the year of assessment to which it relates.

(2) Following the changes to time limits for assessments and claims introduced in *FA 2008, Sch 39*, transitional rules apply to taxpayers who are outside the self assessment regime (*SI 2009/403*; see *CH51560*).

(3) Specific exceptions in respect of business profits and losses include the following:

Provision	Time limit
Averaging of profits of farmers or creative artists (*ITTIOA 2005, s 222(5)*)	First anniversary of the normal self-assessment filing date for the second tax year
Stock transferred to a connected party on cessation of trade to be valued at higher of cost or sale price (*ITTOIA 2005, s 178(4); CTA 2009, s 167(4)*)	(a) Individuals – First anniversary of the normal self-assessment filing date for the tax year of cessation (b) Companies – Two years after the end of the accounting period of cessation
Herd basis (*ITTOIA 2005, s 124(2); CTA 2009, s 122(2)*)	(a) Individuals – First anniversary of the normal self-assessment filing date in which the first relevant period of account ends (b) Companies – Two years after the end of the relevant accounting period
Change of accounting date (*ITTOIA 2005, s 217(2)*)	Filing date for the relevant tax return
Post-cessation relief (*ITTOIA 2005, s 257(4); ITA 2007, s 96(4)*)	First anniversary of the normal self-assessment filing date for the tax year
Furnished holiday lettings: averaging of under-used holiday accommodation (*ITTOIA 2005, s 326(6)*)	First anniversary of normal self-assessment filing date for the tax year
Current and preceding year set-off of trading losses (*ITA 2007, s 64(5)*)	First anniversary of the normal self-assessment filing date for the loss-making year
Three year carry back of trading losses in opening years of trade (*ITA 2007, s 72(3)*)	First anniversary of the normal self-assessment filing date for the tax year in which the loss is made
Relief for trade etc losses against capital gains of the year in which the loss was made or the previous year (*TCGA 1992, s 261B(8)*)	First anniversary of the normal self-assessment filing date for the tax year in which the loss was made

7

Taxation of companies

RATES OF CORPORATION TAX

(*CTA 2010, Pt 2, Ch 2, 3; Pt 3*)

	Financial Year commencing 1 April		
	2012	2011	2010
Small Profits Rate	20%	20%	21%
Small Profits Rate can be claimed by qualifying companies with profits at a rate not exceeding	£300,000	£300,000	£300,000
Marginal Relief Lower Limit	£300,000	£300,000	£300,000
Marginal Relief Upper Limit	£1,500,000	£1,500,000	£1,500,000
Standard fraction	1/100	3/200	7/400
Main rate of Corporation Tax	24%	26%	28%
	2009	2008	2007	2006
Small Profits Rate	21%	21%	20%	19%
Small Profits Rate can be claimed by qualifying companies with profits at a rate not exceeding	£300,000	£300,000	£300,000	£300,000
Marginal Relief Lower Limit	£300,000	£300,000	£300,000	£300,000
Marginal Relief Upper Limit	£1,500,000	£1,500,000	£1,500,000	£1,500,000
Standard fraction	7/400	7/400	1/40	11/400
Main rate of Corporation Tax	28%	28%	30%	30%

Notes

(1) Prior to a change in terminology from 1 April 2010, the 'Small Profits Rate' was known as the 'Small Companies' Rate', 'Marginal Relief' as 'Marginal Small Companies' Relief', and 'Standard fraction' as 'Marginal Small Companies' Relief fraction'.

(2) The Government has announced that the main rate of corporation tax will fall by 2% from 26% to 24% in April 2012, and then to 23% in April 2013 and to 22% in April 2014 (Budget, 21 March 2012).

(3) Legislation will be introduced in *Finance Bill 2012* to introduce the Patent Box, allowing companies to elect for a 10% rate of corporation tax from 1 April 2013 on all profits attributable to qualifying intellectual property (see **Patent Box** below).

Marginal relief

(4) The lower and upper limits for the Small Profits Rate and marginal relief purposes are reduced proportionately for accounting periods of less than 12 months. The limits are also divided by the number of associated companies carrying on a trade or business for all or part of the accounting period *(CTA 2010, s 25)*. The Small Profits Rate does not apply to 'Close Investment Holding Companies' *(CTA 2010, s 18(b))*.

(5) A special rate of tax applies to unit trusts and open-ended investment companies. In such cases, the tax rate for the financial year is the basic income tax rate charged for the tax year beginning on 6 April in that financial year *(CTA 2010, ss 614, 618)*. For financial years 2008 to 2012 the applicable tax rate is 20%.

(6) For companies with ring fence profits from oil-related activities, the Small Profits Rate for financial years 2007 to 2012 is 19% and the ring fence fraction is 11/400 *(FA 2011, s 6)*. The main rate of tax for ring fence profits for financial years 2008 to 2013 is 30%.

(7) Marginal Starting Rate Relief was available for accounting periods starting after 31 March 2000 and ending before 1 April 2006, for companies with taxable profits at an annual rate of between £10,001 and £50,000. For financial year 2005, the starting rate was 0%, and the marginal relief fraction was 19/400.

EFFECTIVE MARGINAL RATES FOR SMALL PROFITS

(CTA 2010, s 19)

Financial Year (Commencing 1 April)	Marginal Small Profits Rate %
2012	25.00
2011	27.50
2010	29.75
2009	29.75
2008	29.75
2007	32.50
2006	32.75

MARGINAL RELIEF

(CTA 2010, s 19)

The corporation tax charged on the company's taxable total profits of the accounting period is reduced by an amount equal to–

$$F \times (U - A) \times \frac{N}{A}$$

Where:

F is the standard fraction,

U is the upper limit,

A is the amount of the augmented profits, and

N is the amount of the taxable total profits.

7 *Taxation of companies*

Notes

(1) 'The standard fraction' means the fraction set by Parliament (*CTA 2010, s 19(3)*) (3/200 for financial year 2011, and 1/100 proposed for 2012).

(2) 'Augmented Profits' is defined as the company's taxable total profits plus any franked investment income received by the company, excluding any franked investment income received by the company from a company which is a 51% subsidiary of the receiving company or a company of which the receiving company is a 51% subsidiary, or from a trading company or relevant holding company that is a quasi-subsidiary of the receiving company. A 'quasi-subsidiary' is a company owned by a consortium of which the recipient company is a member, which is not a 75% subsidiary of any company, where no arrangements exist for it to become a 75% subsidiary of any company (*CTA 2010, ss 32, 33*).

PATENT BOX

(*CTA 2010, Part 8A, as inserted by FB 2012, cl 19, Sch 2*)

- Companies may elect for a special corporation tax rate of 10% to apply to profits attributable to qualifying patents and certain other intellectual property (IP).
- The patent box provisions ('Profits arising from the exploitation of patents etc') apply with effect in relation to accounting periods beginning on or after 1 April 2013, subject to transitional rules.

Notes

(1) *General* – An election is required for the special rate of corporation tax to apply, which is given effect by granting a deduction from trading profits of an amount that gives the same result as reducing the main rate of corporation tax on eligible profits to the lower IP rate of 10%. The legislation provides a formula to calculate the deduction (*CTA 2010, s 357A*).

(2) *Time limit* – The above election must be made (or revoked) by giving notice to HMRC specifying the first accounting period to which it relates, no later than the date by which an amended corporation tax return could be made under *FA 1998, Sch 18, para 15* (*CTA 2010, ss 357G, 357GA*).

(3) *Qualifying companies* – The above election is available to 'qualifying companies' as defined, ie broadly in terms of satisfying a specified ownership requirement in relation to a 'qualifying IP right,' or an 'exclusive licence' in respect of a qualifying IP right (*CTA 2010, Pt 8A, Ch 2*).

(4) *Relevant IP profits* – The 'relevant IP profits' of the trade are those used in the formula mentioned above. The steps necessary to determine the relevant IP profits are set out in the legislation. The legislation also provides for an election (ie a 'streaming' election) to apply an alternative basis for calculating relevant IP profits of the trade (*CTA 2010, Pt 8A, Chs 3, 4*).

(5) *Miscellaneous* – The 'patent box' regime includes provisions dealing with the set-off of amounts in respect of 'relevant IP losses' (eg by matching with relevant IP profits of another trade of the company, or of a later accounting period) for which *CTA 2010, s 357A* would be entitled to a deduction from profits of the trade, subject to transitional rules for the financial years 2013 to 2016. The regime is also subject to anti-avoidance provisions (*CTA 2010, Pt 8A, Chs 5, 6*).

LOANS TO PARTICIPATORS

(CTA 2010, s 455)

- A charge to tax apples if a close company makes a loan or advances money to an individual (or to a company receiving the loan or advance in a fiduciary or representative capacity) who is a participator or an associate of a participator in the company.
- The charge is 25% of the amount of the loan or advance, which is treated as an amount of corporation tax chargeable for the accounting period in which the loan or advance is made.
- The tax, or a proportionate part of it, need not be paid if the loan or advance or part of it has been repaid, released or written off before the tax becomes payable. Where the loan or advance is subsequently repaid, released or written off, there are provisions for the tax to be repaid *(CTA 2010, s 458)*.

BANK PAYROLL TAX

(FA 2010, s 22 and Sch 1)

- Bank payroll tax (BPT) was a one-off tax charge payable by taxable companies such as banks and building societies on the relevant remuneration' of certain employees.
- A fixed BPT rate of 50% was payable on bonuses exceeding £25,000 awarded to relevant banking employees between 12.30pm on 9 December 2009 and 5 April 2010.
- 'Relevant remuneration' for these purposes excludes regular salary or benefits, shares under certain specified share schemes and payments under contractual obligations that arose before 12.30pm on 9 December 2009.
- The tax was due for payment by 31 August 2010. This was also the due date for delivery of a bank payroll tax return to HMRC.

FILING DATES FOR COMPANY TAX RETURNS

(FA 1998, Sch 18, para 14)

The filing date for a company tax return is the later of the following periods:

(a) 12 months from the end of the return period;

(b) If the company's relevant period of account is less than 18 months, 12 months from the end of that period;

(c) If the company's relevant period of account is longer than 18 months, 30 months from the beginning of that period; or

(d) 3 months from the date of a notice by HMRC to deliver the return.

Note

'Relevant period of account' in relation to a return for an accounting period is defined as the period of account of the company in which the last day of that accounting period falls.

7   *Taxation of companies*

DUE AND PAYABLE DATES

(TMA 1970, ss 59D, 59E, 59G–H; SI 1998/3175; ITA 2007, Pt 15, Ch 15; CTA 2010, s 455(3))

Liability	Due Date
Mainstream corporation tax	9 months and 1 day following the end of the accounting period
Mainstream corporation tax in instalments:	See note (2) below
Income tax on interest, annual payments etc.	14 days after end of return period
Charge on loans to participators in close companies	9 months and 1 day after the end of the accounting period in which the loan or advance was made.

Notes

(1) *Managed payment plans* – For corporation tax accounting periods ending from 1 April 2010, provision is made for companies to enter into managed payment plans with HMRC (see *TMA 1970, s 59G*). However, the Government announced in 2010 that this facility would not be introduced for the time being (Budget, 22 June 2010).

(2) *Instalment payments* – Large companies are liable to pay corporation tax in instalments, in accordance with *TMA 1970, s 59E* and *SI 1998/3175*. A 'large' company is one with taxable profits exceeding £1.5m a year, divided by 1 plus the number of any active associated companies. A company is not large for these purposes if its profits are £10,000 or less (reduced proportionately for accounting periods of less than 12 months). In addition, a company is not large if its profits for the accounting period are £10m or less and it was not a large company in the 12 months preceding that accounting period.

The instalment provisions set out the following formula to calculate the amount of the instalments (*SI 1998/3175, regs 5–8*):

$$3 \times CTI/n$$

where

CTI is broadly the amount of the company's total liability for that accounting period; and

n is the number of whole months in the accounting period, plus the 'appropriate decimal' (ie broadly the proportion of a whole 30-day month, rounded to 2 decimal places).

The due dates for the instalment payments are as follows:

1st instalment – 6 months and 13 days from the start of the accounting period (or date of final instalment, if earlier);

2nd instalment (if applicable) – 3 months after 1st instalment;

3rd instalment (if applicable) – 3 months after 2nd instalment; and

final instalment – 3 months and 14 days from the end of the accounting period.

(3) *Income tax on interest, annual payments etc* – Return periods end on 31 March, 30 June, 30 September, 31 December and at the end of an accounting period.

(4) Charge on loans to participators in close companies – Tax is not payable in respect of any loan or advance repaid before the due date.

PENALTIES

(FA 1998, Sch 18; FA 2007, s 97, Sch 24; FA 2008, s 113, Sch 36, s 123, Sch 41)

Offence	Maximum penalty
Failure to notify chargeability	
(FA 2008, s 123; Sch 41, paras 1, 6, 6A; SI 2009/511)	
• Deliberate and concealed act or failure	100% of potential lost revenue
• Deliberate but not concealed act or failure	70% of potential lost revenue
• Any other case	30% of potential lost revenue
Failure to deliver a return	*Flat rate penalty*
(FA 1998, Sch 18, paras 17, 18)	
• Up to 3 months after filing date	£100
	Persistent failure, ie a third successive failure £500
• More than 3 months after filing date	A further £100
	Persistent failure (see above)
	A further £500
	Tax related penalty
• At least 18 months but less than 24 months after end of return period	10% of tax unpaid at 18 months after end of return period
• 24 months or more after end of return period	A further 10% of tax unpaid at 18 months after end of return period
Errors in returns etc	
(FA 2007, s 97; Sch 24, para 4; SI 2008/568)	
• Reasonable care taken	No penalty liability
• Careless inaccuracy	30% of potential lost revenue
• Deliberate but not concealed inaccuracy	70% of potential lost revenue
• Deliberate and concealed inaccuracy	100% of potential lost revenue
Failure to keep and preserve records	Up to £3,000
(FA 1998, Sch 18, para 23)	
Failure to comply with information notice, or obstruction during an inspection	
(FA 2008, s 113, Sch 36, paras 39, 40, 50)	
• Initial failure	£300
• Continued failure	Up to £60 per day
• Continued failure where significant tax is at risk	Penalty may be decided by the Upper Tribunal (See Note 4)
Inaccurate information and documents	Up to £3,000 for each inaccuracy
(FA 2008, Sch 36, para 40A)	

continued

7 Taxation of companies

Offence	Maximum penalty
Failure to notify coming within the charge to corporation tax within 3 months of first accounting period – repealed from 1 April 2010 (*FA 2008, Sch 41, para 25(a)(ii)*) (*FA 2004, s 55; TMA 1970, s 98*)	Up to £300 Up to £60 per day for continued failure
Quarterly Instalment Payments **('Large' companies)** • Deliberate or reckless failure to pay the correct amount on an instalment date; • Fraudulent or negligent claim for repayment (under reg 6(2) of the instalment regulations) (*TMA 1970, s 59E(4); SI 1998/3175, reg 13*)	Up to twice the amount of interest charged on any unpaid amount in respect of the company's total liability for the accounting period

Notes

(1) *Failure to notify* – The failure to notify chargeability provisions took effect from 1 April 2010 (nb penalties were previously charged under *FA 1998, Sch 18, para 2(3)*, up to a maximum of 100% of tax payable for the accounting period and remaining unpaid 12 months after the end of the period).

(2) *Failure to make returns etc* – A new fixed and tax related penalty regime will apply for the late filing of corporation tax returns from a date to be specified by Treasury Order (*FA 2009, s 106, Sch 55*).

(3) *Failure to deliver a return* – The above flat rate penalties do not apply if the return period is one for which the company must deliver accounts under the Companies Act 2006, and the return is filed by the date allowed by Companies House (*FA 1998, Sch 18, para 19*). This has no effect on the tax geared penalties which may arise.

(4) *Information notices and inspections* – In relation to a failure to comply with an information notice, or a deliberate obstruction during an inspection:

    (a) A penalty for obstruction is only due in relation to an inspection which has been approved by the tribunal.

    (b) If the failure or obstruction continues after an initial penalty is charged (under *FA 2008, Sch 36, para 39*), an additional tax-related penalty can be imposed if an HMRC officer has reason to believe that the failure or obstruction may result in a significant loss of tax. However, HMRC must first apply to the Upper Tribunal for the imposition of the additional penalty (see *FA 2008, Sch 36, para 50*).

INTEREST ON OVERDUE TAX

(TMA 1970, ss 87, 87A, 109; SI 1998/3175, reg 7)

Description	Interest runs from
Corporation tax	Due and payable date
Corporation tax payable in instalments	Date instalment is due to be paid
Overdue income tax deducted from certain payments	14 days after end of return period
Overdue tax on loans to participators of close companies	Due and payable date

Notes

(1) *Interest harmonisation* – Following the introduction of a harmonised interest regime in respect of most underpaid and overpaid taxes and duties in *FA 2009*, legislation (in *F(No 3)A 2010, s 25, Sch 9*) makes amendments to *FA 2009* to bring corporation tax (and petroleum revenue tax) into the harmonised interest regime, from a date to be appointed by Treasury Order.

(2) *Surrender of tax refund within a group (CTA 2010, ss 963, 964)* – A group company which is due a tax refund for an accounting period may surrender it to another group member, if both companies give notice to HMRC. The effect is that the recipient company is generally treated as having paid the tax when the surrendering company paid it (or on the due and payable date for the surrendering company, if paid earlier).

INTEREST ON OVERDUE CORPORATION TAX

CTSA (accounting periods ending from 1 July 1999)

Unpaid corporation tax (not underpaid instalments)

From	%
29 September 2009	3.0
24 March 2009 to 28 September 2009	2.5
27 January 2009 to 23 March 2009	3.5
6 January 2009 to 26 January 2009	4.5
6 December 2008 to 5 January 2009	5.5
6 November 2008 to 5 December 2008	6.5
6 January 2008 to 5 November 2008	7.5
6 August 2007 to 5 January 2008	8.5
6 September 2006 to 5 August 2007	7.5
6 September 2005 to 5 September 2006	6.5
6 September 2004 to 5 September 2005	7.5
6 December 2003 to 5 September 2004	6.5
6 August 2003 to 5 December 2003	5.5
6 November 2001 to 5 August 2003	6.5
6 May 2001 to 5 November 2001	7.5
6 February 2000 to 5 May 2001	8.5

7 Taxation of companies

Underpaid instalments (Accounting periods ending from 1 July 1999)

From	%
16 March 2009	1.50
16 February 2009 to 15 March 2009	2.00
19 January 2009 to 15 February 2009	2.50
15 December 2008 to 18 January 2009	3.00
17 November 2008 to 14 December 2008	4.00
20 October 2008 to 16 November 2008	5.50
21 April 2008 to 19 October 2008	6.00
18 February 2008 to 20 April 2008	6.25
17 December 2007 to 17 February 2008	6.50
16 July 2007 to 16 December 2007	6.75
21 May 2007 to 15 July 2007	6.50
22 January 2007 to 20 May 2007	6.25
20 November 2006 to 21 January 2007	6.00
14 August 2006 to 19 November 2006	5.75
15 August 2005 to 13 August 2006	5.50
16 August 2004 to 14 August 2005	5.75
21 June 2004 to 15 August 2004	5.50
17 May 2004 to 20 June 2004	5.25
16 February 2004 to 16 May 2004	5.00
17 November 2003 to 15 February 2004	4.75
21 July 2003 to 16 November 2003	4.50
17 February 2003 to 20 July 2003	4.75
19 November 2001 to 16 February 2003	5.00
15 October 2001 to 18 November 2001	5.50
1 October 2001 to 14 October 2001	5.75
13 August 2001 to 30 September 2001	6.00
21 May 2001 to 12 August 2001	6.25
16 April 2001 to 20 May 2001	6.50
19 February 2001 to 15 April 2001	6.75
20 April 2000 to 18 February 2001	7.00
21 February 2000 to 19 April 2000	8.00
24 January 2000 to 20 February 2000	7.75
15 November 1999 to 23 January 2000	7.50
20 September 1999 to 14 November 1999	7.25
21 June 1999 to 19 September 1999	7.00
19 April 1999 to 20 June 1999	7.25
15 February 1999 to 18 April 1999	7.50
18 January 1999 to 14 February 1999	8.00
1 January 1999 to 17 January 1999	8.25

Interest on overdue corporation tax

Corporation tax pay and file

From	%
29 September 2009	3.00%
24 March 2009 to 29 September 2009	1.75%
27 January 2009 to 23 March 2009	2.75%
6 January 2009 to 26 January 2009	3.50%
6 December 2008 to 25 January 2009	4.25%
6 November 2008 to 5 December 2008	5.00%
6 January 2008 to 5 November 2008	6.00%
6 August 2007 to 5 January 2008	6.75%
6 September 2006 to 5 August 2007	6.00%
6 September 2005 to 5 September 2006	5.25%
6 September 2004 to 5 September 2005	6.00%
6 December 2003 to 5 September 2004	5.25%
6 August 2003 to 5 December 2003	4.25%
6 November 2001 to 5 August 2003	5.00%
6 May 2001 to 5 November 2001	6.00%
6 February 2000 to 5 May 2001	6.75%

Corporation tax pre pay and file

From	%
29 September 2009	3.00%
24 March 2009 to 28 September 2009	2.00%
27 January 2009 to 23 March 2009	2.75%
6 January 2009 to 26 January 2009	3.50%
6 December 2008 to 5 January 2009	4.25%
6 November 2008 to 5 December 2008	5.00%
6 January 2008 to 5 November 2008	5.75%
6 August 2007 to 5 January 2008	6.50%
6 September 2006 to 5 August 2007	5.75%
6 September 2005 to 5 September 2006	5.00%
6 September 2004 to 5 September 2005	5.75%
6 December 2003 to 5 September 2004	5.00%
6 August 2003 to 5 December 2003	4.25%
6 November 2001 to 5 August 2003	5.00%
6 May 2001 to 5 November 2001	5.75%
6 February 2000 to 5 May 2001	6.50%

7 *Taxation of companies*

INTEREST ON TAX REPAYMENTS

(*TA 1988, s 826; SI 1998/3175, reg 8*)

CTSA (accounting periods ending from 1 July 1999)

Overpaid corporation tax

From	%
29 September 2009	0.50
27 January 2009 to 28 September 2009	0.00
6 January 2009 to 26 January 2009	1.00
6 December 2008 to 5 January 2009	2.00
6 November 2008 to 5 December 2008	3.00
6 January 2008 to 5 November 2008	4.00
6 August 2007 to 5 January 2008	5.00
6 September 2006 to 5 August 2007	4.00
6 September 2005 to 5 September 2006	3.00
6 September 2004 to 5 September 2005	4.00
6 December 2003 to 5 September 2004	3.00
6 August 2003 to 5 December 2003	2.00
6 November 2001 to 5 August 2003	3.00
6 May 2001 to 5 November 2001	4.00
6 February 2000 to 5 May 2001	5.00

Overpaid instalments and early payments not due by instalments

From	%
21 September 2009	0.50
16 March 2009 to 20 September 2009	0.25
16 February 2009 to 15 March 2009	0.75
19 January 2009 to 15 February 2009	1.25
15 December 2008 to 18 January 2009	1.75
17 November 2008 to 14 December 2008	2.75
20 October 2008 to 16 November 2008	4.25
21 April 2008 to 19 October 2008	4.75
18 February 2008 to 20 April 2008	5.00
17 December 2007 to 17 February 2008	5.25
16 July 2007 to 16 December 2007	5.50
21 May 2007 to 15 July 2007	5.25
22 January 2007 to 20 May 2007	5.00
20 November 2006 to 21 January 2007	4.75
14 August 2006 to 19 November 2006	4.50
15 August 2005 to 13 August 2006	4.25

Interest on tax repayments

From	%
16 August 2004 to 14 August 2005	4.50
21 June 2004 to 15 August 2004	4.25
17 May 2004 to 20 June 2004	4.00
16 February 2004 to 16 May 2004	3.75
17 November 2003 to 15 February 2004	3.50
21 July 2003 to 16 November 2003	3.25
17 February 2003 to 20 July 2003	3.50
19 November 2001 to 16 February 2003	3.75
15 October 2001 to 18 November 2001	4.25
1 October 2001 to 14 October 2001	4.50
13 August 2001 to 30 September 2001	4.75
21 May 2001 to 12 August 2001	5.00
16 April 2001 to 20 May 2001	5.25
19 February 2001 to 15 April 2001	5.50
21 February 2000 to 18 February 2001	5.75
24 January 2000 to 20 February 2000	5.50
15 November 1999 to 23 January 2000	5.25
20 September 1999 to 14 November 1999	5.00
21 June 1999 to 19 September 1999	4.75
19 April 1999 to 20 June 1999	5.00
15 February 1999 to 18 April 1999	5.25
18 January 1999 to 14 February 1999	5.75
1 January 1999 to 18 January 1999	6.00

Pay and file

From	%
29 September 2009	0.50
27 January 2009 to 28 September 2009	0.00
6 January 2009 to 26 January 2009	0.50
6 December 2008 to 5 January 2009	1.25
6 November 2008 to 5 December 2008	2.00
6 January 2008 to 5 November 2008	2.75
6 August 2007 to 5 January 2008	3.50
6 September 2006 to 5 August 2007	2.75
6 September 2005 to 5 September 2006	2.00
6 September 2004 to 5 September 2005	2.75
6 December 2003 to 5 September 2004	2.00
6 August 2003 to 5 December 2003	1.25
6 November 2001 to 5 August 2003	2.00
6 May 2001 to 5 November 2001	2.75
6 February 2000 to 5 May 2001	3.50

7 *Taxation of companies*

Pre pay and file

From	%
29 September 2009	0.50
24 March 2009 to 28 September 2009	2.00
27 January 2009 to 23 March 2009	2.75
6 January 2009 to 26 January 2009	3.50
6 December 2008 to 5 January 2009	4.25
6 November 2008 to 5 December 2008	5.00
6 January 2008 to 5 November 2008	5.75
6 August 2007 to 5 January 2008	6.50
6 September 2006 to 5 August 2007	5.75
6 September 2005 to 5 September 2006	5.00
6 September 2004 to 5 September 2005	5.75
6 December 2003 to 5 September 2004	5.00
6 August 2003 to 5 December 2003	4.25
6 November 2001 to 5 August 2003	5.00
6 May 2001 to 5 November 2001	5.75
6 February 2000 to 5 May 2001	6.50

TIME LIMITS FOR CLAIMS AND ELECTIONS

With effect from 1 April 2010 and subject to transitional provisions, a claim or election for corporation tax purposes must generally be made in writing within 4 years of the end of the accounting period to which it relates, ie in the absence of any provisions to the contrary (*FA 1998, Sch 18, para 55*, as amended by *FA 2008, s 118, Sch 39*; see also *SI 2009/403*). Previously, the general time limit was 6 years from the end of the accounting period.

Provision	Time limit
Appropriation of asset to trading stock: election to adjust trading profit by the amount of the gain or loss on the deemed disposal at market value (*TCGA 1992, s 161(3)*)	2 years from the end of the accounting period in which the asset is appropriated as trading stock
Reallocation of chargeable gain or an allowable loss within a group (*TCGA 1992, s 171A(5)*)	2 years from the end of the transferring company's accounting period in which the gain or loss accrues
Stock transferred to a connected person on the cessation of trade to be valued at higher of cost or selling price (*CTA 2009, s 167(4)*)	2 years from the end of the accounting period of cessation
Relief for trading losses against total profits of the same, or an earlier, accounting period (*CTA 2010, s 37(7)*)	2 years from the end of the loss making accounting period
Terminal loss relief on the cessation of trade (*CTA 2010, s 39*)	2 years from the end of the loss making accounting period

Time limits for claims and elections

Provision	Time limit
Carry-forward of trading losses (*CTA 2010, s 45*)	No formal claim necessary
Group relief (*FA 1998, Sch 18, para 74*)	Group relief claims must be made or withdrawn by the later of the following:
	(1) 12 months from the filing date for the claimant company's tax return for the accounting period of the claim;
	(2) 30 days after the completion of an enquiry into that return;
	(3) 30 days after the issue of a notice of amendment by HMRC following the completion of an enquiry; or
	(4) 30 days after the determination of any appeal against an HMRC amendment (in (3) above).
Capital allowances (FA 1988, Sch 18, para 82)	As for group relief (see above)
Surrender of company tax refund within group (*CTA 2010, s 963(3)*)	Before the refund is made to the surrendering company
Intangible fixed assets: election to write down cost for tax purposes at a fixed rate (*CTA 2009, s 730*)	2 years from the end of the accounting period in which the company creates or acquires the asset.
Set-off of loss on disposal of shares in unquoted trading company against income of investment company (*CTA 2010, s 70(4)*)	2 years from the end of the accounting period in which the loss was incurred.
Company distributions – election that distribution should not be treated as exempt (*CTA 2009, s 931R*)	Second anniversary of the end of the accounting period in which the distribution is received.
Relief for a non-trading deficit on loan relationships (including any non-trading exchange losses) (*CTA 2009, ss 458(2), 460(1)*)	• Claim to carry forward the deficit to later accounting periods – 2 years from the end of the accounting period following the deficit period.
	• Claim to set off deficit against profits of the deficit period or earlier periods – 2 years from end of period in which deficit arises.

Notes

(1) *Extended time limits* – In some cases, HMRC may allow a longer claim period at its discretion.

(2) *Temporary extension of loss relief carry back provisions* – the loss relief carry back period is extended from 12 months to 3 years, in respect of a trading loss incurred in an accounting period ending after 23 November 2008 and ending before 24 November 2010 (*FA 2009, Sch 6, para 3*).

7   *Taxation of companies*

(3)   *Group relief* – The above references to an enquiry do not include a restricted enquiry into an amendment of a return, (ie where the restriction arises because the time limit for enquiring into that return has expired), where the amendment consists of a group relief claim or the withdrawal of claim (*FA 1998, Sch 18, para 74(4)*).

INDEXATION ALLOWANCE
(*TCGA 1992, Ch IV*)

(a) Retail Prices Index (RPI) Table

	Jan	Feb	Mar	Apr	May	Jun	Jul	Aug	Sep	Oct	Nov	Dec
1982			79.44	81.04	81.62	81.85	81.88	81.90	81.85	82.26	82.66	82.51
1983	82.61	82.97	83.12	84.28	84.64	84.84	85.30	85.68	86.06	86.36	86.67	86.89
1984	86.84	87.20	87.48	88.64	88.97	89.20	89.10	89.94	90.11	90.67	90.95	90.87
1985	91.20	91.94	92.80	94.78	95.21	95.41	95.23	95.49	95.44	95.59	95.92	96.05
1986	96.25	96.60	96.73	97.67	97.85	97.79	97.52	97.82	98.30	98.45	99.29	99.62
1987	100.0	100.4	100.6	101.8	101.9	101.9	101.8	102.1	102.4	102.9	103.4	103.3
1988	103.3	103.7	104.1	105.8	106.2	106.6	106.7	107.9	108.4	109.5	110.0	110.3
1989	111.0	111.8	112.3	114.3	115.0	115.4	115.5	115.8	116.6	117.5	118.5	118.8
1990	119.5	120.2	121.4	125.1	126.2	126.7	126.8	128.1	129.3	130.3	130.0	129.9
1991	130.2	130.9	131.4	133.1	133.5	134.1	133.8	134.1	134.6	135.1	135.6	135.7
1992	135.6	136.3	136.7	138.8	139.3	139.3	138.8	138.9	139.4	139.9	139.7	139.2
1993	137.9	138.8	139.3	140.6	141.1	141.0	140.7	141.3	141.9	141.8	141.6	141.9
1994	141.3	142.1	142.5	144.2	144.7	144.7	144.0	144.7	145.0	145.2	145.3	146.0
1995	146.0	146.9	147.5	149.0	149.6	149.8	149.1	149.9	150.6	149.8	149.8	150.7
1996	150.2	150.9	151.5	152.6	152.9	153.0	152.4	153.1	153.8	153.8	153.9	154.4
1997	154.4	155.0	155.4	156.3	156.9	157.5	157.5	158.5	159.3	159.5	159.6	160.0
1998	159.5	160.3	160.8	162.6	163.5	163.4	163.0	163.7	164.4	164.5	164.4	164.4
1999	163.4	163.7	164.1	165.2	165.6	165.6	165.1	165.5	166.2	166.5	166.7	167.3
2000	166.6	167.5	168.4	170.1	170.7	171.1	170.5	170.5	171.7	171.6	172.1	172.2
2001	171.1	172.0	172.2	173.1	174.2	174.4	173.3	174.0	174.6	174.3	173.6	173.4
2002	173.3	173.8	174.5	175.7	176.2	176.2	175.9	176.4	177.6	177.9	178.2	178.5
2003	178.4	179.3	179.9	181.2	181.5	181.3	181.3	181.6	182.5	182.6	182.7	183.5
2004	183.1	183.8	184.6	185.7	186.5	186.8	186.8	187.4	188.1	188.6	189.0	189.9
2005	188.9	189.6	190.5	191.6	192.0	192.2	192.2	192.6	193.1	193.3	193.6	194.1
2006	193.4	194.2	195.0	196.5	197.7	198.5	198.5	199.2	200.1	200.4	201.1	202.7
2007	201.6	203.1	204.4	205.4	206.2	207.3	206.1	207.3	208.0	208.9	209.7	210.9
2008	209.8	211.4	212.1	214.0	215.1	216.8	216.5	217.2	218.4	217.7	216.0	212.9
2009	210.1	211.4	211.3	211.5	212.8	213.4	213.4	214.4	215.3	216.0	216.6	218.0
2010	217.9	219.2	220.7	222.8	223.6	224.1	223.6	224.5	225.3	225.8	226.8	228.4
2011	229.0	231.3	232.5	234.4	235.2	235.2	234.7	236.1	237.9	238.0	238.5	239.4
2012	238.0	239.9										

Acknowledgement: Office for National Statistics website: www.ons.gov.uk

(b) Indexation formula

The formula for calculating indexation factors is as follows (*TCGA 1992, s 54(1)*):

$$\frac{(RD - RI)}{RI}$$

Where:

RD is the RPI for the month of disposal; and

RI is the RPI for March 1982 (or the month in which the expenditure was incurred, if later).

The resulting figure is applied to each item of qualifying expenditure in the computation, by multiplying the expenditure by the relevant indexation factor as calculated.

Notes

(1) Indexation allowance applies to periods from March 1982 onwards. It is broadly an allowance for inflation, based on the indexed rise in allowable expenditure for capital gains purposes.

(2) Indexation allowance applies to companies within the charge to corporation tax (*TCGA 1992, s 52A*). The allowance is the aggregate of the indexed rise in each item of such expenditure. It can reduce an unindexed gain to nil, but cannot generally be applied to create or increase a loss (*s 53(1)*).

(3) Indexation allowance tables showing the indexed rise in respect of disposals taking place in particular months are published on the HMRC website:

www.hmrc.gov.uk/rates/cg-indexation-allowance/index.htm

(4) As to indexation allowance for individuals, trustees and personal representatives (for whom indexation allowance was abolished for disposals from 6 April 2008, and frozen for disposals between 6 April 1998 and 5 April 2008 (*TCGA 1992, s 54(1)*), see **Capital gains tax: Indexation allowance**.

8

Capital Gains Tax

RATES AND ANNUAL EXEMPTIONS
(TCGA 1992, ss 3, 4, Sch 1)

Tax Year	Annual exempt amount		Rate	
	Individuals, personal representatives (PR's) and trusts for mentally disabled £	General trusts £	Individuals %	Trustees and PR's %
2012–13	10,600	5,300		
– Standard rate			18	28
– Higher rate			28	
2011–12	10,600	5,300		
– Standard rate			18	28
– Higher rate			28	
2010–11 (23 June 2010 to 5 April 2011)	10,100 (whole tax year	5,050 (whole tax year)		
– Standard rate			18	28
– Higher rate			28	
2010–11 (6 April to 22 June 2010)	10,100 (whole tax year)	5,050 (whole tax year)	18	18
2009–10	10,100	5,050	18	18
2008–09	9,600	4,800	18	18
2007–08	9,200	4,600	10/20/40	40
2006–07	8,800	4,400	10/20/40	40

Notes

(1) From 2008–09, an individual who claims to use the remittance basis for a tax year is not entitled to the annual capital gains exemption for that year (*ITA 2007, s 809G*). However the annual exempt amount remains available where the remittance basis applies without a claim – eg where the individual's unremitted foreign income and gains are less than £2,000 for the year (*ITA 2007, s 809D*).

(2) The annual exemption is available to personal representatives in the tax year of death and the following two years (*TCGA 1992, s 3(7)*).

(3) The annual exemption for trustees is divided by the number of qualifying settlements created by one settlor, subject to a lower limit of 10% of the annual exemption for individuals for that tax year (*TCGA 1992, Sch 1, para 2*).

(4) For 2007/08 and earlier tax years, capital gains were taxed as the top slice of income.

(5) A 10% rate of capital gains tax applies from 23 June 2010, in respect of gains qualifying for entrepreneurs' relief (*TCGA 1992, s 169N(3)*; see **Entrepreneurs' relief** below).

CHATTEL EXEMPTION

(*TCGA 1992, s 262*)

	Exemption (max sale proceeds)	Marginal relief (max chargeable gain)
From 1989–90 onwards	£6,000	5/3 of the excess over £6,000

OTHER EXEMPTIONS AND RELIEFS

Entrepreneurs' relief

(*TCGA 1992 ss 169H–169S*)

Date of qualifying business disposal	Lifetime allowance
From 6 April 2011	£10 million
23 June 2010–5 April 2011	£5 million
6 April 2010–22 June 2010	£2 million
6 April 2008–5 April 2010	£1 million

General

(1) The relief broadly applies to qualifying disposals by an individual on or after 6 April 2008 of:
- all or part of a trade carried on alone or in partnership;
- assets of such a trade following cessation; or
- shares or securities in the individual's 'personal company', where the company is a trading company (or the holding company of a trading group) and the individual is an officer or employee of the company (or of a trading group member) (see *TCGA 1992, ss 169H, 169I*).

(2) Entrepreneurs' relief is available where the relevant conditions are met throughout a specific qualifying period of at least one year (see *TCGA 1992, s 169I*).

(3) Trustees can claim relief on the disposal of settlement business assets if a qualifying beneficiary has an interest in possession in the whole or a relevant part of the settled property, where certain conditions are satisfied (see *TCGA 1992, s 169J*).

(4) Transitional rules apply to allow relief to be claimed in some circumstances where a gain made before 6 April 2008 is deferred and becomes chargeable on or after that date (*FA 2008, Sch 3, paras 7, 8*).

8 Capital Gains Tax

(5) The Government will make reforms in the *Finance Bill 2013*, subject to EU State aid approval, so that gains made on shares acquired through exercising EMI options on or after 6 April 2012 will be eligible for entrepreneurs' relief (Budget, 21 March 2012).

Disposals from 6 April 2011

- Gains qualifying for entrepreneurs' relief are charged at the rate of 10%;
- The lifetime limit on total gains eligible for entrepreneurs' relief is increased to £10 million, in respect of qualifying business disposals from 6 April 2011.

Disposals between 23 June 2010 and 5 April 2011

- Gains qualifying for entrepreneurs' relief are charged at the rate of 10%;
- The lifetime limit on total gains eligible for entrepreneurs' relief is £5 million, in respect of qualifying business disposals from 23 June 2010.

Disposals before 23 June 2010

- Chargeable gains are reduced by 4/9ths before being charged to tax at the flat rate of 18%.
- Relief is subject to a lifetime limit of gains of £2 million (from 6 April 2010; prior to this the lifetime limit was £1 million). Disposals before 6 April 2008 are not counted towards this limit.

TAPER RELIEF (TO 5 APRIL 2008)

(TCGA 1992, s 2A, Sch A1 (repealed))

Business assets

Number of complete years from 6/4/98 for which asset held	% of gains chargeable	
	Disposals from 6 April 2002	Disposals between 6 April 2000 and 5 April 2002
0	100.0	100.0
1	50.0	87.5
2	25.0	75.0
3	25.0	50.0
4 or more	25.0	25.0

Non-business assets

Number of complete years from 6/4/98 for which asset held	% of chargeable gains
0	100
1	100
2	100
3	95
4	90
5	85
6	80

continued

Private residence relief

Non-business assets	
Number of complete years from 6/4/98 for which asset held	% of chargeable gains
7	75
8	70
9	65
10 or more	60

ROLLOVER RELIEF

(TCGA 1992, Pt 5, Ch 1)

Qualifying assets *(TCGA 1992, s 155)*:

- Land and buildings occupied (and used) only for the purposes of a trade;
- Fixed plant or machinery (not forming part of a building);
- Ships, aircraft and hovercraft;
- Satellites, space stations and spacecraft (including launch vehicles);
- Goodwill;
- Milk quotas and potato quotas;
- Ewe and suckler cow premium quotas;
- Fish quotas;
- Payment entitlements under the single payment scheme (that is, the scheme of income support for farmers in pursuance of Title III of Council Regulation (EC) No 1782/2003 or, from 1 January 2009 onwards, Council Regulation (EC) No 73/2009) *(Finance Bill 2012, cl 37)*; and
- A Lloyd's members' syndicate rights and assets treated as acquired by a Lloyd's member.

Note

For the purposes of corporation tax, assets in the last 6 categories listed above (goodwill onwards), if owned by a company at any time on or after 1 April 2002, would fall within the intangible assets regime and are therefore excluded from rollover relief (see *TCGA 1992, s 156ZB*).

PRIVATE RESIDENCE RELIEF

(TCGA 1992, ss 222–226B)

(1) Relief is given on the disposal of (or of an interest in) a dwelling house which has been the individual's only or main residence, and on land enjoyed with that residence as its garden or grounds up to the permitted area of half a hectare, or more if required for the reasonable enjoyment of the property.

(2) The relief is time apportioned for periods of occupation, and for certain periods of deemed occupation. The last 36 months of ownership are allowed in any event,

8 Capital Gains Tax

if the property was at some time the individual's only or main residence (*TCGA 1992, s 223(1)*).

(3) Where an individual has two or more residences, they may elect within 2 years which is to be treated as the main residence (TCGA 1992 s 232(5)).

(4) A married couple or civil partnership may have only one main residence at any time (TCGA 1992 s 232(6)).

(5) If the residence has been wholly or partly let as residential accommodation at any time in the period of occupation, the part of the gain, if any, which would otherwise be a chargeable gain by reason of the letting is exempt to the extent of the lower of:

- £40,000 (£20,000 for disposals before 19 March 1991); and
- the amount of the gain otherwise exempt as private residence relief.

(6) In conjunction with the proposed moves to combat avoidance of stamp duty land tax, the Government will consult on the introduction of a capital gains tax charge on residential property owned by non-resident, non-natural persons such as companies or trusts. Legislation will be introduced in the *Finance Bill 2013*, with the measure coming into effect in April 2013. This measure will be consulted on in conjunction with the proposed SDLT enveloping annual charge for high-value residential properties (Budget, 21 March 2012).

ENTERPRISE INVESTMENT SCHEME (EIS)

(TCGA 1992, s 150A, Sch 5B)

(1) A gain on the disposal of EIS shares after the relevant three-year period is exempt to the extent that full income tax relief has been given on the shares.

(2) Reinvestment relief is available for gains on assets where the disposal proceeds are reinvested in new EIS shares upon making a claim. All or part of the original gain can be deferred, and is brought back into charge on the occurrence of a chargeable event.

SEED ENTERPRISE INVESTMENT SCHEME (SEIS)

(FB 2012, cl 38, Sch 6)

It was announced on 29 November 2011 that gains on shares acquired under the new Seed Enterprise Investment Scheme (SEIS) will be exempt from tax.

In addition, an individual realising a gain on any asset disposal in 2012–13 and then investing the proceeds through SEIS in the same year will be able to claim exemption from tax on that gain.

For further details, see **Pensions Investment Income etc: Seed Enterprise Investment Scheme (SEIS)**.

CHARITIES

(TCGA 1992, ss 256, 257)

(1) Gains accruing to charities which are both applicable and applied for charitable purposes are generally exempt for capital gains tax purposes.

(2) Relief from capital gains tax generally applies to gifts to charities and certain other bodies. The relief was extended from 6 April 2002 to asset disposals to Community Amateur Sports Clubs (CASCs).

(3) Although there are some statutory exemptions for gifts and payments to charitable companies and a specific exemption for interest and Gift Aid income of CASCs, a defect in the Gift Aid legislation excludes CASCs from entitlement to claim repayment of income tax under Gift Aid. This is corrected retrospectively with effect from April 2010 (Budget, 21 March 2012; *Finance Bill 2012, cls 51, 52*).

LEASES WHICH ARE WASTING ASSETS

(*TCGA 1992, Sch 8, para 1*)

Depreciation table

Years	%	Monthly increment*	Years	%	Monthly increment*
50 or more	100	–	24	79.622	0.123
49	99.657	0.029	23	78.055	0.131
48	99.289	0.031	22	76.399	0.138
47	98.902	0.032	21	74.635	0.147
46	98.490	0.034	20	72.770	0.155
45	98.059	0.036	19	70.791	0.165
44	97.595	0.039	18	68.697	0.175
43	97.107	0.041	17	66.470	0.186
42	96.593	0.043	16	64.116	0.196
41	96.041	0.046	15	61.617	0.208
40	95.457	0.049	14	58.971	0.221
39	94.842	0.051	13	56.167	0.234
38	94.189	0.054	12	53.191	0.248
37	93.497	0.058	11	50.038	0.263
36	92.761	0.061	10	46.695	0.279
35	91.981	0.065	9	43.154	0.295
34	91.156	0.069	8	39.399	0.313
33	90.280	0.073	7	35.414	0.332
32	89.354	0.077	6	31.195	0.352
31	88.371	0.082	5	26.722	0.373
30	87.330	0.087	4	21.983	0.395
29	86.226	0.092	3	16.959	0.419
28	85.053	0.098	2	11.629	0.444
27	83.816	0.103	1	5.983	0.470
26	82.496	0.110	0	0	0.499
25	81.100	0.116			

8 Capital Gains Tax

Notes

(1) **Formula:** Fraction of expenditure disallowed:

$$\frac{A - B}{A}$$

Where:

A is the percentage for duration of lease at acquisition or expenditure; and

B is the percentage for the duration of the lease at disposal.

(2) *** Fraction of years:** Add one-twelfth of the difference between the percentage for the whole year and the next higher percentage for each additional month. Odd days under 14 are not counted; 14 odd days or more are rounded up to and treated as a month.

SHORT LEASE PREMIUMS

(*ITTOIA 2005, s 277*)

See **Pensions, Investment Income etc** as to the calculation of the proportion of any premium received in respect of a lease of less than 50 years which is partly chargeable to capital gains tax, and that part which is chargeable to income tax as property business profits.

EXEMPT GILT-EDGED SECURITIES

(*TCGA 1992, ss 16(2), 115, Sch 9*)

Gains on the following securities are not chargeable gains and any losses are not allowable losses.

2.50%	Annuities 1905 or after
2.75%	Annuities 1905 or after
2.50%	Consolidated Stock 1923 or after
3.50%	War Loan 1952 or after
4.00%	Consolidated Loan 1957 or after
3.50%	Conversion Loan 1961 or after
3.00%	Treasury Stock 1966 or after
2.50%	Treasury Stock 1975 or after
12.75%	Treasury Loan 1992
8.00%	Treasury Loan 1992
10.00%	Treasury Stock 1992
3.00%	Treasury Stock 1992
12.25%	Exchequer Stock 1992
13.50%	Exchequer Stock 1992
10.50%	Treasury Convertible Stock 1992
2.00%	Index-Linked Treasury Stock 1992
12.50%	Treasury Loan 1993
6.00%	Funding Loan 1993

Exempt gilt-edged securities

13.75%	Treasury Loan 1993
10.00%	Treasury Loan 1993
8.25%	Treasury Stock 1993
14.50%	Treasury Loan 1994
12.50%	Exchequer Stock 1994
9.00%	Treasury Loan 1994
10.00%	Treasury Loan 1994
13.50%	Exchequer Stock 1994
8.50%	Treasury Stock 1994
8.50%	Treasury Stock 1994 'A'
2.00%	Index-Linked Treasury Stock 1994
3.00%	Exchequer Gas Stock 1990–95
12.00%	Treasury Stock 1995
10.25%	Exchequer Stock 1995
12.75%	Treasury Loan 1995
9.00%	Treasury Loan 1992–96
15.25%	Treasury Loan 1996
13.25%	Exchequer Loan 1996
14.00%	Treasury Stock 1996
2.00%	Index-Linked Treasury Stock 1996
10.00%	Conversion Stock 1996
10.00%	Conversion Stock 1996 'A'
10.00%	Conversion Stock 1996 'B'
13.25%	Treasury Loan 1997
10.50%	Exchequer Stock 1997
8.75%	Treasury Loan 1997
8.75%	Treasury Loan 1997 'B'
8.75%	Treasury Loan 1997 'C'
8.75%	Treasury Loan 1997 'D'
8.75%	Treasury Loan 1997 'E'
15.00%	Exchequer Stock 1997
7.00%	Treasury Convertible Stock 1997
6.75%	Treasury Loan 1995–98
15.50%	Treasury Loan 1998
12.00%	Exchequer Stock 1998
12.00%	Exchequer Stock 1998 'A'
9.75%	Exchequer Stock 1998
9.75%	Exchequer Stock 1998 'A'
7.25%	Treasury Stock 1998 'A'
7.25%	Treasury Stock 1998 'B'
12.00%	Exchequer Stock 1998 'B'
4.625%	Index-Linked Treasury Stock 1998

continued

8 Capital Gains Tax

7.25%	Treasury Stock 1998
9.50%	Treasury Loan 1999
10.50%	Treasury Stock 1999
12.25%	Exchequer Stock 1999
12.25%	Exchequer Stock 1999 'A'
12.25%	Exchequer Stock 1999 'B'
2.50%	Index-Linked Treasury Convertible Stock 1999
10.25%	Conversion Stock 1999
6.00%	Treasury Stock 1999
	Floating Rate Treasury Stock 1999
9.00%	Conversion Stock 2000
9.00%	Conversion Stock 2000 'A'
9.00%	Conversion Stock 2000 'B'
9.00%	Conversion Stock 2000 'C'
8.50%	Treasury Loan 2000
8.00%	Treasury Stock 2000
8.00%	Treasury Stock 2000 'A'
13.00%	Treasury Stock 2000
13.00%	Treasury Stock 2000 'A'
7.00%	Treasury Stock 2001
7.00%	Treasury Stock 2001 'A'
14.00%	Treasury Stock 1998–2001
2.50%	Index-Linked Treasury Stock 2001
9.75%	Conversion Stock 2001
10.00%	Treasury Stock 2001
9.50%	Conversion Loan 2001
10.00%	Treasury Stock 2001 'A'
10.00%	Treasury Stock 2001 'B'
	Floating Rate Treasury Stock
12.00%	Exchequer Stock 1999–2002
12.00%	Exchequer Stock 1999–2002 'A'
9.50%	Conversion Stock 2002
10.00%	Conversion Stock 2002
9.00%	Exchequer Stock 2002
7.00%	Treasury Stock 2002
9.75%	Treasury Stock 2002
9.75%	Treasury Stock 2002 'A'
9.75%	Treasury Stock 2002 'B'
9.75%	Treasury Stock 2002 'C'
13.75%	Treasury Stock 2000–2003
13.75%	Treasury Stock 2000–2003 'A'
2.50%	Index-Linked Treasury Stock 2003

Exempt gilt-edged securities

9.75%	Conversion Loan 2003
6.50%	Treasury Stock 2003
8.00%	Treasury Stock 2003
8.00%	Treasury Stock 2003 'A'
10.00%	Treasury Stock 2003
10.00%	Treasury Stock 2003 'A'
10.00%	Treasury Stock 2003 'B'
3.50%	Funding Stock 1999–2004
11.50%	Treasury Stock 2001–2004
9.50%	Conversion Stock 2004
10.00%	Treasury Stock 2004
6.75%	Treasury Stock 2004
5.00%	Treasury Stock 2004
6.75%	Treasury Stock 2004 'A'
4.375%	Index-Linked Treasury Stock 2004
9.50%	Conversion Stock 2004 'A'
12.50%	Treasury Stock 2003–2005
12.50%	Treasury Stock 2003–2005 'A'
10.50%	Exchequer Stock 2005
9.50%	Conversion Stock 2005
9.50%	Conversion Stock 2005 'A'
8.50%	Treasury Stock 2005
8.00%	Treasury Loan 2002–2006
8.00%	Treasury Loan 2002–2006 'A'
2.00%	Index-Linked Treasury Stock 2006
9.75%	Conversion Stock 2006
7.50%	Treasury Stock 2006
7.75%	Treasury Stock 2006
11.75%	Treasury Stock 2003–2007
11.75%	Treasury Stock 2003–2007 'A'
7.25%	Treasury Stock 2007
4.50%	Treasury Stock 2007
8.50%	Treasury Loan 2007
8.50%	Treasury Loan 2007 'A'
8.50%	Treasury Loan 2007 'B'
8.50%	Treasury Loan 2007 'C'
13.50%	Treasury Stock 2004–2008
9.00%	Treasury Loan 2008
9.00%	Treasury Loan 2008 'A'
9.00%	Treasury Loan 2008 'B'
9.00%	Treasury Loan 2008 'C'
9.00%	Treasury Loan 2008 'D'

continued

5.00%	Treasury Stock 2008
2.50%	Index-Linked Treasury Stock 2009
5.75%	Treasury Stock 2009
8.00%	Treasury Stock 2009
4.00%	Treasury Stock 2009
8.00%	Treasury Stock 2009 'A'
4.75%	Treasury Stock 2010
6.25%	Treasury Stock 2010
2.25%	Indexed-Linked Treasury Stock 2011
4.25%	Treasury Gilt 2011
9.00%	Conversion Loan 2011
9.00%	Conversion Loan 2011 'A'
9.00%	Conversion Loan 2011 'B'
9.00%	Conversion Loan 2011 'C'
9.00%	Conversion Loan 2011 'D'
3.25%	Treasury Gilt 2011
5.50%	Treasury Stock 2008–2012
9.00%	Treasury Stock 2012
9.00%	Treasury Stock 2012 'A'
5.00%	Treasury Stock 2012
5.25%	Treasury Gilt 2012
2.50%	Index-Linked Treasury Stock 2013
8.00%	Treasury Stock 2013
4.50%	Treasury Gilt 2013
2.25%	Treasury Gilt 2014
5.00%	Treasury Stock 2014
7.75%	Treasury Loan 2012–2015
2.75%	Treasury Gilt 2015
4.75%	Treasury Stock 2015
8.00%	Treasury Stock 2015
8.00%	Treasury Stock 2015 'A'
2.50%	Treasury Stock 1986–2016
2.50%	Index-Linked Treasury Stock 2016
2.50%	Index-Linked Treasury Stock 2016 'A'
4.00%	Treasury Gilt 2016
2.00%	Treasury Gilt 2016
12.00%	Exchequer Stock 2013–2017
1.25%	Index-Linked Treasury Gilt 2017
8.75%	Treasury Stock 2017
8.75%	Treasury Stock 2017 'A'
5.00%	Treasury Gilt 2018
3.75%	Treasury Gilt 2019

Exempt gilt-edged securities

4.50%	Treasury Gilt 2019
2.50%	Index-Linked Treasury Stock 2020
4.75%	Treasury Stock 2020
3.75%	Treasury Gilt 2020
8.00%	Treasury Stock 2021
3.75%	Treasury Gilt 2021
1.875%	Index-Linked Treasury Gilt 2022
4.00%	Treasury Gilt 2022
2.50%	Index-Linked Treasury Stock 2024
5.00%	Treasury Stock 2025
1.25%	Index-Linked Treasury Gilt 2027
4.25%	Treasury Gilt 2027
6.00%	Treasury Stock 2028
4.125%	Index-Linked Treasury Stock 2030
4.75%	Treasury Gilt 2030
1.25%	Index-linked Treasury Gilt 2032
4.25%	Treasury Stock 2032
4.50%	Treasury Gilt 2034
2.00%	Index-Linked Treasury Stock 2035
4.25%	Treasury Stock 2036
1.125%	Index-Linked Treasury Gilt 2037
4.75%	Treasury Stock 2038
4.25%	Treasury Gilt 2039
0.625%	Index-linked Treasury Gilt 2040
4.25%	Treasury Gilt 4040
0.625%	Index-linked Treasury Gilt 2042
4.50%	Treasury Stock 2042
4.25%	Treasury Gilt 2046
0.75%	Index-Linked Treasury Gilt 2047
4.25%	Treasury Gilt 2049
0.50%	Index-linked Treasury Gilt 2050
1.25%	Indexed-linked Treasury Gilt 2055
4.25%	Treasury Gilt 2055
4.00%	Treasury Gilt 2060
0.5%	Index-linked Treasury Gilt 2060

Securities issued by certain public corporations and guaranteed by the Treasury

3.00%	North of Scotland Electricity Stock 1989–92

8 Capital Gains Tax

IDENTIFICATION OF SECURITIES

(TCGA 1992, ss 104–109)

Disposals by individuals and trustees: 2008–09 onwards

Disposals on or after 6 April 2008 are to be identified with acquisitions in the following order:

(1) Same day acquisitions *(TCGA 1992, s 105(1)(b))* (subject to an election under *s 105A* (see below));

(2) Acquisitions within the following 30 days on the basis of earlier acquisitions in that period, rather than later ones (a FIFO basis) *(s 106A(5))*; and

(3) Securities within the expanded *s 104* holding, which specifically does not include acquisitions under (1) and (2) above, on the basis of later acquisitions before earlier ones (a LIFO basis) *(s 106A)*.

Where the number of securities which comprise the disposal exceed those identified under the above rules, that excess is identified with subsequent acquisitions beyond the 30-day period referred to above, taking the earliest one first.

Disposals by individuals and trustees: years to 2007–08

Pooling for capital gains tax ceased for acquisitions made on or after 6 April 1998.

Disposals from 6 April 1998 are identified with acquisitions in the following order (see CG50564):

(1) Shares acquired on the same day as the disposal (but subject to the effect of an election under *s 105A* (see below));

(2) Shares acquired within 30 days following the disposal, on a 'first in, first out' (FIFO) basis;

(3) Shares acquired after 5 April 1998 (not within (1) and (2) above), on a 'last in, first out' (LIFO) basis;

(4) Shares in a '*section 104*' holding;

(5) Shares in a 1982 holding;

(6) Shares acquired before 6 April 1965 (on a LIFO basis); and

(7) Acquisitions following the disposal (not already identified under (2) above) taking the earliest acquisition first.

An election *(TCGA, s 105A)* could be made for approved-scheme shares (as defined in that section), to be treated as a separate holding from that of the other shares acquired on the same day as the disposal. Where the election was made, the holding of the approved-scheme shares was identified, with the disposal, after the holding of the other shares acquired on the same day.

Disposals by companies

Order of identification:

(1) Any acquisition on the same day *(TCGA, s 105(1)(b))*;

(2) Acquisitions within the previous 10 days *(s 107(3))* (on a 'first in, first out' (FIFO) basis);

(3) Acquisitions since 1 April 1982 ('the *s 104* holding', previously termed 'the new holding') (*s 107(7), (8)*);

(4) Acquisitions in the period 6 April 1965 to 31 March 1982 ('the 1982 holding') (*s 107(7), (9)*), and

(5) Those held on 6 April 1965, in respect of which no election has been made to include them in the pre-1982 pool; these will be identified on a last-in, first-out (LIFO) basis (*s 107(7), (9)*).

For disposals before 5 December 2005, where a company or group of companies held at least 2% of the shares or securities of that class, acquisitions and disposals within one month (for most quoted shares or securities) or six months (for other disposals) could be matched.

Personal representatives' allowable expenses in respect of deaths after 5 April 2004

(*SP 2/04*)

Gross value of estate	Allowable expenditure
Not exceeding £50,000	1.8% of the probate value of assets sold by the personal representatives.
Over £50,000 but not exceeding £90,000	£900, divided among all assets of the estate in proportion to their probate values and allowed in those proportions on assets sold by the personal representatives.
Over £90,000 but not exceeding £400,000	1% of the probate value of assets sold.
Over £400,000 but not exceeding £500,000	£4,000, divided among all assets of the estate in proportion to their probate values and allowed in those proportions on assets sold by the personal representatives.
Over £500,000 but not exceeding £1,000,000	0.8% of the probate value of assets sold.
Over £1,000,000 but not exceeding £5,000,000	£8,000, divided among all assets of the estate in proportion to their probate values and allowed in those proportions on assets sold by the personal representatives.
Over £5,000,000	0.16% of the probate value of the assets sold, subject to a maximum of £10,000.

TIME LIMITS FOR ELECTIONS AND CLAIMS

From 1 April 2010, the general time limit for claims and elections is four years from the end of the chargeable year or period (*TMA 1970, s 43(1)*). HMRC may allow an extension of the normal time limit for certain elections and claims.

For periods up to 31 March 2010 the normal rule is that claims by individuals and trustees must be made within five years from 31 January next following the year to which they relate (for companies the limit was six years from the end of the relevant chargeable period).

8 Capital Gains Tax

Provision	Time limit	References
Asset of negligible value	2 years from end of tax year (or accounting period, if a company) in which deemed disposal/reacquisition takes place	*TCGA 1992, s 24(2)*
Re-basing of all assets to 31 March 1982 values	2 years from end of accounting period of disposal (if a company)	*TCGA 1992, s 35(6)*
50% relief if deferred charge on gains before 31 March 1982 (pre 06/04/08 disposals)	2 years from end of accounting period of disposal (if a company)	*TCGA 1992, s 36, Sch 4 para 9(1)*
Variation within 2 years of death not to constitute a disposal for CGT purposes	6 months from date of variation (nb election not necessary for variations from 1 August 2002; instrument of variation must contain a statement instead (see *s 62(7)*)	*TCGA 1992, s 62(6)*
Employee share schemes – identifying disposals with acquisitions on "same day" transactions	Within 12 months from 31 January next following the tax year of the first disposal	*TCGA 1992, s 105B(2)*
Earn-out right to be treated as a security	Within 12 months from 31 January next following the tax year in which the right is conferred (or 2 years from end of accounting period, if a company)	*TCGA 1992, s 138A(5)*
Replacement of business assets (roll-over relief)	4 years from the end of the tax year (or accounting period) Prior to 1 April 2010: 5 years from 31 January next following the tax year (or 6 years from the end of the accounting period if a company) **Note:** Replacement asset to be purchased between 12 months before and 3 years after disposal of old asset (see *TCGA 1992, s 152(3)*)	*TCGA 1992, s 152(1)*
Asset appropriated to trading stock: trading profits to be adjusted by gain or loss on the deemed disposal at market value	Within 12 months from 31 January next following the year of assessment in which the period of account when the asset is appropriated to trading stock ends (or 2 years from the end of the accounting period in which the asset is appropriated to trading stock, if a company)	*TCGA 1992, s 161(3A)*
Disapplication of incorporation relief under TCGA 1992, s 162	2 years from 31 January following the end of the year of assessment in which the business is transferred If all the new assets have been disposed of by the end of the year of assessment following the one in which the business transfer took place, the time limit is 12 months from 31 January next following the tax year of the business transfer	*TCGA 1992, s 162A(3), (4)*

100

Time limits for elections and claims

Provision	Time limit	References
Hold-over of relief for gifts of business assets	4 years from the end of the tax year. Prior to 1 April 2010: 5 years from 31 January next following the tax year	TCGA 1992, s 165(1)
Entrepreneurs' relief	Within 12 months from 31 January following the tax year in which the qualifying business disposal is made	TCGA 1992, s 169M(3)
Deemed disposal/ reacquisition on expiry of mineral lease	4 years from the relevant date. Prior to 1 April 2010: 6 years from the relevant event	TCGA 1992, s 203(2)
Main residence notification	2 years from a change in combination of residences (eg acquisition of a second private residence)	TCGA 1992, s 222(5)
Small part disposals of land: consideration to be deducted from allowable expenditure on a subsequent disposal	Within 12 months from 31 January next following the tax year of disposal (or 2 years from end of accounting period of disposal, if a company)	TCGA 1992, s 242(2A)
Irrecoverable loan to a trader	4 years from the end of the tax year (or accounting period). Prior to April 2010: 5 years from 31 January next following the tax year (or 6 years from the end of the accounting period, if a company)	TCGA 1992, s 253(3)
Hold-over relief for gifts on which IHT is immediately chargeable etc	4 years from the end of the tax year. Prior to 1 April 2010: 5 years from 31 January next following the tax year	TCGA 1992, s 260(1)
Trading losses relieved against gains	12 months from 31 January next following the tax year in which loss arose	TCGA 1992, s 261B(8)
Post-cessation expenses relieved against gains	12 months from 31 January next following the tax year in which expenses paid	TCGA 1992, s 261D(6)
Delayed remittances of foreign gains	4 years from the end of the tax year (or accounting period). Prior to 1 April 2010: 5 years from 31 January next following the tax year (or 6 years from the end of the accounting period, if a company)	TCGA 1992, s 279(5)
Loss on disposal of right to deferred unascertainable consideration to be treated as accruing in an earlier year	Within 12 months from 31 January next following the year of the loss	TCGA 1992, s 279D(8)

8 *Capital Gains Tax*

INDEXATION ALLOWANCE

(TCGA 1992, ss 53, 54)

Indexation allowance was introduced in 1982. It is broadly an allowance for inflation, based on the indexed rise in allowable expenditure for capital gains purposes. The allowance is the aggregate of the indexed rise in each item of such expenditure.

The formula for calculating indexation factors is as follows (*TCGA 1992, s 54(1)*):

$$\frac{(RD - RI)}{RI}$$

Where: RD is the Retail Prices Index (RPI) for the month of disposal; and

RI is the RPI for March 1982 or the month in which the expenditure was incurred, if later).

The resulting figure is applied to each item of qualifying expenditure in the computation, by multiplying the expenditure by the relevant indexation factor.

Indexation allowance was abolished for disposals from 6 April 2008, except for disposals made by companies within the charge to corporation tax (*TCGA 1992, s 52A*).

For individuals, trustees and personal representatives, indexation allowance was frozen for disposals between 6 April 1998 and 5 April 2008. The table below shows the indexation factors up to April 1998, which can be applied to disposals up to 5 April 2008 in order to reduce gains, but not to create or increase a loss.

Indexation: March 1982–April 1998

Date cost incurred	1982	1983	1984	1985	1986	1987
Jan		0.968	0.872	0.783	0.689	0.626
Feb		0.960	0.865	0.769	0.683	0.620
Mar	1.047	0.956	0.859	0.752	0.681	0.616
Apr	1.006	0.929	0.834	0.716	0.665	0.597
May	0.992	0.921	0.828	0.708	0.662	0.596
Jun	0.987	0.917	0.823	0.704	0.663	0.596
Jul	0.986	0.906	0.825	0.707	0.667	0.597
Aug	0.985	0.898	0.808	0.703	0.662	0.593
Sep	0.987	0.889	0.804	0.704	0.654	0.588
Oct	0.977	0.883	0.793	0.701	0.652	0.580
Nov	0.967	0.876	0.788	0.695	0.638	0.573
Dec	0.971	0.871	0.789	0.693	0.632	0.574

Companies

Date cost incurred	1988	1989	1990	1991	1992	1993
Jan	0.574	0.465	0.361	0.249	0.199	0.179
Feb	0.568	0.454	0.353	0.242	0.193	0.171
Mar	0.562	0.448	0.339	0.237	0.189	0.167
Apr	0.537	0.423	0.300	0.222	0.171	0.156
May	0.531	0.414	0.288	0.218	0.167	0.152
Jun	0.525	0.409	0.283	0.213	0.167	0.153
Jul	0.524	0.408	0.282	0.215	0.171	0.156
Aug	0.507	0.404	0.269	0.213	0.171	0.151
Sep	0.500	0.395	0.258	0.208	0.166	0.146
Oct	0.485	0.384	0.248	0.204	0.162	0.147
Nov	0.478	0.372	0.251	0.199	0.164	0.148
Dec	0.474	0.369	0.252	0.198	0.168	0.146

Date cost incurred	1994	1995	1996	1997	1998
Jan	0.151	0.114	0.083	0.053	0.019
Feb	0.144	0.107	0.078	0.049	0.014
Mar	0.141	0.102	0.073	0.046	0.011
Apr	0.128	0.091	0.066	0.040	
May	0.124	0.087	0.063	0.036	
Jun	0.124	0.085	0.063	0.032	
Jul	0.129	0.091	0.067	0.032	
Aug	0.124	0.085	0.062	0.026	
Sep	0.121	0.080	0.057	0.021	
Oct	0.120	0.085	0.057	0.019	
Nov	0.119	0.085	0.057	0.019	
Dec	0.114	0.079	0.053	0.016	

COMPANIES

(1) Indexation allowance continues to be available for corporation tax purposes after April 2008.

(2) The RPI is published by the Office for National Statistics (www.ons.gov.uk).

(3) Monthly RPIs are also published on HMRC's website. Tables showing the indexed rise to be used in calculating the indexation allowance in respect of assets disposed of in a particular month can be found on HMRC's website (www.hmrc.gov.uk/rates/cg-indexation-allowance/index.htm).

9

Inheritance tax

(IHTA 1984, s 7, Sch 1)

INHERITANCE TAX (IHT) THRESHOLDS AND RATES (LIFETIME TRANSFERS AND TRANSFERS ON DEATH OR WITHIN 7 YEARS BEFORE DEATH)

Period	Upper limit £	Rate of tax	Grossing up rate for each £ over the upper limit
6 April 2009–5 April 2015	325,000	20% on gross lifetime transfers over the cumulative upper limit	¼ for net lifetime transfers
2008–09	312,000		
2007–08	300,000		
2006–07	285,000		
2005–06	275,000		
2004–05	263,000		
2003–04	255,000		
2002–03	250,000		
2001–02	242,000		
2000–01	234,000		
1999–2000	231,000		
1989–99	223,000		
1997–98	215,000		
1996–97	200,000		
1995–96	154,000	40% on transfers on death over the cumulative upper limit	2/3 for net transfers on death (not bearing own tax)
10 March 1992 to 5 April 1995	150,000		
6 April 1991 to 9 March 1992	140,000		
1990–91	128,000		
1989–90	118,000		
15 March 1988 to 5 April 1989	110,000		
17 March 1987 to 14 March 1988	90,000		
18 March 1986 to 16 March 1987	71,000		

Inheritance tax (IHT) thresholds and rates (lifetime transfers and transfers on death etc)

Note

(1) IHT threshold (or 'nil rate band') is set at £325,000 for the tax years 2010–11 to 2014–15 inclusive (*FA 2010, s 8*).

(2) The IHT threshold can normally be expected to increase annually by reference to the Retail Prices Index (RPI). However, it was announced in Budget 2011 that, from April 2012, the default indexation factor for direct taxes, including IHT, will move from the RPI to the Consumer Price Index (CPI). As the IHT nil rate band is frozen until 5 April 2015 (see below), the CPI will have no effect until after that date.

(3) A lower IHT rate of 36% can apply to a deceased person's estate, where 10% or more of the estate has been left to charities and/or registered community amateur sports clubs, with effect for deaths on or after 6 April 2012 (*IHTA 1984, Sch 1A*) (see **Gifts to charities, below**).

Capital transfer tax (inheritance tax thresholds) – 13 March 1975 to 17 March 1986

From	To	Limit
06.04.1985	17.03.1986	£67,000
13.03.1984	05.04.1985	£64,000
15.03.1983	12.03.1984	£60,000
09.03.1982	14.03.1983	£55,000
26.03.1980	08.03.1982	£50,000
27.10.1977	25.03.1980	£25,000
13.03.1975	26.10.1977	£15,000

Estate duty (Inheritance tax thresholds) – 16 August 1914 to 12 March 1975

England, Wales and Scotland

From	To	Limit
22.03.1972	12.03.1975	£15,000
31.03.1971	21.03.1972	£12,500
16.04.1969	30.03.1971	£10,000
04.04.1963	15.04.1969	£5,000
09.04.1962	03.04.1963	£4,000
30.07.1954	08.04.1962	£3,000
10.04.1946	29.07.1954	£2,000
16.08.1914	09.04.1946	£100

9 Inheritance tax

Northern Ireland

From	To	Limit
22.03.1972	12.03.1975	£15,000
05.05.1971	21.03.1972	£12,500
04.06.1969	04.05.1971	£10,000
22.05.1963	03.06.1969	£5,000
04.07.1962	21.05.1963	£4,000
01.11.1954	03.07.1962	£3,000
29.08.1946	31.10.1954	£2,000
16.08.1914	28.08.1946	£100

ANNUAL AND SMALL GIFT EXEMPTION

(IHTA 1984, ss 19, 20)

Period	Annual exemption	Small Gift exemption (to the same person)
From 6 April 1981	£3,000	£250
6 April 1980 to 5 April 1981	£2,000	£250
6 April 1976 to 5 April 1980	£2,000	£100

Note

To the extent that the annual exemption is unused for a particular tax year, it can be carried forward to the next following year, but not beyond (*IHTA 1984, s 19(2)*).

GIFTS IN CONSIDERATION OF MARRIAGE/CIVIL PARTNERSHIP

(IHTA 1984, s 22)

Donor	Limit
Parent of party to the marriage/civil partnership	£5,000
Remoter ancestor than parent of party to the marriage/civil partnership	£2,500
Party to the marriage/civil partnership	£2,500
Any other person	£1,000

Note

If the value transferred by the gift is greater than the amount of the available exemption, it is an exempt transfer up to the amount of the available exemption, and the excess is chargeable.

NON-UK DOMICILED SPOUSE / CIVIL PARTNER GIFT EXEMPTION

(IHTA 1984, s 18)

Period	Limit
Transfers on or after 9 March 1982	£55,000

Note

(1) The exemption was extended to civil partners with effect from 5 December 2005 (*SI 2005/3229*).

(2) Subject to consultation, the Government intends to bring forward proposals in the *Finance Bill 2013* to increase the IHT-exempt amount that a UK-domiciled individual can transfer to their non-UK domiciled spouse or civil partner, and to allow individuals who are domiciled outside the UK and who have a UK-domiciled spouse or civil partner to elect to be treated as domiciled in the UK for the purposes of IHT (Budget, 21 March 2012).

AGRICULTURAL AND BUSINESS PROPERTY RELIEF

(*IHTA 1984, Pt V, Chs 1, 2*)

Agricultural property (notes (1), (2))		**Business Property**	
Nature of property	**Disposals from 6 April 1996 %**	**Nature of property**	**Disposals from 6 April 1996 %**
Vacant possession or right to obtain it within 12 months	100	Business or interest in a business (note (4))	100
Tenanted land with vacant possession value (note (3))	100	Quoted company: controlling shareholding	50
Agricultural land let on or after 1 September 1995	100	Unquoted company: controlling shareholding (note (4))	100
Any other circumstances	50	Unquoted company: shareholding more than 25% (note (4))	100
		Unquoted company: shareholding 25% or less (note (5))	100
		Unquoted securities: control holding	100
		Settled property used in life tenant's business (note (6))	100/50
		Land, buildings, machinery or plant used by transferor's company or partnership	50

Notes

(1) IHT due or paid from 23 April 2003 in respect of agricultural property located in a qualifying EEA state at the time of the chargeable event is eligible for relief (*FA 2009, s 122*).

(2) If land is let to graze animals or take grass from land for a season, and vacant possession reverts to the landowner within a year, any agricultural property relief due will be at the 100% rate (*IHTM24142*).

9 Inheritance tax

(3) Land let on a tenancy commencing before 10 March 1981 may qualify for relief at 100% in certain circumstances, ie broadly if the transferor owned the land before 10 March 1981, the land would have qualified for relief (under *FA 1975, Sch 8*) had it been transferred before that date, and the transferor did not have vacant possession (or entitlement to it) from then until the date of death/transfer (*IHTA 1984, s 116(2), (3)*).

(4) The rate of relief was increased from 50% with effect from 10 March 1992.

(5) The rate of relief was increased from 50% with effect from 6 April 1996.

(6) The higher rate applies if the settled property is transferred with the business on death (see *IHTM25243*).

QUICK SUCCESSION RELIEF

(*IHTA 1984, s 141*)

Years between transfers		Percentage
More than	Not more than	(applied to formula – see below) %
0	1	100
1	2	80
2	3	60
3	4	40
4	5	20

Note

Formula:

$$\text{Percentage} \times \text{Tax charge on earlier transfer} \times \frac{\text{Increase in value of transferee's estate}}{\text{Value of earlier chargeable transfer}}$$

TAPER RELIEF

(*IHTA 1984, s 7(4)*)

Years between gift and death	% of full charge at death rates
0–3	100
3–4	80
4–5	60
5–6	40
6–7	20

Notes

(1) The relief provides for a reduced tax charge on gifts made within 7 years before death. The amount of relief depends on the length of time the deceased survived following the transfer. The tax is reduced by applying the percentages in the preceding table.

(2) Taper relief does not apply where the tapered tax would otherwise have been less than the tax which would have been chargeable on the original transfer using half death rates (IHTA 1984, s 7(5)).

PRE-OWNED ASSETS

(*FA 2004, s 84, Sch 15*)

General

An income tax charge arises where an individual continues to benefit from property previously owned by them. The charge arises in respect of the following:

- land;
- chattels; and
- intangible property (in a settlement where the settlor retains an interest).

No tax is payable if the aggregate amount attributable to a chargeable person does not exceed £5,000. However, if benefits exceed £5,000, the charge is on the full amount.

Land

The chargeable amount is the 'appropriate rental value' less any amount paid under a legal obligation in respect of the occupation of the land. The 'appropriate rental value' is calculated using the following formula:

$$R \times \frac{DV}{V}$$

Where: R is the rental value of the relevant land for the taxable period;

DV is the value at the valuation date of the interest in the relevant land that was disposed of by the chargeable person or, where the disposal was a non-exempt sale, the appropriate proportion of that value; and

V is the value of the relevant land at the valuation date.

The 'taxable period' is the year of assessment, or part of a year of assessment, during which the relevant conditions are met.

The 'rental value' is based on the assumption of a letting from year to year where the tenant pays the taxes, rates and charges and the landlord is responsible for repairs and insurance. Land may be valued on a five-yearly rather than an annual valuation (*SI 2005/724, reg 4*).

Chattels

The chargeable amount is the 'appropriate amount' less any amount paid under a legal obligation to the owner of the chattel. The 'appropriate amount' is:

$$N \times \frac{DV}{V}$$

Where: N is the notional interest for the taxable period, at the prescribed rate, on the value of the chattel at the valuation date;

DV is the value at the valuation date of the interest in the relevant chattel that was disposed of by the chargeable person or, where the disposal was a non-exempt sale, the appropriate proportion of that asset; and

V is the value of the chattel at the valuation date.

9 Inheritance tax

Intangible property in settlor-interested settlements

The chargeable amount in relation to the relevant property is:

$$N - T$$

Where: N is the notional amount of interest for the taxable period, at the prescribed rate, on the value of the property at the valuation date; and

T is the amount of income tax or capital gains tax payable by the chargeable person in the taxable period by virtue of gains from contracts of life assurance, income from settlements where the settlor retains an interest, transfer of assets abroad, the charge on settlors with an interest in settlements and the attribution of gains to settlors with an interest in non-resident or dual resident settlements for capital gains tax purposes.

Note

The 'prescribed rate' to be applied to the values of chattels and intangibles when quantifying the cash value of the benefit enjoyed is the official rate of interest at the valuation date, being the first day of each taxable period (usually 6 April) (SI 2005/724, regs 2, 3).

DELIVERY OF ACCOUNTS: DUE DATES

(*IHTA 1984, s 216*)

Type of transfer	Due Date
Chargeable lifetime transfer	Later of:
	– 12 months after end of month in which transfer occurred
	– 3 months after person became liable
Transfers on death	Later of:
	– 12 months after end of month in which death occurred
	– 3 months after personal representatives first act in that capacity
Potentially exempt transfers which have become chargeable	12 months after end of month in which the transferor died
Gifts subject to reservation included in donor's estate at death	12 months after end of month in which death occurred
National heritage property or woodlands (on disposal)	6 months after end of month in which chargeable event occurred

Excepted estates

DELIVERY OF ACCOUNTS: EXCEPTED TRANSFERS, ESTATES AND SETTLEMENTS

(IHTA 1984, ss 216, 256; SI 2008/605; SI 2004/2543 (as amended); SI 2008/606)

EXCEPTED TRANSFERS

From 6 April 2007

(SI 2008/605, reg 4)

For chargeable transfers from 6 April 2007, no account is necessary where:

- the transfer is in cash or quoted shares or securities and the value of the transfer and other chargeable transfers made in the preceding seven years does not exceed the IHT threshold; or
- the value of the transfer (ignoring business and agricultural property relief) and other chargeable transfers made in the preceding seven years does not exceed 80% of the IHT threshold, and the value of the transfer does not exceed the net amount of the threshold available to the transferor at the time of the transfer.

Similar rules apply in determining whether the termination of an interest in possession in settled property is excepted from the requirement to deliver an account *(SI 2008/605, reg 5)*.

Before 6 April 2007

(SI 2002/1731)

Certain small lifetime transfers and terminations of interests in possession were (from 6 April 1981) excused from delivering an IHT account. The excepted transfer limits for periods to 5 April 2007 are as follows:

(a) Total chargeable transfers in the tax year – £10,000; and

(b) Total transferred by that and all previous chargeable transfers in the last 10 years – £40,000

EXCEPTED ESTATES

Deaths from	Before	Excepted estate limit	Assets held outside UK – limit	Total value of settled property	Specified transfers – limit	Specified exempt transfers – limit
6/4/2012	5/4/2013	325,000	100,000	150,000	150,000	1,000,000
6/4/2011	5/4/2012	325,000	100,000	150,000	150,000	1,000,000
6/4/2010	5/4/2011	325,000	100,000	150,000	150,000	1,000,000
6/4/2009	5/4/2010	325,000	100,000	150,000	150,000	1,000,000
6/4/2008	5/4/2009	312,000	100,000	150,000	150,000	1,000,000
6/4/2007	5/4/2008	300,000	100,000	150,000	150,000	1,000,000
1/9/2006	5/4/2007	285,000	100,000	150,000	150,000	1,000,000
6/4/2006	31/8/2006	285,000	75,000	100,000	100,000	1,000,000

continued

9   *Inheritance tax*

Deaths from	Before	Excepted estate limit	Assets held outside UK – limit	Total value of settled property	Specified transfers – limit	Specified exempt transfers – limit
6/4/2005	5/4/2006	275,000	75,000	100,000	100,000	1,000,000
6/4/2004	5/4/2005	263,000	75,000	100,000	100,000	1,000,000
6/4/2003	5/4/2004	240,000	75,000	100,000	100,000	–
6/4/2002	5/4/2003	220,000	75,000	100,000	100,000	–
6/4/2000	5/4/2002	210,000	50,000	–	75,000	–
6/4/1998	5/4/2000	180,000	50,000	–	75,000	–
6/4/1996	5/4/1998	180,000	30,000	–	50,000	–
6/4/1995	5/4/1996	145,000	15,000	–	–	–
6/4/1991	5/4/1995	125,000	15,000	–	–	–

Notes

(1) *General* – The current excepted estate provisions are contained in *SI 2004/2543* (as amended by *SI 2005/3230, SI 2006/2141, SI 2011/214 and SI 2011/2226*), which originally came into force from 1 November 2004 with effect for deaths occurring from 6 April 2004. The regulations essentially provide for three categories of excepted estate:

   (a) The 'low value' estate;

   (b) The 'exempt estate'; and

   (c) The 'foreign domiciliaries' estate.

(2) *IHT threshold and transferable nil rate band* – The low value and exempt estate categories were expanded by *The Inheritance Tax (Delivery of Accounts) (Excepted Estates) (Amendment) Regulations, SI 2011/214*, with effect for deaths occurring from 6 April 2010, to take account of the 'transferable nil rate band' provisions *(IHTA 1984, s 8A)*.

The regulations provide, inter alia, for the 'IHT threshold' (as defined) to be increased to £650,000 (for 2011–12), subject to a claim being made to increase the nil rate band by 100% on the basis of the full nil rate band being available to transfer from not more than one earlier deceased spouse or civil partner, and subject to certain other conditions being satisfied. Where a claim for unused nil rate band is required, an excepted estate return (form IHT205, or C5 in Scotland) must also be made.

(3) *IHT and alternatively secured pension funds* – The excepted estates provisions were amended by *The Inheritance Tax (Delivery of Accounts) (Excepted Estates) (Amendment) (No. 2) Regulations 2011 (SI 2011/2226)* with effect for deaths occurring from 6 April 2011, to reflect the repeal of the IHT provisions on alternatively secured pension funds *(IHTA 1984, ss 151A–151C)*.

(4) *Further guidance* – For HMRC guidance on excepted estates, see HMRC Inheritance Tax Manual IHTM06011 et seq.

EXCEPTED SETTLEMENTS

(IHTA 1984, ss 216, 256; SI 2008/606)

From 6 April 2007

No account is necessary of settled property in which no qualifying interest in possession subsists for chargeable events from 6 April 2007, broadly where:

Either:

- Cash has always been the only property comprised in the settlement;
- The settlor has added no further property to the settlement;
- The trustees have been UK resident since the settlement commenced;
- The gross value of settled property has not exceeded £1,000 since the settlement commenced; and
- There are no related settlements.

or

- The settlor was UK domiciled when the settlement was made, and remained so until the chargeable event, or until death (whichever is earlier);
- The trustees have been UK resident since the settlement commenced; and
- There are no related settlements; and *either*
- For ten-year anniversary IHT charge purposes, the value of the notional aggregate chargeable transfer (in *IHTA 1984, s 66(3)*) does not exceed 80% of the nil rate band; *or*
- On a chargeable event before the settlement's first ten-year anniversary, the value of the notional aggregate chargeable transfer (in *IHTA 1984, s 68(4)*) does not exceed 80% of the nil rate band; *or*
- On a chargeable event between ten-year anniversaries, the value of the notional aggregate chargeable transfer (in *IHTA 1984, s 66(3)*, taking account of *s 69*) does not exceed 80% of the nil rate band; *or*
- Where an IHT charge arises in respect of an 'age 18 to 25' trust (under *IHTA 1984, s 71E*), the value of the notional aggregate chargeable transfer (as adjusted in accordance with *IHTA 1984, s 71F(8)*) does not exceed 80% of the nil rate band.

Before 6 April 2007

For chargeable events occurring between 6 April 2002 and 5 April 2007, no account is necessary of settled property in which no qualifying interest in possession subsists broadly in the following circumstances (*SI 2002/1732*):

- Cash is the only asset in the settlement;
- The settlor added no further assets since making the settlement;
- The trustees have been UK resident since the settlement commenced;
- The gross value of settled assets at the time of the chargeable event does not exceed £1,000; and
- There are no related settlements.

9 *Inheritance tax*

Note

Further guidance – For HMRC guidance on excepted settlements, see HMRC Inheritance Tax Manual, IHTM06120 et seq.

DUE DATES FOR PAYMENT

(IHTA 1984, s 226)

Transfer	Due Date
Chargeable transfers other than death made between:	
6 April and 30 September	30 April in following year
1 October and 5 April	6 months after end of month in which transfer was made
Chargeable transfers which have conditional exemptions for heritage	6 months after end of month in which chargeable event occurred
Charge to tax on disposals of trees or underwood	
Transfers on death	Earlier of :
	– 6 months after of month in which death occurs; or
	– delivery of account by personal representatives
Chargeable transfers and potentially exempt transfers within 7 years of death	6 months after end of month in which death occurs

PENALTIES

(IHTA 1984, ss 216, 217, 218, 219, 219A, 245, 245A, 247; FA 2007, Sch 24; FA 2008, Schs 36, 40)

Offence		Penalty
Failure to deliver account *(IHTA 1984, s 245(2)(a); see also IHTM36023)*	Account outstanding at the statutory filing date	Fixed penalty of £100 (but not exceeding tax due)
Failure to deliver account: proceedings for declaring the failure not started *IHTA 1984, s 245(3)(b)*	Account outstanding 6 months after the statutory filing date	A further fixed penalty of £100 (but not exceeding tax due)
Failure to deliver account: proceedings for declaring the failure started (IHTA 1984, s 245(2)(b))	Daily penalty until accounts received (from day after failure declared by a court or the tribunal)	Up to £60 a day

Penalties

Offence		Penalty
Failure to deliver account (IHTA 1984, s 245(4A))	Account still outstanding 12 months after the statutory filing date	Up to £3,000
Failure by professional person to deliver a return of a settlement by a UK-domiciled person but with non-resident trustees *(IHTA 1984, s 218)* *(IHTA 1984, s 245A)*	Account outstanding at end of statutory period (three months from making of settlement)	Up to £300
	Daily penalty until accounts received (from day after failure declared by a court or the tribunal)	Up to £60 per day
Failure to report an instrument of variation which increases the IHT liability *(IHTA 1984, s 218A)* *(IHTA 1984, s 245A)*	Copy of instrument outstanding at end of statutory filing date	Up to £100
	Daily penalty until copy of instrument received (from day after failure declared by a court or the tribunal)	Up to £60 a day
	Penalty for failure to comply within 18 months of deed of variation being executed	Up to £3,000
Failure to comply with a notice requiring information (where notice given from 1 April 2010) *(FA 2008, Sch 36, paras 39, 40, 50; SI 2009/3054)*	Fixed penalty	£300
	Daily penalty after failure declared by a court or the tribunal	Up to £60 a day
	Continued failure where significant tax is at risk	Penalty may be decided by the Upper Tribunal
Inaccurate information and documents *(FA 2008, Sch 36, para 40A)*	Tax-geared penalty	Up to £3,000 for each inaccuracy
Failure to comply with a notice requiring documents, accounts or particulars (where notice was given before 1 April 2010) *(IHTA 1984, s 219A; SI 2009/3054)*	Penalty	Up to £50
	Daily penalty after failure declared by a court or the tribunal	Up to £30 a day
Person assisting in or inducing the provision of incorrect information etc. *(IHTA 1984, s 247(4))*	Penalty	Up to £3,000

continued

9 Inheritance tax

Offence		Penalty
Error in IHT account or return etc (*FA 2007, Sch 24, para 1*))	Careless action	30% of potential lost revenue (subject to any reductions for disclosure)
	Deliberate but not concealed action	70% of potential lost revenue (subject to any reductions for disclosure)
	Deliberate and concealed action	100% of potential lost revenue (subject to any reductions for disclosure)
Error in taxpayer's document attributable to another person (*FA 2007, Sch 24, para 1A*))	Penalty	100% of potential lost revenue (subject to any reductions for disclosure)

INTEREST RATES

(*IHTA 1984, s 233*)

Interest period	Interest rate (%)	Interest rate repaid (%)	Days
From 29 Sept 2009	3%	0.5%	–
24 March 2009 to 28 Sept 2009	0%	0%	189
27 Jan 2009 to 23 March 2009	1%	1%	56
6 Jan 2009 to 26 Jan 2009	2%	2%	21
6 Nov 2008 to 5 Jan 2009	3%	3%	61
6 Jan 2008 to 5 Nov 2008	4%	4%	304
6 August 2007 to 5 Jan 2008	5%	5%	153
6 Sept 2006 to 5 August 2007	4%	4%	334
6 Sept 2005 to 5 Sept 2006	3%	3%	365
6 Sept 2004 to 5 Sept 2005	4%	4%	365
6 Dec 2003 to 5 Sept 2004	3%	3%	275
6 August 2003 to 5 Dec 2003	2%	2%	122
6 Nov 2001 to 5 August 2003	3%	3%	638
6 May 2001 to 5 Nov 2001	4%	4%	184
6 Feb 2000 to 5 May 2001	5%	5%	455
6 March 1999 to 5 Feb 2000	4%	4%	337
6 Oct 1994 to 5 March 1999	5%	5%	1612
6 Jan 1994 to 5 Oct 1994	4%	4%	273
6 Dec 1992 to 5 Jan 1994	5%	5%	396
6 Nov 1992 to 5 Dec 1992	6%	6%	30
6 July 1991 to 5 Nov 1992	8%	8%	489
6 May 1991 to 5 July 1991	9%	9%	61

Distribution of intestate estates

Interest period	Interest rate (%)	Interest rate repaid (%)	Days
6 March 1991 to 5 May 1991	10%	10%	61
6 July 1989 to 5 March 1991	11%	11%	608
6 Oct 1988 to 5 July 1989	9%	9%	273

INTEREST ON IHT PAID IN YEARLY INSTALMENTS

(IHTA 1984, ss 227, 234)

Month of death	Due date	Interest starts from
January	31 July	1 August
February	31 August	1 September
March	30 September	1 October
April	31 October	1 November
May	30 November	1 December
June	31 December	1 January
July	31 January	1 February
August	28/29 February	1 March
September	31 March	1 April
October	30 April	1 May
November	31 May	1 June
December	30 June	1 July

Note

For IHT payable by ten equal yearly instalments, the first instalment is due six months from the end of the month in which the individual died. The second instalment is due on the same day twelve months after the first payment, and subsequent instalments are due on the same day each year. The preceding table shows how to work out the due date. Interest commences from the following day.

DISTRIBUTION OF INTESTATE ESTATES

The following provisions relate to England and Wales only

(Administration of Estates Act 1925, s 46)

(1) Spouse or civil partner and issue survive	
Spouse or civil partner receives	*Issue receives*
• All personal chattels; • £250,000 absolutely (or the entire interest where this is less); and • Life interest in one-half of residue (if any).	• One half of residue (if any) on statutory trusts (plus the other half of residue on statutory trusts upon the death of the spouse).

continued

9 Inheritance tax

(2) Spouse or civil partner survives without issue, but a surviving parent or brother or sister or issue of a brother or sister

Spouse or civil partner receives	Residuary estate to
• All personal chattels; • £450,000 absolutely (or entire estate where this is less); and • One half of residue (if any) absolutely.	• The deceased's parent(s). • If no parent survives: on trust for the deceased's brothers and sisters of the whole blood (and the issue of any such deceased brother or sister).

Note – The above fixed sums of £250,000 and £450,000 apply for deaths on or after 1 February 2009 (*The Family Provision (Intestate Succession) Order, SI 2009/135*). Previously, the fixed sums were £125,000 and £200,000 respectively.

(3) Spouse or civil partner survives but no issue, parents, brothers or sisters or their issue

Whole estate to surviving spouse or civil partner.

(4) No spouse or civil partner survives

Estate held in the following order with no class beneficiaries participating unless all those in a prior class have predeceased. Statutory trusts may apply except under (b), (e) and (h):

(a) Issue of deceased.

(b) Parent(s).

(c) Brothers and sisters (or issue).

(d) Half-brothers and half-sisters (or issue).

(e) Grandparent(s).

(f) Uncles and aunts (or issue).

(g) Half-brothers and half-sisters of deceased's parents (or issue).

(h) The Crown, the Duchy of Lancaster or the Duke of Cornwall.

Notes

(1) **General** – The distribution of a deceased individual's estate, and the IHT liability in respect of the estate, can be affected if the individual died without having made a valid will. The above applies in respect of deaths on or after 1 February 2009.

(2) **Civil partners** – The Administration of Estates Act 1925 was extended (by the Civil Partnership Act 2004, Sch 4, paras 7–12) to include the remaining surviving civil partner, who effectively acquires the same rights as a spouse in cases of intestacy.

(3) **Survivorship** – The above provisions in favour of the deceased's spouse or civil partner are subject to a 28 day survival period (*AEA 1925, s 46(2A)*).

(4) **Further information** – The above is an outline of the intestacy provisions. Further information is available in HMRC's IHT manual (at IHTM12101 onwards), and from the Justice website:

www.justice.gov.uk/guidance/courts-and-tribunals/courts/probate/why-make-a-will.htm

GIFTS TO CHARITIES ETC

(IHTA 1984, s 7(2), Sch 1A, as inserted by FB 2012, cl 207, Sch 32)

- A lower rate of IHT of 36% (as opposed to the 40% rate normally charged on death on the net value of the estate above the available nil rate band) is chargeable on a deceased person's estate broadly where 10% or more of the net estate has been left to charities and/or registered community amateur sports clubs.

- The lower rate is available in relation to deaths occurring on or after 6 April 2012.

Notes

(1) *General* – The reduced IHT rate is subject to a 'charitable giving' condition that the 'donated amount' is at least 10% of the 'baseline amount' (as defined) for one or more components of the estate.

(2) *Components* – The three components of the estate as defined for these purposes are the survivorship or a special destination (or corresponding provisions in a non-UK jurisdiction), settled property and general components. The general component excludes gifts with reservation.

(3) *Election* – An election is available to merge estate components in appropriate circumstances. The election must be made by all of the 'appropriate persons' (as defined) in respect of the components concerned. Alternatively, an election is available to 'opt out' of the lower rate for one or more components of the estate. In both cases, the election must be made by written notice within two years after the deceased's death (and may be withdrawn within two years and one month after death, or such longer period as HMRC may allow).

10

Capital Allowances

PLANT AND MACHINERY
(*CAA 2001, Pt 2*)

Writing down allowances (WDAs)
(*CAA 2001, s 56*)

	Main rate (%)	Special rate (%)
From April 2012	18	8
April 2008 to April 2012	20	10
Before April 2008	25	–

Notes

(1) The above changes in WDA rates from 1 April 2012 (corporation tax) or 6 April 2012 (for income tax) were made by *FA 2011, s 10*.

(2) For chargeable periods which straddle the above relevant dates, the rate of WDA is a hybrid of the rates before and after the changes.

Annual investment allowance (AIA)
(*CAA 2001, s 51A*)

Expenditure incurred	Maximum allowance £
From April 2012	25,000
April 2010 to April 2012	100,000
April 2008 to April 2010	50,000

Notes

(1) The reduction in AIA from 1 April 2012 (for corporation tax) or 6 April 2012 (for income tax) was made by *FA 2011, s 11*.

(2) The AIA is given for a chargeable period. As a general rule, the annual limit is proportionately increased or decreased for chargeable periods longer or shorter than 12 months.

(3) For chargeable periods which straddle the above relevant dates, the maximum AIA entitlement is calculated by splitting the chargeable period into two chargeable periods, the first ending with the date before the relevant date, and the second

Plant and machinery

commencing from the relevant date. The maximum AIA available is then calculated according to the transitional rules.

First year allowances (FYAs)

(*CAA 2001, s 52*)

FYAs at a rate of 100%, are available for the following types of expenditure incurred by businesses of any size, subject to general exclusions listed below (see **First year allowances: general exclusions**).

Expenditure	Legislation (*CAA 2001*)
Certain energy–saving plant or machinery (see note i below)	s 45A
Cars with low CO_2 emissions	s 45D
Goods vehicles with zero emissions (see note ii below)	s 45DA
Plant or machinery for gas refuelling stations (see note iii below)	s 45E
Plant or machinery for use by a company wholly in a ring fence trade	s 45F
Environmentally beneficial plant or machinery (see note iv below)	s 45H
Certain new investment by companies in new plant or machinery in designated assisted areas in Enterprise Zones (for further details, see **Enterprise Zones** below)	s 45K

Notes

(i) *Energy-saving plant or machinery*:

- No 100% FYAs will be available on expenditure on plant or machinery which generates electricity or heat (or produces biogas or biofuels) attracting tariff payments under the Feed-in Tariff (FiT) or Renewable Heat Incentive (RHI) schemes. This will apply from 1 April 2012 (for corporation tax) or 6 April 2012 (for income tax), except in the case of combined heat and power equipment (CHP) where the restriction applies from April 2014. 100% FYAs may still be claimed (subject the other conditions of the FYA scheme) in respect of expenditure on such equipment as long as no tariffs are paid. Any FYAs granted, in respect of expenditure incurred from April 2012 (or April 2014 for CHP installations), will be withdrawn if FITs or RHI tariffs are paid subsequently (*CAA 2001, s 45AA, as inserted by FB 2012, cl 45*).

- Other changes to the scheme for 100% FYAs on energy-saving and water-efficient technologies will be made with effect from a date to be appointed by Treasury order during summer 2012, adding Heat Pump Driven Air curtains; removing Combustion Trim Controls, Energy Saving Controls for Desiccant Air Dryers and Sequence Controls; and revising approval criteria for other items.

(ii) *Zero–emission goods vehicles* –

- 100% FYAs are generally available for business expenditure on registered new and unused (not second hand) zero-emission goods vehicles, for a period of 5 years from 1 April 2010 (corporation tax) and 6 April 2010 (income tax) (*CAA 2001, s 45DA*).

- Expenditure on zero-emissions goods vehicles does not qualify for 100% FYAs broadly if the person who incurred it is (or forms part of) an undertaking

10 Capital Allowances

that is a 'firm in difficulty' and/or is subject to an outstanding recovery order. In addition, expenditure is excluded if incurred for a qualifying activity in the fishery or aquacultural sectors, or which manages the waste of undertakings. Expenditure is also excluded if taken into account for the purposes of a 'relevant grant' or 'relevant payment' made towards it (*CAA 2001, s 45DB*).

There is a cap on the amount of expenditure on zero-emission goods vehicles that qualifies for FYAs, of €85 million per undertaking over the five year life of the allowances (*CAA 2001, s 212T*).

(iii) *Gas refuelling equipment* – Legislation will be introduced in the *Finance Bill 2013* to extend the 100% FYA for plant and machinery used in gas, biogas and hydrogen refuelling stations for two years beyond the current expiry date, to 31 March 2015 (Budget, 21 March 2012).

(iv) *Tax credits for environmentally beneficial plant or machinery* – Note that legislation will be introduced in the *Finance Bill 2013* to extend the availability of first-year tax credits, for companies surrendering losses attributable to their expenditure on designated energy-saving or environmentally beneficial plant or machinery, for a further five years from 1 April 2013.

Temporary first year allowances (FYAs)

(*FA 2009, s 24*)

A temporary FYA at 40% is available for expenditure on plant and machinery in the 12 months ended 31 March 2010 (for corporation tax) or 5 April 2010 (for income tax).

First year allowances: general exclusions

(*CAA 2001, s 46(2)*)

No first year allowances are available for the following types of expenditure:

1. expenditure incurred in the chargeable period in which the qualifying activity is permanently discontinued;
2. cars (other than those with low CO_2 emissions);
3. certain ships (within *CAA 2001, s 94*);
4. certain railway assets;
5. expenditure that would be long–life asset expenditure but for transitional provisions (in *CAA 2001, Sch 3, para 20*);
6. expenditure on the provision of plant or machinery for leasing (whether in the course of a trade or otherwise) (subject to exceptions in *CAA 2001, s 46(5)*);
7. certain anti–avoidance cases where the obtaining of a FYA is linked to a change in the nature or conduct of a trade;
8. plant and machinery was initially acquired for purposes other than those of the qualifying activity;
9. plant or machinery that was provided for long funding leasing starts to be used for other purposes; and
10. plant and machinery that was acquired by way of a gift.

CARS

(CAA 2001, ss 45D, 52, Pt 2, Ch 10A)

The rate of capital allowances is based on the car's carbon dioxide emissions, as summarised below:

CO$_2$ emissions		Capital allowances
From 2009–2010 to 2012–13	From 2013–2014 to 2014–15	
Up to 110g/km	Up to 95g/km	FYAs at 100% available
Up to 160g/km	Up to 130g/km	Main rate pool applies
Over 160g/km	Over 130g/km	'Special rate' pool applies

Notes

(1) The 100% FYA for business cars with CO$_2$ emissions up to 110g/km applies only for expenditure up to 31 March 2013 on cars which are new and unused (not second hand). *(CAA 2001, s 45D)*. In the *Finance Bill 2013* the Government will extend the 100% FYA for a further two years to 31 March 2015, but the CO$_2$ emissions threshold below which cars are eligible for the FYA will also be reduced from 110 g/km to 95 g/km, and leased business cars will no longer be eligible for the FYA (Budget, 21 March 2012).

(2) *Cars with private use* – The main or special rates apply as above (depending on CO$_2$ emissions) but the car is retained in a single asset pool (see HMRC Capital Allowances Manual, *CA23535*). Allowances are restricted for private use.

(3) *Leased cars* – A 15% disallowance of relevant payments applies if CO$_2$ emissions exceed 160g/km, to be reduced to 130g/km from April 2013 *(ITTOIA 2005, ss 48–49*, to be amended by *Finance Bill 2013*; Budget, 21 March 2012).

(4) *Prior to April 2009* – A standard rate of WDA applied, and allowances were restricted to £3,000 for cars costing £12,000 or more. A proportion of the hire cost of cars was disallowed for tax purposes where the retail price when new exceeded £12,000 *(CAA 2001, Pt 2, Ch 8)*.

(5) *Capital allowances rates* – For WDA rates in respect of the main rate pool and special rate pool, see **Writing down allowances** (WDAs) above.

(6) The *Finance Bill 2013* will provide that, with effect from April 2013, the CO$_2$ emissions threshold for the main rate of capital allowances for business cars will reduce from 160 g/km to 130 g/km. The threshold above which the lease rental restriction applies will also reduce from 160 g/km to 130 g/km (Budget, 21 March 2012).

Integral features

(CAA 2001, ss 33A–B, 104A(1), 104D)

Expenditure on integral features is excluded from the main capital allowances pool. WDAs are given at the special rate (see above) on the reducing balance of the pool. The following fall within the definition of integral features:

- electrical systems (including lighting systems);
- cold water systems;
- space or water heating systems, powered systems of ventilation, air cooling or air purification, and any floor or ceiling comprised in such systems;

10 Capital Allowances

- lifts, escalators and moving walkways; and
- external solar shading.

Notes

(1) The above items do not include any asset whose principal purpose is to insulate or enclose the interior of a building, or to provide an interior wall, floor or ceiling intended to remain permanently in place (*CAA 2001, 33(A)(6)*).

(2) Expenditure on integral features (eg repairs) is treated as being on the replacement of the integral feature, if the expenditure exceeds 50% of the item's replacement cost (*s 33B*).

(3) Expenditure incurred on or after 1 April 2012 (for corporation tax) or 6 April 2012 (for income tax) on solar panels (whether integral or not) will be designated as special rate expenditure (*FB 2012, cl 45*).

Fixtures

(*CAA 2001, Pt 2, Ch 14*)

Special provisions apply to determine entitlement to capital allowances on plant or machinery that becomes a fixture (*CAA 2001, s 172 et seq*). The availability of capital allowances to a purchaser of fixtures on or after 1 April 2012 (for corporation tax) or 6 April 2012 (for income tax) is conditional on either (a) the seller and purchaser using one of two pre-existing procedures (a joint election under CAA 2001, ss 198–199 or determination by the First Tier Tribunal) to fix the value of the fixtures transferred within two years of the transfer, or (b) the past owner providing a written statement of the amount of the disposal value of fixtures which he had some time earlier been required to bring into account. After a transitional period of two years, from 1 or 6 April 2014 it will also be necessary to show that previous business expenditure on qualifying fixtures had been pooled before a subsequent transfer on to another person (*CAA 2001, s 187A, as inserted by FB 2012, Sch 10*).

INDUSTRIAL AND AGRICULTURAL BUILDINGS ALLOWANCES

(*CAA 2001, Pt 3; FA 2008, ss 84–85*)

Financial year commencing	Tax year	Percentage %
1 April 2011 and later	2011–12 and later	0 (abolished)
1 April 2010	2010–11	25%
1 April 2009	2009–10	50%
1 April 2008	2008–09	75%
1 April 2007 and earlier	2007–08 and earlier	100%

Note

Industrial buildings allowances (including those for qualifying hotels) and agricultural buildings allowances were abolished in *Finance Act 2008* with effect from 1 April 2011 (for corporation tax) and 6 April 2011 (for income tax), subject to a transitional phasing out period. For the purposes of reducing allowance entitlement during that period, the above percentages are applied to the allowances that would otherwise be available in respect of the qualifying expenditure.

OTHER ALLOWANCES

(CAA 2001, ss 298–306; Pts 3A, 4A, 5–10)

Allowances	Date of expenditure	Initial allowance	Writing down allowance
Assured tenancy	10 March 1982 to 31 March 1992	–	4% (Note 1)
Business premises renovation	From 11 April 2007	100%	25% (Notes 1, 2)
Dredging	From 1 April 1986	–	4% (Note 1)
Enterprise zones	Expenditure on industrial or commercial buildings if: (a) incurred within 10 years of site being included within the enterprise zone; or (b) contracted within that 10-year period and incurred within 20 years after site being included in the zone.	100%	25% (Notes 1, 3)
Flat conversion	From 11 May 2001 to 31 March or 5 April 2013	100%	25% (Notes 1, 4)
Know–how	From 1 April 1986	–	25% (Note 5)
Mineral extraction	From 1 April 1986	–	10% (acquisition of mineral asset); or 25% (other expenditure)
Patents	From 1 April 1986	–	25% (Note 5)
Research and development	From 5 November 1962	100%	

Notes

(1) The writing down allowances cross-referenced to this note are given on a 'straight line' basis rather than a 'reducing balance' basis.

(2) The business premises renovation allowance has been extended to 2017 and a number of changes have been made to ensure that it continues to comply with the rules for EU State Aid (Budget, 21 March 2012).

(3) Allowances for industrial and commercial buildings in 'old' 10-year enterprise zones were abolished with effect from 1 April 2011 (corporation tax) and 6 April 2011 (income tax) (FA 2008, s 84). The last such enterprise zone to be designated was Tyne Riverside (North Tyneside and South Tyneside) on 21 October 1996.

(4) The flat conversion allowance will be withdrawn for expenditure after 31 March 2013 (for corporation tax) and 5 April 2013 (for income tax) *(FB 2012, cl 225, Sch 38)*.

(5) Capital allowances for know-how and patents still apply for income tax, but were replaced for most corporation tax purposes by the Intangible Assets regime with effect from 1 April 2002.

10 Capital Allowances

TIME LIMITS FOR ELECTIONS AND CLAIMS

(FA 1998, Sch 18, Part IX; CAA 2001, s 3; s 85(2); ss 198, 201, 260(6), 266, 569–570)

Claim	Time Limit
Capital allowances: general *(CAA 2001, s 3; FA 1998, Sch 18, Part IX)*	Later of: (1) 12 months after the filing date for the return in respect of the tax year or accounting period to which the claim relates; (2) 30 days after a closure notice issued on completion of an enquiry; (3) 30 days after notice of amendment to a return issued following completion of an enquiry; or (4) 30 days after the determination of any appeal against an HMRC amendment.
'Short life' asset election (income tax) *(CAA 2001, s 85(2))*	12 months from 31 January next following the tax year in which the relevant chargeable period ends (ie generally the chargeable period in which the qualifying expenditure was incurred)
'Short life' asset election (corporation tax) *(CAA 2001, s 85(2))*	2 years from the end of the relevant chargeable period (ie generally the chargeable period in which the qualifying expenditure was incurred)
Purchase of interest in land that includes a fixture – election to fix apportionment of disposal proceeds *(CAA 2001, ss 198, 201)*	2 years from the date of purchase
Lease of interest in land that includes a fixture – election to fix apportionment of disposal proceeds (CAA 2001, ss 199, 201)	2 years from the date the lease is granted
Set–off of capital allowances on special leasing (corporation tax) *(CAA 2001, s 260(6))*	2 years from end of accounting period
Business successions – transfers between connected parties of plant and machinery at tax–written down value *(CAA 2001, s 266)*	2 years from the date on which the succession took place
Connected parties and controlled sales treated as being at market value: election for sale to be treated as being for an alternative amount *(CAA 2001, s 570(5))*	2 years from the date of sale

Note

Capital allowances claims: general – Capital allowances must be claimed. Most capital allowances are claimed in the tax return (*CAA 2001, s 3*). However, the claims rules for income tax (*TMA 1970, s 42*) and corporation tax (*FA 1998, Sch 18, paras 54–60*) apply in certain instances (*CAA 2001, s 3(4), (5)*):

- Special leasing plant and machinery allowances claims;
- Claims to carry back balancing allowances in respect of mining concerns (these cease to have effect with the abolition of industrial buildings allowances from 1 or 6 April 2011); and
- Claims for patent allowances on non–trading expenditure (in income tax cases).

ENTERPRISE ZONES

(*CA 2001, ss 45K–45N as inserted by FB 2012, cl 44, Sch 11*)

Enhanced Capital Allowances (ECAs) are available to trading companies investing in new plant and machinery in certain designated areas in Enterprise Zones with effect from 1 April 2012.

Notes

(1) *General* – First-year allowances (FYAs) of 100% are available for a limited period to companies (but not unincorporated businesses) investing in new and unused plant or machinery for use primarily in designated assisted areas within Enterprise Zones. To qualify for 100% FYAs under these provisions, the expenditure must be incurred for the purposes of a qualifying activity. The expenditure must be new investment rather than replacement, and must not be on a means of transport or transport equipment for the purposes of a business in the road freight or air transport sectors. There is a cap on the amount of expenditure on new plant or machinery in designated assisted areas that qualifies for FYAs, of €125 million for each 'investment project' (as defined).

(2) *Scope* – The FYAs apply to expenditure incurred in the 5 year period from 1 April 2012 to 31 March 2017 inclusive. The expenditure must be incurred at a time when the designated area is in an assisted area (as defined by the *Assisted Areas Order, SI 2007/107*), and certain defined conditions must be met.

(3) *Assisted areas* – The following Enterprise Zones will qualify for 100% FYAs (Autumn Statement, 29 November 2011):

- Black Country
- Humber Renewable Energy Super Cluster
- Liverpool
- North Eastern
- Sheffield
- Tees Valley

The following additional designated area will qualify for 100% FYAs (Speech by Chief Secretary to the Treasury, 9 March 2012):

- the designated Paull site with Humber Green Port Corridor

The following additional designated areas will qualify for 100% FYAs (Budget, 21 March 2012):

10 Capital Allowances

- a designated site in the London Royal Docks Enterprise Zone
- designated sites in enterprise areas in Scotland, including Irvine, Nigg and Dundee
- a designated site at Deeside in North Wales

A full list of current zones and maps is to be published on the Treasury website (Budget, 21 March 2012).

(4) *Exclusions* – Expenditure in such designated assisted areas does not qualify for 100% FYAs broadly if the company that incurred it is (or forms part of) an undertaking that is a 'firm in difficulty' and/or is subject to an outstanding recovery order. In addition, expenditure is excluded if incurred for a qualifying activity in the fishery or aquacultural sectors, managing the waste of undertakings, or engaged in any of the coal, steel, shipbuilding or synthetic fibres sectors or in the primary production of agricultural products. Expenditure is also excluded if taken into account for the purposes of a 'relevant grant' or 'relevant payment' made towards it.

11

Stamp Taxes

STAMP DUTY LAND TAX (SDLT)

SDLT on land or property

(FA 2003, s 55; FA 2010, s 7)

Effective Date	Residential property	Non-residential or mixed property	Rate %
From 22 March 2012	Up to £125,000	Up to £150,000	0
	£125,001–£250,000*	£150,001–£250,000	1
	£250,001–£500,000	£250,001–£500,000	3
	£500,001–£1000,000	£500,001 and over	4
	£1,000,001–£2,000,000	n/a	5
	£2,000,001 and over	n/a	7
From 6 April 2011 to 21 March 2012	Up to £125,000	Up to £150,000	0
	£125,001–£250,000*	£150,001–£250,000	1
	£250,001–£500,000	£250,001–£500,000	3
	£500,001–£1000,000	£500,001 and over	4
	£1,000,001 and over	n/a	5
1 January 2010 to 5 April 2011	Up to £125,000	Up to £150,000	0
	£125,001–£250,000*	£150,001–£250,000	1
	£250,001–£500,000	£250,001–£500,000	3
	£500,001 and over	£500,001 and over	4
3 September 2008 to 31 December 2009	Up to £175,000	Up to £150,000	0
	£175,001–£250,000	£150,001–£250,000	1
	£250,001–£500,000	£250,001–£500,000	3
	£500,001 and over	£500,001 and over	4
23 March 2006 to 2 September 2008	Up to £125,000	Up to £150,000	0
	£125,001–£250,000	£150,001–£250,000	1
	£250,001–£500,000	£250,001–£500,000	3
	£500,001 and over	£500,001 and over	4
17 March 2005 to 22 March 2006	Up to £120,000	Up to £150,000	0
	£120,001–£250,000	£150,001–£250,000	1
	£250,001–£500,000	£250,001–£500,000	3
	£500,001 and over	£500,001 and over	4
1 December 2003 to 16 March 2005	Up to £60,000	Up to £150,000	0
	£60,001–£250,000	£150,001–£250,000	1
	£250,001–£500,000	£250,001–£500,000	3
	£500,001 and over	£500,000 and over	4

11 Stamp Taxes

Notes

(1) *Calculation of SDLT* – SDLT on chargeable transactions is calculated as a percentage of the amount of relevant consideration for the land or property (*FA 2001, s 55(1)*).

(2) *Acquisitions of multiple dwellings* – On or after 19 July 2011, relief can be claimed for transactions which include the acquisition of interests in more than one dwelling. The rate of SDLT is determined by reference to the consideration divided by the number of dwellings, but subject to a minimum rate of 1%.

(3) *Anti-avoidance* – The following measures are designed to combat avoidance of SDLT by the 'enveloping' of high value properties into companies (Budget, 21 March 2012):

- With effect from 21 March 2012, residential properties over £2,000,000 purchased by non-natural persons (such as companies or trusts) will be liable to SDLT at 15%.
- The Government will consult on the introduction of an annual charge on residential properties valued at over £2 million owned by non-natural persons, to be introduced with effect from April 2013.
- The Government will also consult on extending the capital gains tax regime to gains on disposals of UK residential property by non-resident, non-natural persons, to be introduced with effect from April 2013.

The Government has introduced an additional measure, with effect from 21 March 2012, designed to put beyond doubt that an SDLT avoidance scheme that relies on the sub-sales rules does not work. The change makes it explicit that the grant or assignment of an option cannot be a 'transfer of rights' (*FB 2012, cl 210*). The Government will also consult on the wider approach to addressing SDLT sub-sales avoidance (Budget, 21 March 2012).

*   First time buyers – See below.

Land in disadvantaged areas

(*FA 2003, s 57, Sch 6*)

Effective Date	Residential property	Non-residential or mixed property	Rate %
From 22 March 2012 to 5 April 2013	Up to £150,000	up to £150,000	0
	£150,001–£250,000		1
	£250,001–£500,000		3
	£500,001–£1,000,000		4
	£1,00,001–£2,000,000		5
	£2,000,001 and over		7
From 6 April 2011 to 21 March 2012	£150,000	up to £150,000	0
	£150,001–£250,000*	£150,001–£250,000	1
	£250,001–£500,000	£250,001–£500,000	3
	£500,000–£1,000,000	£500,001 and over	4
	£1,000,001 and over	n/a	5
17 March 2005 to 5 April 2011	£150,000	up to £150,000	0
	£150,001–£250,000	£150,001–£250,000	1
	£250,001–£500,000	£250,001–£500,000	3
	£500,001 and over	£500,001 and over	4

Notes

(1) *General* – Disadvantaged area relief is not available for non-residential land transactions with an effective date on or after 17 March 2005. However, the relief remains available for the completion of contracts entered into and substantially performed on or before 16 March 2005, or for the completion or substantial performance of other contracts entered into on or before 16 March 2005, where certain conditions are satisfied (see *SDLTM20110*).

(2) *Abolition of the relief* – The Government has announced that this relief is to be abolished with effect from 6 April 2013 (Budget, 21 March 2012).

First time buyers

(FA 2003, s 57AA)

SDLT exemption applies to purchases of residential property if the chargeable consideration is more than £125,000 but not more than £250,000 and the purchaser is a first time buyer, where the effective date of the transaction is on or after 25 March 2010 but before 25 March 2012. The relief applies irrespective of whether or not the property is in a disadvantaged area. The Government confirmed on 29 November 2011 (Autumn Statement) that this exemption would not continue beyond 24 March 2012.

Lease rentals

(FA 2003, s 56, Sch 5)

Effective Date	Residential property	Non-residential or mixed property	Rate %
From 1 January 2010	£125,000	£150,000	0
	over £125,000	over £150,000	1
3 September 2008 to 31 December 2009	£175,000	£150,000	0
	over £175,000	over £150,000	1
23 March 2006 to 2 September 2008	£125,000	£150,000	0
	over £125,000	over £150,000	1
17 March 2005 to 22 March 2006	£120,000	£150,000	0
	over £120,000	over £150,000	1
1 December 2003 to 16 March 2005	£60,000	£150,000	0
	over £60,000	over £150,000	1

Notes

(1) *General* – Where the chargeable consideration includes rent, SDLT is payable on the lease premium and on the 'net present value' (NPV) of the rent payable. Online SDLT calculators are available on the HMRC website in respect of both new leases and freehold transactions: (www.hmrc.gov.uk/sdlt/calculate/calculators.htm).

(2) *Annual rent* – Where the annual rent for the lease of non-residential property amounts to £1,000 or more, the 0% SDLT band is unavailable in respect of any lease premium *(FA 2003, Sch 5, para 9A)*. Prior to 12 March 2008, this rule also applied to residential properties, if the annual rent exceeded £600.

(3) *First time buyers* – SDLT exemption applies to the acquisition of residential property on a freehold property or lease premium where the chargeable consideration (excluding rent) is more than £125,000 but not more than £150,000, the purchaser is a first time buyer, and the effective date of the transaction is on or after 25 March 2010 but before 25 March 2012 (*FA 2003, s 57AA*). SDLT on rent is as above.

Stamp duty on land transactions before 1 December 2003

SDLT was introduced from 1 December 2003. Stamp duty rates and tables in respect of freehold property and leasehold property transactions prior to SDLT taking effect are available on the HMRC website: www.hmrc.gov.uk/sd/land/landtransfers-rates.htm.

STAMP DUTY

(*FA 1986, s 67; FA 1999, s 112, Schs 13, 15*)

Stamp duty in respect of land transactions was replaced by SDLT with effect from 1 December 2003, subject to transitional provisions for land transactions effected in pursuance of a contract entered into on or before 10 July 2003 (ie the date of Royal Assent to Finance Act 2003); see SDLT above. However:

- Stamp duty remains chargeable in respect of certain transfers on sale, including the conveyance or transfer of stock or marketable securities (0.5%). However, stamp duty is not payable on transfers of stock or marketable securities on or after 13 March 2008 if the consideration is £1,000 or less, and the instrument is certified at £1,000 (*FA 1999, Sch 13, paras 1(3A), 3*).

- A special stamp duty rate of 1.5% applies to depositary receipts in certain circumstances (*FA 1986, s 67*). A stamp duty rate of 1.5% also applies in respect of bearer instruments in certain circumstances (*FA 1999, Sch 15*).

- Fixed stamp duty is charged without reference to the value of transactions. For instruments executed from 1 October 1999, the amount of every fixed duty is £5 (*FA 1999, s 112(2)*). Fixed duties were generally abolished for most instruments executed from 13 March 2008. However, fixed duty has been retained for certain instruments effecting land transactions (*FA 2008, Sch 32, para 22*).

Stamp duty which is not fixed ('ad valorem' stamp duty) is rounded up to the nearest multiple of £5 (*FA 1999, s 112(1)(b)*).

EXEMPT INSTRUMENTS

(*FA 1985, s 87; SI 1987/516*)

A. The vesting of property subject to a trust in the trustees of the trust on the appointment of a new trustee, or in the continuing trustees on the retirement of a trustee.

B. The conveyance or transfer of property the subject of a specific devise or legacy to the beneficiary named in the will (or his nominee).

C. The conveyance or transfer of property which forms part of an intestate's estate to the person entitled on intestacy (or his nominee).

D. The appropriation of property within section 84(4) of the Finance Act 1985 (death: appropriation in satisfaction of a general legacy of money) or section 84(5) or (7) of that Act (death: appropriation in satisfaction of any interest of surviving spouse or civil partner and in Scotland also of any interest of issue).

E. The conveyance or transfer of property which forms part of the residuary estate of a testator to a beneficiary (or his nominee) entitled solely by virtue of his entitlement under the will.

F. The conveyance or transfer of property out of a settlement in or towards satisfaction of a beneficiary's interest, not being an interest acquired for money or money's worth, being a conveyance or transfer constituting a distribution of property in accordance with the provisions of the settlement.

G. The conveyance or transfer of property on and in consideration only of marriage to a party to the marriage (or his nominee) or to trustees to be held on the terms of a settlement made in consideration only of the marriage.

GG. The conveyance or transfer of property on and in consideration only of the formation of a civil partnership to a party to the civil partnership (or his nominee) or to trustees to be held on the terms of a settlement made in consideration only of the civil partnership.

H. The conveyance or transfer of property within section 83(1) or (1A) of the Finance Act 1985 (transfers in connection with divorce or dissolution of civil partnership etc).

I. The conveyance or transfer by the liquidator of property which formed part of the assets of the company in liquidation to a shareholder of that company (or his nominee) in or towards satisfaction of the shareholder's rights on a winding-up.

J. The grant in fee simple of an easement in or over land for no consideration in money or money's worth.

K. The grant of a servitude for no consideration in money or money's worth.

L. The conveyance or transfer of property operating as a voluntary disposition inter vivos for no consideration in money or money's worth nor any consideration referred to in section 57 of the Stamp Act 1891 (conveyance in consideration of a debt etc).

M. The conveyance or transfer of property by an instrument within section 84(1) of the Finance Act 1985 (death: varying disposition).

N. The declaration of any use or trust of or concerning a life policy, or property representing, or benefits arising under, a life policy.

Notes

(1) Instruments of transfer executed from 1 May 1987 which effect one or more of the transactions specified above and which are properly certified (eg a gift of ordinary shares between family members) are exempt from fixed stamp duty, and do not need to be presented to HMRC for the payment of duty, or for adjudication.

(2) Category N was inserted by the *Stamp Duty (Exempt Instruments) (Amendment) Regulations, SI 1999/2539, reg 5* with effect from 1 October 1999.

11 Stamp Taxes

(3) Category GG was inserted by *Tax and Civil Partnership (No 2) Regulations, SI 2005/3230 reg 2*, with effect from 5 December 2005.

(4) The above are in addition to various other stamp duty exemptions, including an exemption from ad valorem duty for transfers of stock or marketable securities where the consideration is certified as not exceeding £1,000 (*FA 1999, Sch 13, para 1(3A)*). For further information on stamp duty exemptions and generally, see *Stamp Taxes* by Kevin Griffin (Bloomsbury Professional).

STAMP DUTY RESERVE TAX (SDRT)

(*FA 1986, Pt IV; FA 1999, Sch 19, Pt II*)

Charge	Rate
General share transactions (*FA 1986, s 87*)	0.5%
Transfer of securities into depository receipt schemes and clearance services (*FA 1986, ss 93, 96*)	1.5%
Charge in respect of units in unit trusts and shares in open–ended investment companies (*FA 1999, Sch 19, para 3*)	0.5%

Notes

(1) Stamp duty reserve tax (SDRT) was introduced in 1986 to cater for paperless share transactions. SDRT operates alongside the stamp duty charge on share transfers.

(2) The above charges are rounded to the nearest penny, taking any ½p as nearest to the next whole penny above (*FA 1986, s 99(13)*).

ADMINISTRATION

SDLT penalties – general

(*FA 2003, Schs 10, 11; FA 2008, Sch 36, paras 39, 40, 40A, 50*)

Offence	Penalty
Failure to deliver a return by the filing date (*FA 2003, Sch 10, paras 3, 4*)	Up to 3 months late – £100
	Over 3 months late – £200
	Over 12 months – tax related penalty not exceeding the tax chargeable
Failure to comply with a notice to deliver a return (*FA 2003, Sch 10, para 5*)	Up to £60 for each day on which the failure continues
Failure to keep and preserve records (*FA 2003, Sch 10, para 11; Sch 11, para 6*)	Up to £3,000 (unless other satisfactory documentary evidence provided)

Offence	Penalty
Failure to comply with an information notice, or Deliberate obstruction of HMRC officer in the course of a tribunal approved inspection *(FA 2008, Sch 36, paras 39, 40, 50)*	• Initial penalty £300 • Up to £60 for each day on which the failure or obstruction continues • Tax related penalty if HMRC officer has reason to believe that a significant loss of tax will result from continued failure or obstruction.
Inaccurate information and documents *(FA 2008, Sch 36, para 40A)*	Up to £3,000 for each inaccuracy

Notes

(1) The penalty for failure to comply with an information notice or the deliberate obstruction of an HMRC officer during a tribunal approved inspection applies with effect from 1 April 2010 *(FA 2009, s 96, Sch 48; SI 2009/3054, art 2)*. For information notices issued before 1 April 2010, penalties may be charged as follows *(FA 2003, Sch 10, para 16; SI 2009/3054, art 7)*:

- Initial penalty £50; and
- Up to £30 (if determined by HMRC) or £150 (if determined by courts) for each day on which the failure continues.

(2) The tax related penalty for failure to comply with an information notice, or the deliberate obstruction of an HMRC officer in the course of a tribunal approved inspection, requires HMRC to make an application to the Upper Tribunal within certain time limits *(FA 2008, Sch 36, para 50(1))*.

SDLT AND SDRT PENALTIES – ERRORS

(FA 2007, Sch 24)

Unprompted disclosure	**Penalty**
Careless error	0% to 30% of potential lost revenue
Deliberate but not concealed error	20% to 70% of potential revenue lost
Deliberate and concealed error	30% to 100% of potential revenue lost
Prompted disclosure	
Careless error	15% to 30% of potential lost revenue
Deliberate but not concealed error	35% to 70% of potential lost revenue
Deliberate and concealed error	50% to 100% of potential lost revenue

Notes

(1) The above penalties apply with effect for inaccuracies in returns or other documents to be filed on or after 1 April 2010 *(SI 2009/571, art 5)*.

(2) A penalty may also be charged if an error in a return is attributable to another person *(FA 2007, Sch 24, para 1A)*. Penalties in such circumstances range from 30% to 100% for unprompted disclosure, and 50% to 100% for prompted disclosure. They apply where the inaccuracy is contained in a return or other document which is due to be filed from 1 April 2010, and which relates to a tax period beginning from 1 April 2009.

11 Stamp Taxes

STAMP DUTY PENALTIES – LATE STAMPING

(SA 1891, s 15B)

Offence	Penalty
Document not presented within 30 days after: • Execution in the UK; or • It is first received in the UK (if executed outside the UK)	The lower of: • £300; or • the amount of duty
Document presented more than 1 year after the above 30 day period	The greater of: • £300; or • the amount of duty

Notes

(1) The above penalties apply with effect for instruments executed from 1 October 1999.

(2) Penalties are rounded down to the nearest multiple of £5 (STM 3.27).

STAMP TAXES – INTEREST ON LATE PAYMENTS AND OVERPAYMENTS

(SA 1891, s 15A; FA 1999, s 110; FA 2003, ss 87, 89; SI 1986/1711, regs 13, 14)

Period	Late payment Rate %	Overpayments Rate %
From 29 September 2009	3.00	0.50
24 March 2009 to 28 September 2009	2.50	0.00
27 January 2009 to 23 March 2009	3.50	0.00
6 January 2009 to 26 January 2009	4.50	0.75
6 December 2008 to 5 January 2009	5.50	1.50
6 November 2008 to 5 December 2008	6.50	2.25
6 January 2008 to 5 November 2008	7.50	3.00
6 August 2007 to 5 January 2008	8.50	4.00
6 September 2006 to 5 August 2007	7.50	3.00
6 September 2005 to 5 September 2006	6.50	2.25
6 September 2004 to 5 September 2005	7.50	3.00
6 December 2003 to 5 September 2004	6.50	2.25
6 August 2003 to 5 December 2003	5.50	1.50
6 November 2001 to 5 August 2003	6.50	2.25
6 May 2001 to 5 November 2001	7.50	3.00
6 February 2000 to 5 May 2001	8.50	4.00

Notes

(1) *General* – Interest on unpaid stamp duty applies from the end of 30 days after the date on which the document was executed until the duty is paid, with effect for

instruments executed from 1 October 1999. The interest is rounded down to the nearest multiple of £5, and no interest is payable (or repayable) on amounts of less than £25. Interest on repayment of overpaid duty applies in relation to documents executed from 1 October 1999.

(2) *SDLT* – Interest on unpaid SDLT runs from the end of 30 days after the 'relevant date' (generally the effective date of the transaction) until the tax is paid. The relevant dates for repayment of overpaid SDLT are from the date on which the payment is lodged with HMRC until the date when the repayment order is issued.

(3) *SDRT* – Interest on SDRT is charged from the 'accountable date' to the date of payment. If SDRT is overpaid then any repayment of SDRT will be made with interest from the date that it was paid, However, no interest is added to SDRT repayments under £25.

12

VAT

RATES
(*VATA 1994, s 2(1)*)

Effective date	Standard rate %
04/01/11	20.0
01/01/10	17.5
01/12/08	15.0
01/04/91	17.5

Notes

(1) *Reduced rate* – A reduced VAT rate of 5% applies with effect for certain supplies made, and acquisitions taking place, after 31 October 2001 (*VATA 1994, s 29A, Sch 7A*).

(2) *VAT increase* – The rate of VAT was increased from 17.5% to 20% in relation to any supply made from 4 January 2011, and any acquisition or importation taking place from that date (*F(No 2)A 2010, s 3*). Anti-avoidance provisions introduce a supplementary VAT charge of 2.5% on certain supplies that span the date of the change in VAT rate (*F(No 2)A 2010, Sch 2*).

VAT fraction

VAT percentage (%)	VAT fraction
20.0	1/6
17.5	7/47
15.0	3/23
5.0	1/21

Note

The VAT fraction is used to calculate the VAT element of VAT-inclusive goods and services at the appropriate rate.

FORTHCOMING CHANGES

(*Budget, 21 March 2012*)

Changes will be made with effect from 1 October 2012 to address various anomalies and loopholes in the VAT legislation, including:

- applying VAT to approved alterations to listed buildings to bring them into line with the VAT treatment of alterations to non-listed buildings, and repairs and maintenance for all buildings; and

- providing consistency of treatment between self-storage and other forms of storage.
- applying VAT, in the minority of cases where it does not already apply, to hot food and to sports drinks;
- putting beyond doubt the fact that VAT applies to the rental of hairdressers' chairs and the sale of cold food for consumption on the supplier's premises (even if those premises are shared with other suppliers); and
- ensuring that the purchase of holiday caravans is taxed consistently at the standard rate.

Transitional arrangements will be available for alteration works to listed buildings already underway. Anti-forestalling legislation, effective from 21 March 2012, will apply to changes to the VAT treatment of self-storage and alteration works to listed buildings.

ZERO-RATED SUPPLIES

(*VATA 1994, Sch 8*)

Group Number	Subject matter
1	Food
2	Sewerage services and water
3	Books, etc
4	Talking books for the blind and handicapped and wireless sets for the blind
5	Construction of buildings, etc
6	Protected buildings
7	International services
8	Transport
9	Caravans and houseboats
10	Gold
11	Bank notes
12	Drugs, medicines, aids for the handicapped, etc
13	Imports, exports etc
15	Charities etc
16	Clothing and footwear
17	Emissions allowances – repealed for supplies made after 31 October 2010 (see Note (1))

Notes

(1) *Emissions allowances (Group 17)* – Added by *SI 2009/2093, art 4*, with effect from 31 July 2009 but repealed for supplies made after 31 October 2010 and replaced by the reverse charge (*SI 2010/2549*).

(2) *Group 14* – deleted by *SI 1999/1642*, with effect from 1 July 2009.

12 VAT

(3) *'Qualifying aircraft'* – The definition of aircraft which may be supplied at the zero rate was amended (by *F(No3)A 2010, s 21*) with effect in relation to supplies made from 1 January 2011. Zero-rating applies from that date to supplies of aircraft 'used by an airline operating for reward chiefly on international routes' (*VATA 1994, Sch 8, Group 8, Note A1(b)*). This change removes aircraft weight and design/adaptation criteria for all supplies other than to state institutions, to bring UK legislation into line with EU legislation.

(4) *Group 3* – From 19 July 2011, zero-rating is withdrawn from printed matter where the printed matter is ancillary to a differently rated service, and where, if the service and printed matter had been supplied by a single company, the two supplies would have been treated as a single standard-rated, reduced-rated or exempt supply (FA 2011, s 74).

REDUCED RATE SUPPLIES
(*VATA 1994, Sch 7A*)

Group Number	Subject matter
1	Supplies of domestic fuel or power
2	Installation of energy-saving materials (see note 2 below)
3	Grant-funded installation of heating equipment or security goods or connection of gas supply.
4	Women's sanitary products
5	Children's car seats (see note 3 below)
6	Residential conversions
7	Residential renovations and alterations
8	Contraceptive products (from 1 July 2006: *SI 2006/1472*)
9	Welfare advice or information (from 1 July 2006: *SI 2006/1472*)
10	Installation of mobility aids for the elderly (from 1 July 2007: *SI 2007/1601*)
11	Smoking cessation products (for 1 year from 1 July 2007: SI 2007/1601; from 1 July 2008: *SI 2008/1410*)

Notes

(1) *General* – The reduced VAT rate (5%) applies with effect for certain supplies made, and acquisitions taking place, after 31 October 2001 (*VATA 1994, s 29A*).

(2) *Energy-saving materials in charitable buildings* – the *Finance Bill 2013* will remove charitable buildings from the scope of the reduced rate of VAT for the supply and installation of energy-saving materials. The reduced rate of VAT will continue to apply to the supply and installation of energy-saving materials in residential accommodation, including accommodation operated by charities (Budget, 21 March 2012).

(3) *Children's car seats (Group 5)* – Extended to related base units from 1 July 2009 (*SI 2009/1359*).

EXEMPT SUPPLIES

(*VATA 1994, Sch 9*)

Group Number	Subject matter
1	Land
2	Insurance
3	Postal services
4	Betting, gaming and lotteries
5	Finance
6	Education
7	Health and welfare
8	Burial and cremation
9	Subscriptions to trade unions, professional and other public interest bodies
10	Sport, sports competitions and physical education
11	Works of art etc
12	Fund-raising events by charities and other qualifying bodies
13	Cultural services etc (from 1 June 1996: *SI 1996/1256*)
14	Supplies of goods where input tax cannot be recovered (from 1 March 2000: *SI 1999/2833*)
15	Investment gold (from 1 January 2000: *SI 1999/3116*)

Note

Postal services – The definition of postal service was restricted from 31 January 2011 to supplies of public postal services and incidental goods made by a universal service provider (ie the Royal Mail): *F(No 3)A 2010, s 22*.

REGISTRATION LIMITS

UK taxable supplies

(*VATA 1994, Sch 1 para 1*; Supplement to Notices 700/1 and 700/11)

Effective date	Turnover: (a) Past year exceeded; or (b) Next 30 days will exceed:	Exception: Turnover for next year will not exceed:
	£	£
01/04/12	77,000	75,000
01/04/11	73,000	71,000
01/04/10	70,000	68,000
01/05/09	68,000	66,000
01/04/08	67,000	65,000
01/04/07	64,000	62,000

12 VAT

Notes

(1) *Taxable supplies* – Turnover includes zero-rated sales, but not exempt, non-business or outside the scope supplies. Supplies of capital assets (excluding any supplies of land on which the option to tax has been exercised) do not count towards the turnover limit. The same applies to any taxable supplies which would not be taxable supplies apart from *VATA 1994, s 7(4)* (ie in connection with 'distance selling'). Any supplies or acquisitions to which *VATA 1994, s 18B(4)* (last acquisition or supply of goods before removal from fiscal warehousing) applies, and supplies treated as made by him under *s 18C(3)* (self-supply of services on removal of goods from warehousing), are also disregarded (*VATA 1994, Sch 1, para 1(7)–(9)*).

(2) *Compulsory registration* – A person who makes taxable supplies but is not registered under *VATA 1994* becomes liable to be registered if (a) the one year or (b) 30 day turnover limits above are exceeded (*Sch 1, para 1*). However, the one-year turnover test in (a) above is subject to an exception (see note 4 below).

(3) *Going concerns* – If all or part of a business carried on by a taxable person is transferred to another person as a going concern, and the transferee is not registered under *VATA 1994* at the time of transfer, the transferee becomes liable to be registered if: (a) the one year; or (b) 30 day limits above are exceeded (*Sch 1, para 2*). However, the one-year turnover test in (a) above is subject to an exception (see note 4 below).

(4) *Exception* – A person does not become liable to be registered under the mandatory (see note 2) or going concern (see note 3) provisions under the one-year turnover test in (a) above if HMRC are satisfied that the value of his taxable supplies in the one year period beginning when he would otherwise become liable to be registered does not exceed the exception limits in the table above (*Sch 1, para 3*).

(5) *Non-UK established businesses* – Up to 30 November 2012, businesses without a UK establishment who make taxable supplies of goods or services in the UK are allowed to use the UK VAT registration. From 1 December 2012, non-UK established businesses making UK taxable supplies must register for UK VAT regardless of the value of taxable supplies they make in the UK (*FB 2012, cl 201*).

Supplies from other EU member states ('distance selling')

(*VATA 1994, Sch 2; HMRC Notice 700/1, Section 5*)

(1) A taxable person in another EU state which supplies and delivers goods to non-VAT registered customers in the UK broadly becomes liable to register here on any day if, in the period beginning with 1 January of the year in which that day falls, the value of its relevant supplies exceeds £70,000.

(2) This limit has not changed since it was introduced on 1 January 1993.

(3) Special rules apply to the sale of excise goods (eg alcohol and tobacco) (see *HMRC Notice 700/1, section 5.6*).

Acquisitions from other EU member states

(VATA 1994, Sch 3; HMRC Notice 700/1, Section 6)

Effective date	Registration threshold
	£
1/4/12	77,000
1/4/11	73,000
1/4/10	70,000
1/5/09	68,000
1/4/08	67,000
1/4/07	64,000
1/4/06	61,000

Notes

(1) Where an unregistered business or organisation, which does not make or intend to make any taxable supplies in the UK, buys goods from a VAT registered supplier in another EU state to bring to the UK, these are known as relevant acquisitions. This would typically apply to a business making exempt supplies only or using the goods to make non-business supplies only.

(2) The business must register for VAT where the value of relevant acquisitions exceeds the registration limit in the calendar year to 31 December, or if there are reasonable grounds for believing that the value of relevant acquisitions will exceed the registration limit in the next 30 days.

DEREGISTRATION LIMITS

De-registration: UK taxable supplies

(VATA 1994, Sch 1, para 4)

Effective date	Turnover threshold
	£
1/4/12	75,000
1/4/11	71,000
1/4/10	68,000
1/5/09	66,000
1/4/08	65,000
1/4/07	62,000
1/4/06	59,000

Notes

(1) *General* – The turnover threshold applies to the value of taxable supplies in the next 12 months.

(2) *Voluntary deregistration* – A business can ask HMRC to cancel its VAT registration if its annual VAT taxable turnover falls, or is expected to fall in the next 12

12 VAT

months, below the threshold for deregistration. Registration cannot be cancelled if the reduction in turnover is due to the intention of the business to stop trading or suspend making taxable supplies for 30 days or more in the next 12 months. (*HMRC Notice 700/11. para 2.2*)

(3) *Compulsory deregistration* – A business which is registered due to making taxable supplies in the UK must cancel the registration in certain circumstances, eg ceasing to make taxable supplies, or if the business intended to make taxable supplies but no longer intends doing so (*HMRC Notice 700/11, para 2.1*).

Deregistration: Supplies from other EU member states

(*VATA 1994, Sch 2, para 2; HMRC Notice 700/11, para 3*)

(1) *General* – If the business was registered because it exceeded the distance sales threshold (currently £70,000), then it may apply to cancel its registration where:

  (a) the value of its distance sales in the year ending 31 December did not exceed the threshold; and

  (b) the value of its distance sales in the year following, beginning 1 January, will not exceed the threshold.

(2) *Compulsory deregistration* – If the business was registered due to making distance sales from other EC member states, the registration must be cancelled if either the business ceases to make distance sales, or if the business intended to make distance sales but no longer intends to do so and is not eligible or liable for registration as a result of any taxable supplies, acquisitions or relevant supplies (*HMRC Notice 700/11, para 3.1*).

(3) *Voluntary deregistration* – If the business is applying for voluntary deregistration, was registered because the UK was the place of supply for its distance sales, and had opted and made supplies, the business remains registered in the UK for at least two calendar years from the date of first supply following registration. However, if the business opted but did not start to make supplies, the business may apply for cancellation of registration (*HMRC Notice 700/11, para 3.2*).

Acquisitions from other EU member states

(*VATA 1994, Sch 3, para 2; HMRC Notice 700/11, para 4.2*)

Effective date	Relevant acquisitions threshold £
1/4/12	77,000
1/4/10	70,000
1/5/09	68,000
1/4/08	67,000
1/4/07	64,000
1/4/06	61,000

Notes

(1) *General* – If the business was registered because it had previously exceeded the relevant acquisitions threshold, then it may apply to cancel its registration where:

   (a) the value of its relevant acquisitions in the year ending 31 December did not exceed the threshold; and

   (b) the value of its relevant acquisitions in the year following, beginning 1 January, will not exceed the threshold.

(2) *Compulsory deregistration* – If the business was registered due to making relevant acquisitions from other EC member states, the registration must be cancelled if the business ceases to make relevant acquisitions, or if the business intended to make relevant acquisitions but no longer intends doing so and is not eligible or liable for registration as a result of any taxable supplies, distance sales or relevant supplies (*HMRC Notice 700/11, para 4.1*).

(3) *Voluntary deregistration* – An application for voluntary registration may be made if the business was registered because the acquisition threshold was previously exceeded, the value of relevant acquisitions in the year ending 31 December did not exceed the threshold, and the value of relevant acquisitions in the following year will not exceed the threshold. However, a business which voluntarily registered for relevant acquisitions will remain registered in the UK for at least two calendar years unless entitlement to be registered has ceased (*HMRC Notice 700/11, para 4.2*).

ANNUAL ACCOUNTING SCHEME

(*VAT Regulations 1995 (SI 1995/2518), regs 52, 53; HMRC Notice 732*)

Effective date	Joining threshold £	Leaving threshold £
1/4/06	1,350,000	1,600,000
1/4/04	660,000	825,000
1/4/01	600,000	750,000

Notes

(1) *Joining threshold* – A business can use the scheme if estimated taxable supplies for the coming year are not expected to exceed the above joining threshold, subject to certain other criteria (see *SI 1995/2518, reg 52*, and *HMRC Notice 732, paras 2.1 and 2.6*).

(2) *Leaving threshold* – A business must leave the scheme if at the end of the current accounting year (or transitional accounting period) the value of taxable supplies in that year (or period) exceeds the leaving threshold (*SI 1995/2518, reg 53*).

CASH ACCOUNTING SCHEME

(*VAT Regulations 1995 (SI 1995/2518), regs 58, 60; HMRC Notice 731*)

Effective date	Joining threshold (Column 1) £	Leaving threshold (Column 2) £
1/4/07	1,350,000	1,600,000
1/4/04	660,000	825,000
1/4/01	600,000	750,000

Notes

(1) *Joining threshold* – A business can use the scheme if estimated taxable supplies in the next year is not expected to exceed the above joining threshold, and subject to certain other criteria (see *SI 1995/2518, reg 58*, and *HMRC Notice 731, para 2.1*).

(2) *Leaving threshold* – A business must leave the scheme if the value of taxable supplies for a 12 month period (ending at the end of a tax period) has exceeded the above leaving threshold (*SI 1995/2518, reg 60*; see also *HMRC Notice 731, para 6.2*).

(3) *'One-off' sales increases* – A business may remain on cash accounting where it exceeds the amount in column 2 above because of a one-off increase in sales resulting from a genuine commercial activity, provided there are reasonable grounds for believing that the value of its taxable supplies in the next 12 months will be below the amount in column 1 (see *HMRC Notice 731, para 2.6*).

FLAT-RATE SCHEME FOR SMALL BUSINESSES

(*VAT Regulations 1995 (SI 1995/2518), regs 55K, 55L, 55M; SI 2010/2940, regs 2, 4; HMRC Notice 733*)

Category of business	From 4 January 2011 %	1 January 2010 to 3 January 2011 %	1 December 2008 to 31 December 2009 %
Accountancy or book-keeping	14.5	13.0	11.5
Advertising	11.0	10.0	8.5
Agricultural services	11.0	10.0	7.0
Any other activity not listed elsewhere	12.0	10.5	9.0
Architect, civil and structural engineer or surveyor	14.5	13.0	11.0
Boarding or care of animals	12.0	10.5	9.5
Business services that are not listed elsewhere	12.0	10.5	9.5
Catering services including restaurants and takeaways	12.5	11.0	10.5

Flat-rate scheme for small businesses

Category of business	From 4 January 2011 %	1 January 2010 to 3 January 2011 %	1 December 2008 to 31 December 2009 %
Computer and IT consultancy or data processing	14.5	13.0	11.5
Computer repair services	10.5	9.5	10.0
Dealing in waste or scrap	10.5	9.5	8.5
Entertainment or journalism	12.5	11.0	9.5
Estate agency or property management services	12.0	10.5	9.5
Farming or agriculture that is not listed elsewhere	6.5	6.0	5.5
Film, radio, television or video production	13.0	11.5	9.5
Financial services	13.5	12.0	10.5
Forestry or fishing	10.5	9.5	8.0
General building or construction services*	9.5	8.5	7.5
Hairdressing or other beauty treatment services	13.0	11.5	10.5
Hiring or renting goods	9.5	8.5	7.5
Hotel or accommodation	10.5	9.5	8.5
Investigation or security	12.0	10.5	9.0
Labour-only building or construction services*	14.5	13.0	11.5
Laundry or dry-cleaning services	12.0	10.5	9.5
Lawyer or legal services	14.5	13.0	12.0
Library, archive, museum or other cultural activity	9.5	8.5	7.5
Management consultancy	14.0	12.5	11.0
Manufacturing fabricated metal products	10.5	9.5	8.5
Manufacturing food	9.0	8.0	7.0
Manufacturing that is not listed elsewhere	9.5	8.5	7.5
Manufacturing yarn, textiles or clothing	9.0	8.0	7.5
Membership organisation	8.0	7.0	5.5
Mining or quarrying	10.0	9.0	8.0
Packaging	9.0	8.0	7.5
Photography	11.0	10.0	8.5
Post offices (from 1/4/04, previously Postal and courier services at 5.5)	5.0	4.5	2.0
Printing	8.5	7.5	6.5
Publishing	11.0	10.0	8.5
Pubs	6.5	6.0	5.5

continued

12 VAT

Category of business	From 4 January 2011	1 January 2010 to 3 January 2011	1 December 2008 to 31 December 2009
	%	%	%
Real estate activity not listed elsewhere	14.0	12.5	11.0
Repairing personal or household goods	10.0	9.0	7.5
Repairing vehicles	8.5	7.5	6.5
Retailing food, confectionary, tobacco, newspapers or children's clothing	4.0	3.5	2.0
Retailing pharmaceuticals, medical goods, cosmetics or toiletries	8.0	7.0	6.0
Retailing that is not listed elsewhere	7.5	6.5	5.5
Retailing vehicles or fuel	6.5	6.0	5.5
Secretarial services	13.0	11.5	9.5
Social work	11.0	10.0	8.0
Sport or recreation	8.5	7.5	6.0
Transport or storage, including couriers, freight, removals and taxis (couriers prior to 1/4/04 covered by Postal and courier services)	10.0	9.0	8.0
Travel agency	10.5	9.5	8.0
Veterinary medicine	11.0	10.0	8.0
Wholesaling agricultural products	8.0	7.0	5.5
Wholesaling food	7.5	6.5	5.0
Wholesaling that is not listed elsewhere	8.5	7.5	6.0

* 'Labour-only building or construction services' means building or construction services where the value of materials supplied is less than 10% of relevant turnover from such services; any other building or construction services are 'general building or construction services'.

Notes

(1) *Eligibility* – The flat-rate scheme is open to businesses who expect taxable supplies in the next year to be no more than £150,000 excluding VAT (from 10 April 2003). (HMRC Notice 733, para 3.1) In addition, up to 1 April 2009 when this requirement was removed, total business income in that next year must not exceed £187,500 including VAT. Admission to the scheme is also subject to certain other criteria (see *SI 1995/2518, reg 55L* and *HMRC Notice 733, para 3.6*).

(2) *Withdrawal* – From 4 January 2011 a business must leave the scheme if either its tax inclusive annual flat rate turnover (excluding sales of capital assets) exceeds £230,000 at any anniversary of the start date, or if its tax inclusive turnover in the next 30 days alone can reasonably be expected to exceed £230,000. Prior to 4 January 2011, both exit thresholds were £225,000. A business may leave the scheme voluntarily at any time on giving notice. (see *SI 1995/2518, reg 55M*)

Capital goods scheme (CGS)

(3) *Discount* – A newly registered business is generally entitled to a 1% discount on the normal percentage until the day before its first anniversary of becoming VAT registered (see *SI 1995/2518, reg 55JB*; *HMRC Notice 733, para 4.5*).

PARTIAL EXEMPTION DE MINIMIS LIMITS

(*VAT Regulations, SI 1995/2518, regs 106, 107*; *HMRC Notice 706*)

Exempt input tax not exceeding:
• £625 per month on average; and
• 50% of total input tax for the period concerned

Notes

(1) Businesses which have both taxable and exempt income can treat all their exempt input tax as taxable input tax and recover it all, provided the exempt input tax is below the de minimis limit. The input tax claimed in each tax period is provisional until any under or over recovery of input tax is accounted for in an annual adjustment.

(2) For VAT periods starting on or after 1 April 2010, two new optional de minimis tests are available, and also the opportunity for a business to treat itself as de minimis throughout a tax year if it was de minimis in the previous tax year – but still subject to an annual adjustment at the end of the tax year, which could make the business partly exempt and subject to an input tax payback (see *SI 1995/2518, reg 107*; *VAT Information Sheet 04/10*).

CAPITAL GOODS SCHEME (CGS)

(*VAT Regulations 1995, SI 1995/2518, Part XV*; *HMRC Notice 706/2*)

Assets included in the scheme

- Land and buildings – costing £250,000 or more (excluding VAT)

- Computers and computer equipment and from 1 January 2011 this was extended to include ships, boats and aircraft costing more than £50,000 (excluding VAT)

The CGS requires the adjustment of input tax recovered by partially exempt traders and from 1 January 2011, businesses that have business/non-business use on property, computers, aircraft, ships and boats.

12 VAT

Adjustment periods

(SI 1995/2518, reg 114)

Asset	No of intervals in adjustment period
Computers	5
An interest in land, buildings or civil engineering works acquired when the interest (eg a lease) had less than 10 years to run	5
All other assets	10

Notes

(1) *Land and buildings* – In addition to the purchase or construction of a building, the capital goods scheme can apply to alterations, constructions of extensions or annexes, refurbishments and civil engineering works (*SI 1995/2518, reg 113*). Prior to 1 January 2011 building alterations and constructions of extensions or annexes were only included where additional floor space of 10% or more was created by the works.

(2) *Adjustments* – Input tax is initially recovered under the normal partial exemption rules. Section 6 of *HMRC Notice 706/2* ('Capital goods scheme') explains how to make subsequent adjustments under the scheme.

VAT INVOICES

(SI 1995/2518, reg 14)

A VAT invoice must show the following:

- A sequential number based on one or more series which uniquely identifies the document
- The time of the supply
- The date of the issue of the document
- The name, address and registration number of the supplier
- The name and address of the person to whom the goods or services are supplied
- A description sufficient to identify the goods or services supplied
- For each description, the quantity of the goods or the extent of the services, and the rate of VAT and the amount payable, excluding VAT, expressed in any currency.
- The gross total amount payable, excluding VAT, expressed in any currency
- The rate of any cash discount offered
- The total amount of VAT chargeable, expressed in sterling
- The unit price

- Where the VAT invoice includes zero-rated or exempt goods or services, the total of those values separately showing clearly that there is no VAT payable on them

- Where a margin scheme is applied under *VATA 1994, s 50A* (see Note 3 below) or *s 53* (certain supplies made by a tour operator), a relevant reference or any indication that a margin scheme has been applied

- Where a VAT invoice relates in whole or part to a supply where the person supplied is liable to pay the tax (ie a reverse charge), a relevant reference or any indication that the supply is one where the customer is liable to pay the tax.

Notes

(1) *Retailers' invoices* – A retailer who makes a sale of goods or services for £250 or less (including VAT) can issue a simplified invoice (where the customer asks for a VAT invoice), if the supply is other than to a person in another member state. The VAT invoice need only contain the following particulars (*SI 1995/2518, reg 16*):

- The name, address and registration number of the retailer;
- The time of the supply;
- A description sufficient to identify the goods or services supplied;
- The total amount payable including VAT; and
- For each rate of VAT chargeable, the gross amount payable including VAT, and the VAT rate applicable.

(2) *Invoices to persons in other EU member states* – Where a VAT invoice is provided for a person in another EU member state, separate requirements apply as to the particulars which must be included in the invoice, unless HMRC allow otherwise (*SI 1995/2518, reg 14(2); VAT Information Sheet 10/07*).

(3) *Margin schemes* – *VATA 1994, s 50A* applies to supplies of works of art, antiques or collectors' items, motor vehicles, second-hand goods, and any supply of goods through a person who acts as an agent, but in his own name, in relation to the supply. An invoice in relation to such supplies must include a relevant reference. Similar provisions apply to certain supplies made by tour operators (*VATA 1994, s 53*).

(4) *Relevant reference* – A 'relevant reference' is: (a) a reference to the appropriate provision of Council Directive 2006/112/EC; (b) a reference to the corresponding provision of the Act; or (c) any other reference that a margin scheme has been applied or that a reverse charge may apply. Examples of relevant references or indications that a margin scheme has been applied are if the invoice includes: 'This invoice is for a second-hand margin scheme supply' or 'This is a tour operators' margin scheme supply' (*SI 1995/2518, reg 14(8)*; see *VAT Information Sheet 10/07*).

12 VAT

ADVISORY FUEL RATES
(*www.hmrc.gov.uk/cars/advisory_fuel_current.htm*)

Date of journey	Cylinder capacity	Petrol	Diesel	LPG
From 1 March 2012	Up to 1,400cc	15p		10p
	1,401 to 2,000cc	18p		12p
	Over 2,000cc	26p		18p
	Up to 1,600cc		13p	
	1,601 to 2,000cc		15p	
	Over 2,000cc		19p	
From 1 December 2011 to 29 February 202	Up to 1,400cc	15p		10p
	1,401 to 2,000cc	18p		12p
	Over 2,000cc	26p		18p
	Up to 1,600cc		12p	
	1,601 to 2,000cc		15p	
	Over 2,000cc		18p	
From 1 September 2011 to 30 November 2011	Up to 1,400cc	15p		11p
	1,401 to 2,000cc	18p		12p
	Over 2,000cc	26p		18p
	Up to 1,600cc		12p	
	1,601 to 2,000cc		15p	
	Over 2,000cc		18p	
From 1 June 2011 to 31 August 2011	Up to 1,400cc	15p		11p
	1,401–2,000 cc	18p		13p
	Over 2,000cc	23p		18p
	Up to 1,600cc		12p	
	1,601–2,000 cc		15p	
	Over 2,000cc		18p	
From 1 March 2011 to 31 May 2011	1400cc or less	14p	13p	10p
	1401cc to 2000cc	16p	13p	12p
	Over 2000cc	23p	16p	17p
From 1 December 2010 to 28 February 2011	1400cc or less	13p	12p	9p
	1401cc to 2000cc	15p	12p	10p
	Over 2000cc	21p	15p	15p
From 1 June 2010 to 30 November 2010	1400cc or less	12p	11p	8p
	1401cc to 2000cc	15p	11p	10p
	Over 2000cc	21p	16p	14p

Private fuel scale charges

Date of journey	Cylinder capacity	Petrol	Diesel	LPG
From 1 December 2009 to 31 May 2010	1400cc or less	11p	11p	7p
	1401cc to 2000cc	14p	11p	8p
	Over 2000cc	20p	14p	12p
From 1 July to 30 November 2009	1400cc or less	10p	10p	7p
	1401cc to 2000cc	12p	10p	8p
	Over 2000cc	18p	13p	12p
From 1 January to 30 June 2009	1400cc or less	10p	11p	7p
	1401cc to 2000cc	12p	11p	9p
	Over 2000cc	17p	14p	12p
From 1 July to 31 December 2008	1400cc or less	12p	13p	7p
	1401cc to 2000cc	15p	13p	9p
	Over 2000cc	21p	17p	13p
From 1 January to 30 June 2008	1400cc or less	11p	11p	7p
	1401cc to 2000cc	13p	11p	8p
	Over 2000cc	19p	14p	11p

Notes

(1) The advisory fuel rates for company cars published by HMRC apply for income tax and National Insurance contributions purposes. HMRC also apply these rates for VAT purposes, ie a business can reclaim the VAT element on the amount attributable to fuel of mileage allowances paid to employees or subcontractors.

(2) Earlier advisory fuel rates can be found at www.hmrc.gov.uk/cars/advisory-fuel-archive-2002-07.htm

PRIVATE FUEL SCALE CHARGES

(*VATA 1994, ss 56(7), 57*)

Fuel scale charge from 1 May 2011 to 30 April 2012

Shown here on a VAT-inclusive basis (*SI 2012/882*)

See also www.hmrc.gov.uk/vat/forms-rates/rates/rates-thresholds.htm#8 and Notes below.

Description of vehicle: vehicle's CO_2 emissions figure	12 month period £	3 month period £	1 month period £
120 or less	665	166	55
125	1,000	250	83
130	1,065	266	88
135	1,135	283	94
140	1,200	300	100
145	1,270	316	105
150	1,335	333	111

continued

12 VAT

Description of vehicle: vehicle's CO_2 emissions figure	12 month period £	3 month period £	1 month period £
155	1,400	350	116
160	1,470	366	122
165	1,535	383	127
170	1,600	400	133
175	1,670	416	138
180	1,735	433	144
185	1,800	450	150
190	1,870	467	155
195	1,935	483	161
200	2,000	500	166
205	2,070	517	172
210	2,135	533	177
215	2,200	550	183
220	2,270	567	189
225 or more	2,335	583	194

Fuel scale charge from 1 May 2011 to 30 April 2012

Description of vehicle: vehicle's CO_2 emissions figure	12 month period £	3 month period £	1 month period £
120 or less	630	157	52
125	945	236	78
130	1,010	252	84
135	1,070	268	89
140	1,135	283	94
145	1,200	299	99
150	1,260	315	105
155	1,325	331	110
160	1,385	346	115
165	1,450	362	120
170	1,515	378	126
175	1,575	394	131
180	1,640	409	136
185	1,705	425	141
190	1,765	441	147
195	1,830	457	152
200	1,890	472	157
205	1,955	488	162
210	2,020	504	168
215	2,080	520	173
220	2,145	536	178
225 or more	2,205	551	183

Private fuel scale charges

Fuel scale charge from 1 May 2010 to 30 April 2011

Description of vehicle: vehicle's CO_2 emissions figure	12 month period £	3 month period £	1 month period £
120 or less	570	141	47
125	850	212	70
130	850	212	70
135	910	227	75
140	965	241	80
145	1,020	255	85
150	1,080	269	89
155	1,135	283	94
160	1,190	297	99
165	1,250	312	104
170	1,305	326	108
175	1,360	340	113
180	1,420	354	118
185	1,475	368	122
190	1,530	383	127
195	1,590	397	132
200	1,645	411	137
205	1,705	425	141
210	1,760	439	146
215	1,815	454	151
220	1,875	468	156
225	1,930	482	160
230 or more	1,985	496	165

Fuel scale charge from 1 May 2009 to 30 April 2010

Description of vehicle: vehicle's CO_2 emissions figure	12 month period £	3 month period £	1 month period £
120 or less	505	126	42
125	755	189	63
130	755	189	63
135	755	189	63
140	805	201	67
145	855	214	71
150	905	226	75
155	960	239	79

continued

12 VAT

Description of vehicle: vehicle's CO$_2$ emissions figure	12 month period £	3 month period £	1 month period £
160	1,010	251	83
165	1,060	264	88
170	1,110	276	92
175	1,160	289	96
180	1,210	302	100
185	1,260	314	104
190	1,310	327	109
195	1,360	339	113
200	1,410	352	117
205	1,465	365	121
210	1,515	378	126
215	1,565	390	130
220	1,615	403	134
225	1,665	416	138
230	1,715	428	142
235 or more	1,765	441	147

Fuel scale charge from 1 May 2008 to 30 April 2009

Description of vehicle: vehicle's CO$_2$ emissions figure	12 month period £	3 month period £	1 month period £
120 or less	555	138	46
125	830	207	69
130	830	207	69
135	830	207	69
140	885	221	73
145	940	234	78
150	995	248	82
155	1,050	262	87
160	1,105	276	92
165	1,160	290	96
170	1,215	303	101
175	1,270	317	105
180	1,325	331	110
185	1,380	345	115
190	1,435	359	119
195	1,490	373	124
200	1,545	386	128
205	1,605	400	133
210	1,660	414	138

Description of vehicle: vehicle's CO_2 emissions figure	12 month period £	3 month period £	1 month period £
215	1,715	428	142
220	1,770	442	147
225	1,825	455	151
230	1,880	469	156
235 or more	1,935	483	161

Notes

(1) *General* – If a business pays for any fuel used for private motoring by its owners, directors or employees, it has to pay VAT on the VAT-inclusive fuel scale charge listed above at the rate applicable at the time the charge is due. To calculate standard rate VAT from the VAT inclusive amount, multiply the VAT inclusive scale charge by the appropriate VAT fraction.

(2) *CO_2 emissions figures* – Where the CO_2 emissions figure of a vehicle is not a multiple of five, the figure is rounded down to the next multiple of five to determine the level of the charge. For a bi-fuel vehicle which has two CO_2 emissions figures, the lower of the two figures should be used. For cars which are too old to have a CO_2 emissions figure, HMRC have prescribed a level of emissions by reference to the vehicle's engine capacity. (*HMRC Notice 700/64, para 9.3*)

(3) *Further information* – Information on fuel scale charges and motor expenses generally is contained in *HMRC Notice 700/64*.

EU COUNTRY CODES

(*VAT Regulations, SI 1995/2518, reg 2*)

EU country	Country code
Austria	AT
Belgium	BE
Bulgaria (from 1/1/07)	BG
Cyprus	CY
Czech Republic	CZ
Denmark (except the Faroe Islands and Greenland)	DK
Estonia	EE
Finland (but excluding the Åland Islands)	FI
France (including Monaco but excluding Guadeloupe, Martinique, Réunion, St. Pierre and Miquelon, and French Guiana)	FR

continued

12 VAT

EU country	Country code
Germany (except Büsingen and the Isle of Heligoland)	DE
Greece	EL
Hungary	HU
Ireland	IE
Italy (except the communes of Livigno and Campione d'Italia and the Italian waters of Lake Lugano)	IT
Latvia	LV
Lithuania	LT
Luxembourg	LU
Malta	MT
Netherlands (except Bonaire, Sint Eustatius and Saba – former components of the Netherlands Antilles)	NL
Poland	PL
Portugal (including the Azores and Madeira)	PT
Romania (from 1/1/07)	RO
Slovak Republic	SK
Slovenia	SI
Spain (including the Balearic Islands but excluding Ceuta, Melilla and the Canary Islands)	ES
Sweden	SE
United Kingdom	GB

Notes

(1) Cyprus – those areas under the control of the Government of the Republic of Cyprus and including the UK Sovereign Base Areas of Akrotiri and Dhekelia.

(2) United Kingdom – The UK and the Isle of Man are part of the EU VAT area, but sales to the UK and/or the Isle of Man should not be included on the EC Sales List (ESL).

(3) The following are not part of the EU VAT area:

- The Åland Islands
- Andorra
- The Channel Islands
- The overseas departments of France (Guadeloupe, Martinique, Reunion, St. Pierre and Miquelon, and French Guiana)
- Gibraltar
- Liechtenstein
- Mount Athos (Agion Poros)

- San Marino
- Vatican City

(4) HMRC have published a list of EU country VAT number formats and links to foreign language enquiry letters (www.hmrc.gov.uk/vat/managing/international/esl/country-codes.htm; see also *HMRC Notice 725*).

CIVIL PENALTIES, SURCHARGES AND INTEREST

Note

HMRC (or the tribunal) may reduce certain civil penalties to such amount (including nil) as they think proper (*VATA 1994, s 70*). For guidance on the penalties which can be mitigated, and the potential levels of mitigation, see VCP11713 and VCP11740 et seq.

Errors in returns, etc

(*FA 2007, s 97, Sch 24*)

Behaviour	Unprompted disclosure Maximum penalty	Unprompted disclosure Minimum penalty	Prompted disclosure Maximum penalty	Prompted disclosure Minimum penalty
Careless	30%	0%	30%	15%
Deliberate but not concealed	70%	20%	70%	35%
Deliberate and concealed	100%	30%	100%	50%

Notes

(1) *General* – For penalties to apply, the inaccuracy must be careless or deliberate and result in an underpayment of tax. Where a document contains more than one inaccuracy, a penalty is payable for each inaccuracy (*FA 2007, Sch 24, paras 1, 4(1)*).

(2) *Scope* – For VAT purposes, penalties can apply in relation to the following:
- VAT returns under regulations made under *VATA 1994, Sch 11, para 2*;
- Returns, statements or declaration in connection with a claim; and
- Any document which is likely to be relied upon by HMRC to determine, without further inquiry, a question about (a) a person, P's liability to tax, (b) payments by P by way of or in connection with tax, (c) any other payment by P (including penalties), or (d) repayments, or any other kind of payment or credit, to P.

(3) *Commencement* – The above penalties generally apply to returns for tax periods commencing from 1 April 2008, and for which the filing date is on or after 1 April 2009 (*SI 2008/568*). Exceptions to this general rule include those below; the filing date for these documents must be on or after 1 April 2009 (see CH81012):
- Claims under the Thirteenth Council Directive (arrangements for the refund of VAT to persons not established in Community territory) must be for years commencing on or after 1 July 2008.

12 VAT

- Claims under the Eighth Council Directive (arrangements for the refund of VAT to taxable persons not established in the territory of the country) must be for years commencing on or after 1 January 2009.

(3) *Type and quality of disclosure* – The maximum penalties above are subject to potential reduction, depending on whether the disclosure of the inaccuracy is 'prompted' or 'unprompted', and reflecting the quality of the disclosure.

(4) *Error by another person* – A penalty can also apply to an error in a taxpayer's document which is attributable to another person (*FA 2007, Sch 24, para 1A*). Penalties range from 30% to 100% for unprompted disclosure, and 50% to 100% for prompted disclosure.

(5) *Special reductions and suspensions* – HMRC may reduce a penalty in 'special circumstances', and penalties may be suspended at HMRC's discretion in appropriate cases (*FA 2007, Sch 24, paras 11, 14*).

Under-assessment by HMRC

(*FA 2007, Sch 24, paras 2, 4C*)

- *General* – A penalty can be charged on a person if an HMRC assessment understates the tax payable, and the person fails to take reasonable steps to notify HMRC of the under-assessment within 30 days from the date of the assessment.
- *Level of penalty* – The maximum penalty payable is 30% of the potential lost revenue. The penalty may be reduced in the same way as for errors in returns where the person would otherwise be liable to a penalty at the 30% rate.
- *Commencement* – The penalty provisions generally apply to assessments for tax periods commencing from 1 April 2008 (*SI 2008/568, art 2(b)*).
- *Special reductions* – HMRC may reduce a penalty because of 'special circumstances' (*FA 2007, Sch 24, para 11*).

Failure to notify

(*FA 2008, Sch 41, paras 1, 6*)

Behaviour	Unprompted disclosure		Prompted disclosure	
	Maximum penalty	Minimum penalty	Maximum penalty	Minimum penalty
Non-deliberate	30%	0% or 10%*	30%	10% or 20%*
Deliberate but not concealed	70%	20%	70%	35%
Deliberate and concealed	100%	30%	100%	50%

* *Non-deliberate failure* – In cases involving a maximum penalty of 30%, the minimum penalties of 0% (for unprompted disclosure) and 10% (for prompted disclosure) potentially apply if HMRC become aware of the failure less than 12 months after the tax first becomes unpaid by reason of the failure. In any other case, the higher minimum percentages (ie 10% or 20%) apply (*FA 2008, Sch 41, para 13(5), (6)*).

Notes

(1) *General* – The notification requirements for which the above penalties apply include the following (*FA 2008, Sch 41, para 1*):

- Obligations to notify liability to register, and to notify material change in the nature of supplies made by a person exempted from registration (*VATA 1994, Sch 1, paras 5, 6, 7, 14(2), 14(3)*);
- Obligation to notify liability to register (under *VATA 1994, Sch 2 para 3*);
- Obligations to notify liability to register and to notify acquisition affecting exemption from registration (under *VATA 1994, Sch 3, paras 3, 8(2)*);
- Obligations to notify liability to register, and to notify relevant change in supplies made by person exempted from registration (under *VATA 1994, Sch 3A, paras 3, 4, 7(2), 7(3)*); and
- Obligation to give notification of acquisition of goods from another member state (*VATA 1994, Sch 11, para 2(4)*).

(2) *Commencement* – The above penalty regime applies where the obligation to notify arises from 1 April 2010 (*SI 2009/511, art 3*).

(3) *Type and quality of disclosure* – The maximum penalties above are subject to potential reduction, generally depending on whether the disclosure of the inaccuracy is 'prompted' or 'unprompted', and reflecting the quality of the disclosure.

(4) *Special reductions and reasonable excuse* – HMRC may reduce a penalty in 'special circumstances', and penalties do not arise if HMRC or the tribunal are satisfied that there is a 'reasonable excuse' for the act or failure (*FA 2008, Sch 41, paras 14, 20*).

Default surcharge

(*VATA 1994, ss 59–59B, 71; HMRC Notice 700/50*)

Defaults	Surcharge	Surcharge period
First default	No surcharge Surcharge Liability Notice issued.	12 months
Second default in a surcharge period	2% (unless it is less than £400)*	12 months from the date of the most recent default
Third default in a surcharge period	5% (unless it is less than £400)*	12 months from the date of the most recent default
Fourth default in a surcharge period	10%	12 months from the date of the most recent default
Fifth and subsequent defaults in a surcharge period	15%	12 months from the date of the most recent default

* HMRC do not issue a surcharge at the 2% and 5% rates if it is calculated to be less than £400 (*HMRC Notice 700/50, para 4.5*)

12 VAT

Notes

(1) *General* – A default surcharge can apply to the failure to submit a return or amount of VAT payable on time, or the amount due under the payment on account scheme on time. The surcharge is calculated as a percentage of the unpaid VAT in default.

(2) *Small businesses* – HMRC apply special arrangements to 'small businesses' (ie those with a taxable turnover of £150,000 or less) to help when the business first has difficulties paying VAT on time. HMRC will send a letter offering help and support rather than a Surcharge Liability Notice following the first default (*HMRC Notice 700/50, para 4.2*).

(3) *Minimum surcharge* – There is a minimum surcharge of £30 for surcharges calculated at the 10% or 15% rates (*VATA 1994, s 59(4); see HMRC Notice 700/50, para 4.5*).

(4) *Reasonable excuse* – A surcharge liability does not arise if HMRC or the tribunal are satisfied that there is a reasonable excuse for the return or VAT payment being late (*VATA 1994, s 59(7)*). As to circumstances which cannot constitute a 'reasonable excuse' for these purposes, see *VATA 1994, s 71(1)*.

(5) *Payments on account* – Surcharges can apply to late payments on account; see *VATA 1994, s 59A* and *HMRC Notice 700/50, para 4.4*).

(6) *Further information* – For further information on default surcharges, and on VAT penalties generally, see www.hmrc.gov.uk/vat/managing/problems/penalties.htm.

Unauthorised issue of VAT invoice

(FA 2008, Sch 41, paras 2, 6)

- *General* – A penalty is payable by a person who makes an unauthorised issue of a VAT invoice, ie where an 'unauthorised person' (eg a person not registered under *VATA 1994*) issues an invoice showing an amount of VAT or a VAT inclusive amount).

- *Commencement* – The provisions apply to any unauthorised issue of an invoice taking place from 1 April 2010 (*SI 2009/511, art 3*).

- *Level of penalty* – The same penalties apply as for failure to notify (see **Failure to notify** above), except that the lower penalties for non-deliberate behaviour (ie 0% (unprompted) and 10% (prompted)) do not apply.

- *Special reductions and reasonable excuse* – HMRC may reduce a penalty in 'special circumstances' and penalties do not arise if HMRC or the tribunal are satisfied that there is a 'reasonable excuse' for the act or failure (*FA 2008, Sch 41, paras 14, 20*).

Incorrect certificates as to zero-rating etc

(VATA 1994, s 62)

- *General* – The penalty is charged in respect of incorrect certificates within *VATA 1994, s 62(1)*, or in respect of acquisitions of goods from other member states within the fiscal warehousing regime; see *s 62(1A)*.

- *Person liable* – The person giving or preparing the certificate is liable to the penalty.
- *Level of penalty* – The penalty is equal to the difference between the VAT chargeable if the certificate had been correct and any VAT actually charged, or (in respect of acquisitions from other member states within the fiscal warehousing regime) the amount of VAT actually chargeable on the acquisition.

Inaccuracies in EC sales statements, etc

(*VATA 1994, s 65*)

- *General* – A penalty may be charged for material inaccuracies in EC sales statements, or in statements relating to *VATA 1994, s 55A* ('Customers to account for tax on supplies of goods or services of a kind used in missing trader intra-community fraud').
- *Amount of penalty* – A penalty of £100 is charged for a material inaccuracy on a statement submitted within 2 years after a penalty notice has been issued by HMRC. The penalty applies if the trader submits a third EC sales statement containing a material inaccuracy within the 2-year period, and only relates to the third list containing an inaccuracy (see VCP11044).

Failure to submit EC sales statements, etc

(*VATA 1994, s 66*)

- *General* – A penalty may be charged for the late submission of EC sales statements, or of statements relating to *VATA 1994, s 55A* ('Customers to account for tax on supplies of goods or services of a kind used in missing trader intra-community fraud').
- *Level of penalties* – Penalties may be charged if HMRC has served a default notice and the statement to which the notice relates is not submitted within 14 days after the notice is served. The penalty is the greater of £50 or the following daily penalties (each up to a maximum of 100 days):
  - First default (or the default to which the notice relates) – £5 per day;
  - Second default – £10 per day; and
  - Any other case – £15 per day.

Breach of walking possession agreements

(*VATA 1994, s 68*)

- *General* – A penalty can be imposed for the breach of an undertaking contained in a walking possession agreement (nb a penalty under *VATA 1994, s 68* does not extend to Scotland).
- *Amount of penalty* – The person in default is liable to a penalty equal to 50% of VAT due or any amount recoverable as if it were VAT due.

Breaches of regulatory provisions

(VATA 1994, s 69; VCP11100 et seq)

- *General* – Subject to certain exceptions in *VATA 1994, s 69(4)* (eg if the trader is liable to a default surcharge for the same failure), the penalty for a failure to comply with any regulatory requirement is determined according to the number of occasions in the previous 2 years on which the person has failed to comply with that requirement. The regulatory requirements in question are listed in *VATA 1994, s 69* (eg failure to notify HMRC of cessation of trading by a registered person, or failure to comply with any requirement set out in the VAT Regulations and any other regulations made under *VATA 1994*).
- *Amount of penalty* – The penalty is generally the greater of £50 and an amount equal to the prescribed rate multiplied by the number of days on which the failure continues, up to a maximum of 100. The 'prescribed rate' depends upon the number of failures to comply, as follows:
    - No previous failure to comply in the above period – £5
    - One previous failure in that period – £10
    - Any other case – £15
- *Late payments or late submission of VAT returns* – Where the breach is a late payment failure or the late furnishing of a return, the prescribed penalty rate is the greater of the penalty above, and the amounts as follows (*VATA 1994, s 69(5)*):
    - No previous failure in the above period – One-sixth of 1% of the VAT due or assessed in respect of that period
    - One previous failure in that period – One-third of 1% of the VAT due
    - Any other case – One-half of 1% of the VAT due

    A late payment or filing penalty cannot be assessed if a default surcharge is to be assessed for the same failure (VCP11134).

Failure to preserve records

(VATA 1994, s 69(2))

- *General* – HMRC may require records to be preserved for a period specified in writing, but not exceeding 6 years (*VATA 1994, Sch 11, para 6(3)*). A penalty may be charged for a failure to comply.
- *Amount of penalty* – The penalty for failing to comply with a requirement imposed under *VAT 1994, Sch 11, para 6(3)* is £500, unless HMRC or the tribunal is satisfied that there is a reasonable excuse for the failure.

Failure to keep records or provide information: specified gold transactions

(VATA 1994, s 69A)

- *General* – The provisions apply to a person who fails to comply with certain record and information requirements in respect of specified gold transactions (ie in respect of regulations made under *FA 1999, s 13(5)(a)* or *(b)*).

- *Penalty* – The maximum penalty is 17.5% of the value of the transactions to which the failure relates, unless HMRC or the tribunal is satisfied that there is a reasonable excuse for the failure.

Breach of HMRC direction to keep records

(VATA 1994, s 69B, Sch 11, para 6A(1), (6))

- *General* – Penalties can arise in respect of the following compliance failures:

    (a) To comply with a HMRC direction to keep specified records;

    (b) To comply with a requirement by HMRC to preserve records for a period of up to 6 years.

- *Penalties* – The penalties for failing to comply with the above requirements (unless HMRC or the tribunal is satisfied that there is a reasonable excuse for the failure) are as follows:

    (a) In respect of (a) above – The penalty is £200 for each day the failure continues (up to a maximum of 30 days);

    (b) In respect of (b) above – The penalty is £500.

Evasion of import VAT (and other relevant duties)

(FA 2003, ss 24(2)(d), 25)

- *General* – A penalty can be imposed where a person engages in conduct to evade import VAT, or by which he contravenes a legislative duty, obligation, requirement or condition in relation to import VAT.

- *Penalty* – The penalty for evasion involving dishonesty is an amount equal to the import VAT evaded or sought to be evaded.

- Other relevant duties – The same penalty provisions that apply to import VAT apply to other relevant duties.

Contravention of relevant rules

(FA 2003, ss 26, 27, 29; Customs (Contravention of a Relevant Rule) Regulations 2003, SI 2003/3113)

- *General* – A penalty can arise for contravening a 'relevant rule' (see *FA 2003, s 26(8), SI 2003/3113, reg 3 and Schedule*).

- *Penalty* – A penalty of up to £2,500 (or other amount prescribed by Treasury Order) can be imposed (unless HMRC or the tribunal are satisfied that there is a reasonable excuse for the failure, or unless the penalty is reduced or cancelled by HMRC or the tribunal).

Online filing – Failure of a specified person to file VAT returns electronically (prescribed accounting periods ending from 31 March 2011)

(*Value Added Tax Regulations 1995, SI 1995/2518, reg 25A*)

Annual VAT exclusive turnover	Penalty	Annual VAT exclusive turnover	Penalty
£22,800,001 and above	£400	£100,001 to £5,600,000	£200
£5,600,001 to £22,800,000	£300	£100,000 and under	£100

Notes

(1) *Specified person* – A 'specified person' is one who became VAT registered on or after 1 April 2010, or is registered before that date and at 31 December 2009 or any later date has an annual turnover of £100,000 or more (exclusive of VAT), whether or not that person's turnover subsequently falls below that level, and who in either case is notified by HMRC as being a specified person. A 'specified person' is charged a penalty if they submit a paper return for any accounting period ending on or after 31 March 2011.

(2) *Commencement* – Specified persons can be liable to penalties in relation to returns made for prescribed accounting periods ending on or after 31 March 2011 (SI 1995/2518, reg 25A(15)).

(3) *Digital by default* – All VAT registered persons are required to submit online VAT returns from 1 April 2012. Those first required to do so from that date will be charged a penalty if they submit a paper return for any accounting period ending on or after 31 March 2013.

(4) *Exceptions* – A person who has a reasonable excuse for failing to comply is not liable to a penalty. There is also an exemption for businesses run by individuals who have a religious conscience objection to the use of computers and the internet.

Disclosure of tax avoidance schemes

(*VATA 1994, Sch 11A, paras 10, 11; The VAT (Disclosure of Avoidance Schemes) Regulations 2004, SI 2004/1929; Value Added Tax (Disclosure of Avoidance Schemes) (Designations) Order 2004, SI 2004/1933; HMRC Notice 700/8*).

(1) *General* – A penalty can apply to the failure to disclose the following (within the statutory time limit in *SI 2004/1929, reg 2;* see *HMRC Notice 700/8, section 5*):
- The use of a designated avoidance scheme, unless the taxable person has already notified HMRC; or
- A notifiable scheme that is not a designated scheme.

(2) *Amount of penalty* – The penalties for failing to comply with the notification requirements (unless there is a reasonable excuse for the failure) are as follows:
- Notifiable scheme that is not a designated scheme – £5,000; or
- Designated scheme – 15% of the VAT saving.

Interest on underpaid VAT (default interest)

(VATA 1994, s 74; HMRC Departmental interest rates; HMRC Notice 700/43)

Period from	Interest rate applicable
	%
29/9/09	3.00
24/3/09	2.50
27/1/09	3.50
6/1/09	4.50
6/12/08	5.50
6/11/08	6.50
6/1/08	7.50
6/8/07	8.50
6/9/06	7.50
6/9/05	6.50
6/9/04	7.50
6/12/03	6.50

Notes

(1) *General* – Default interest is charged where appropriate on any amount of VAT which has been underdeclared or overclaimed, from the time the amount should have been paid to the time it is assessed. It is intended to provide 'commercial restitution' for the loss of understated or overclaimed VAT and should not be considered a penalty (see *HMRC Notice 700/43, para 1.2*).

(2) *Payment of interest* – If all the VAT liable to interest is not paid within 30 days of a notification from HMRC, further interest is chargeable. Interest continues to be charged on a monthly basis until all the VAT liable to interest is paid. HMRC will issue notification of these additional interest charges on a Notice of Assessment of Further Interest Form (*HMRC Notice 700/43, para 2.8*).

Interest on overpaid VAT in certain cases of official error

(VATA 1994, s 78; HMRC Departmental interest rates – 'Statutory interest')

Period from	Interest rate
	%
29/9/09	0.5
27/1/09	0.0
6/1/09	1.0
6/12/08	2.0
6/11/08	3.0
6/1/08	4.0
6/8/07	5.0
6/9/06	4.0
6/9/05	3.0
6/9/04	4.0
6/12/03	3.0

12 VAT

Notes

(1) In addition to interest relating to errors, HMRC also pay interest if the mistake meant that the recipient had to wait an unreasonable time before receiving payment of an amount related to VAT. A separate claim must be made for any interest from HMRC, as it is not paid automatically (see www.hmrc.gov.uk/vat/managing/problems/corrections/receiving-interest.htm).

(2) An interest claim (under *VATA 1994, s 78*) must be made not more than 4 years after the end of the applicable period to which it relates (*s 78(11)*).

13

Other taxes and duties

INSURANCE PREMIUM TAX (IPT)

(*FA 1994, Pt III, Schs 6A–7A; IPT Regulations 1994, SI 1994/1774*)

Rates of IPT

(*FA 1994, ss 51, 51A*)

Period	Standard Rate %	Higher Rate %
From 4 January 2011	6.0	20.0
1 July 1999 to 3 January 2011	5.0	17.5
1 April 1997 to 30 June 1999	4.0	17.5
1 October 1994 to 31 March 1997	2.5	–

Notes
(1) Insurance premium tax (IPT) was introduced in 1994. It is charged on premiums received by insurers under taxable insurance contracts from 1 October 1994.
(2) The higher rate of IPT applies to insurance sold in certain circumstances relating to motor cars or motorcycles, certain electrical or mechanical domestic appliances and travel insurance (*FA 1994, Sch 6A*).

LANDFILL TAX

(*FA 1996, Pt III, Sch 5; FA 2011, s 25; SI 1996/1527; SI 2011/1017*)

Rates

(*FA 1996, s 42*)

Disposals made or treated as made	Standard rate per tonne £	Lower rate per tonne £	Maximum credit %
From 1 April 2013	72	2.50	6.2
1 April 2012–31 March 2013	64	2.50	6.2
1 April 2011–31 March 2012	56	2.50	6.2
1 April 2010–31 March 2011	48	2.50	5.5
1 April 2009–31 March 2010	40	2.50	6.0
1 April 2008–31 March 2009	32	2.50	6.0
1 April 2007–31 March 2008	24	2.00	6.6

13 Other taxes and duties

Notes

(1) Landfill Tax was introduced from 1 October 1996. It applies to waste disposals by way of landfill at a licensed site, unless specifically exempted. Landfill site operators are taxed on disposals of waste by reference to the weight and type of waste concerned. Inactive or inert waste (as listed in the *Landfill Tax (Qualifying Material) Order, SI 2011/1017* (replacing *SI 1996/1528* with effect from 1 April 2011) is taxed at a reduced rate.

(2) It was announced in the June 2010 Budget that the standard rate of landfill tax would rise by £8 per tonne on 1 April each year up to and including 2014. The Government also announced a floor under the standard rate of landfill tax so that the rate will not fall below £80 per tonne from 2014–15 to 2019–20.

(3) The lower rate is currently £2.50 a tonne and this rate will remain frozen for 2013–14 (Budget, 21 March 2012).

(4) The lower rate of landfill tax relates to listed inactive (or inert) wastes. The standard rate applies to all other taxable waste.

(5) Registered landfill site operators can claim a tax credit worth 90% of any qualifying contributions made to approved environmental bodies, subject to a maximum percentage of their landfill tax liability during the contribution year. (*Landfill Tax Regulations, SI 1996/1527, reg 31*).

AGGREGATES LEVY

(*FA 2001, Pt 2, Schs 4–10; FA 2011, s 24; Aggregates Levy Regulations 2002, SI 2002/761*)

Rates

(*FA 2001, s 16*)

Period	Rate per tonne £
From 1 April 2013	2.10
1 April 2009–31 March 2013	2.00
1 April 2008–31 March 2009	1.95
1 April 2002–31 March 2008	1.60

Notes

(1) Aggregates levy was introduced on 1 April 2002. It is charged on aggregate (broadly rock, sand and gravel) subjected to commercial exploitation.

(2) The levy is charged at a rate per tonne, and the amount of levy charged on a part of a tonne of aggregate shall be the proportionately reduced amount (*FA 2001, s 16(4)*).

(3) The statutory rate per tonne is currently stated to be £2.10 (*FA 2001, s 16(4)*), increased from £2.00 with effect from 1 April 2011, but it was announced in Budget 2011 that this increase was being deferred. The Government has now announced that this increase is to be further deferred until 1 April 2013 (Budget, 21 March 2012).

CLIMATE CHANGE LEVY

(FA 2000 s 30, Sch 6; Climate Change Levy (General) Regulations 2001, SI 2001/838)

Rates

(FA 2000, Sch 6, para 42; FA 2011, s 23)

Taxable commodity supplied	Rate at which levy payable if supply is not a reduced-rate supply						
	From 1 April 2013	1 April 2012–31 March 2013	1 April 2011–31 March 2012	1 April 2009–31 March 2011	1 April 2008–31 March 2009	1 April 2007–31 March 2008
Electricity	£0.00509 per kilowatt hour (kWh)	£0.00509 per kilowatt hour (kWh)	£0.00485 per kilowatt hour (kWh)	£0.00470 per kilowatt hour (kWh)	£0.00456 per kilowatt hour (kWh)	£0.00441 per kilowatt hour (kWh)
Gas supplied by a gas utility or any gas supplied in a gaseous state that is of a kind supplied by a gas utility	£0.00182 per kWh (£0.00064 in N. Ireland to 31/10/13)	£0.00177 per kWh (£0.00062 in N. Ireland)	£0.00169 per kWh (£0.00059 in N. Ireland)	£0.00164 pence per kWh	£0.00159 per kWh	£0.00154 per kWh
Any petroleum gas, or other gaseous hydrocarbon, supplied in a liquid state	£0.01172 per kilogram	£0.01137 per kilogram	£0.01083 per kilogram	£0.01050 per kilogram	£0.01018 pence per kilogram	£0.00985 per kilogram
Any other taxable commodity	£0.01429 per kilogram	£0.01387 per kilogram	£0.01321 per kilogram	£0.01281 per kilogram	£0.01242 pence per kilogram	£0.01201 per kilogram

Notes

(1) *General* – Climate change levy (CCL) was introduced from 1 April 2001, as part of a range of measures designed to help the UK meet its legally binding commitment to reduce greenhouse gas emissions. CCL is chargeable on the industrial and commercial supply of taxable commodities for lighting, heating and power by consumers in specified business sectors.

(2) *Reduced-rate supplies* (FA 2000, Sch 6, para 42(1)) – CCL is charged at 20% of the full rate for energy intensive industries that have entered into a negotiated energy efficiency Climate Change Agreement (35% for supplies on or after 1 April 2011 (FA 2010, s 18)).

(3) *Half rate* – Prior to 1 April 2006, a 50% reduction in the levy (half-rate) was available to horticultural suppliers if certain conditions were satisfied (FA 2000, Sch 6, para 43). This half-rate was removed by FA 2006, s 172.

13 Other taxes and duties

ROAD FUEL DUTY

(Hydrocarbon Oil Duties Act 1979 (HODA 1979); FA 2011, ss 19, 20; FA 2009, ss 15, 16; FA 2010, ss 12, 13)

Description	From 1 August 2012	23 March 2011 to 31 July 2011	1 January 2011 to 22 March 2011	1 October 2010 to 31 December 2010	1 April 2010 to 30 September 2010	1 September 2009 to 31 March 2010	1 April 2009 to 31 August 2009
Unleaded petrol and bioethanol *(HODA 1979, s 6(1A)(a))*	60.97p	57.95p	58.95p	58.19p	57.19p	56.19p	54.19p
Heavy oil and biodiesel *(HODA 1979, s 6(1A)(c)*	60.97p	57.95p	58.95p	58.19p	57.19p	36.19p	34.19p
Natural road fuel gas (including biogas) *(HODA 1979, s 8(3)(a))*	29.07p per kg	24.70p per kg	26.15p per kg	25.05p per kg	23.60p per kg	22.16p per kg	19.26p per kg
Other road fuel gas (eg liquefied petroleum gas) *(HODA 1979, s 8(3)(b))*	37.34p per kg	31.61p per kg	33.04p per kg	31.95p per kg	30.53p per kg	27.67p per kg	24.82p per kg

Notes

(1) Figures shown in pence per litre (unless otherwise stated).

(2) The rate of duty on bioethanol is, since 1 April 2010, the same as that on unleaded petrol (FA 2010, s 12(5)). The rate for unleaded petrol is set out in HODA 1979, s 6(1A)(a)).

(3) The rate of duty on biodiesel is, since 1 April 2010, the same as that on heavy oil (FA 2010, s 12(3)). The rate for heavy oil is set out in HODA 1979, s 6(1A)(c).

VEHICLE EXCISE DUTY

(Vehicle Excise and Registration Act 1994 (VERA 1994), ss, 2, 4, Sch 1; FA 2008, s 17; FA 2009, ss 13, 14; FA 2011, ss 21, 22)

Light passenger vehicles – General rates

(VERA 1994, Sch 1, para 1B)

Band	CO$_2$ (g/km)	From 1 April 2012 Alternative fuel car (Tax Class 59) Reduced £	From 1 April 2012 Petrol car (Tax Class 48) and Diesel Car (Tax Class 49) Standard £	From 1 April 2011 Alternative fuel car (Tax Class 59) Reduced £	From 1 April 2011 Petrol car (Tax Class 48) and Diesel Car (Tax Class 49) Standard £	From 1 April 2010 Alternative fuel car (Tax Class 59) Reduced £	From 1 April 2010 Petrol car (Tax Class 48) and Diesel Car (Tax Class 49) Standard £	1 May 2009 to 31 March 2010 Alternative fuel car (Tax Class 59) Reduced £	1 May 2009 to 31 March 2010 Petrol car (Tax Class 48) and Diesel Car (Tax Class 49) Standard £
A	Up to 100	0	0	0	0	0	0	0	0
B	101 to 110	10	20	10	20	10	20	15	35
C	111 to 120	20	30	20	30	20	30	15	35
D	121 to 130	90	100	85	95	80	90	100	120
E	131 to 140	110	120	105	115	100	110	100	120
F	141 to 150	125	135	120	130	115	125	105	125
G	151 to 165	160	170	155	165	145	155	130	150
H	166 to 175	185	195	180	190	170	180	155	175
I	176 to 185	205	215	200	210	190	200	155	175
J	186 to 200	240	250	235	245	225	235	200	215
K	201 to 225	260	270	250	260	235	245	200	215
L	226 to 255	450	460	435	445	415	425	390	405
M	Over 255	465	475	450	460	425	435	390	405

13 Other taxes and duties

Notes

(1) The above rates apply for vehicle licences lasting 12 months. The rate for a six month licence is 55% of the annual rate (*VERA 1994, s 4(2)*).

(2) Band K includes cars that have a CO_2 figure over 225g/km but were registered before 23 March 2006 (*VERA 1994, Sch 1, para 1B*).

Light passenger vehicles – First year rates

(*VERA 1994, Sch 1, para 1B*)

Band	CO_2 (g/km)	From 1 April 2012 Alternative fuel car (Tax Class 59) Reduced £	From 1 April 2012 Petrol car (Tax Class 48) and Diesel car (Tax Class 49) Standard £	From 1 April 2011 Alternative fuel car (Tax Class 59) Reduced £	From 1 April 2011 Petrol car (Tax Class 48) and Diesel car (Tax Class 49) Standard £
A	Up to 100	0	0	0	0
B	101 to 110	0	0	0	0
C	111 to 120	0	0	0	0
D	121 to 130	0	0	0	0
E	131 to 140	110	120	105	115
F	141 to 150	125	135	120	130
G	151 to 165	160	170	155	165
H	166 to 175	265	275	255	265
I	176 to 185	315	325	305	315
J	186 to 200	450	460	435	445
K	201 to 225	590	600	570	580
L	226 to 255	805	815	780	790
M	Over 255	1,020	1,030	990	1,000

Notes

(1) From 1 April 2010, anyone buying a new car will pay a different rate of vehicle tax for the first tax disc (ie taken out at first registration). These are known as 'first year rates'. From the second tax disc onwards, the normal standard or reduced rate of vehicle tax will apply.

(2) Six month licences are not applicable to vehicles being registered for the first time in bands A to D. Six month tax discs are only available where the vehicle tax rate is more than £50 (*VERA 1994, s 3(2)*). Vehicle tax in bands A to D is free on first registration from 1 April 2010. In addition, from 1 April 2010 six-month tax discs are not available for vehicles being registered in bands H to M, as the first year rate for these vehicles is higher than the normal standard rate (*VERA 1994, s 3(7)*). However, a six month tax disc is available when re-taxing the vehicle.

Other vehicles

(*VERA 1994, Sch 1, paras 1, 1J, 2*)

Category	From 1 April 2012 £	From 1 April 2011 £	From 1 April 2010 £	1 May 2009– 31 March 2010 £
Light goods vehicles (Tax Class 39) (weighing no more than 3,500kg revenue weight) (*Sch 1, para 1J*)	215	200	200	185
Lower-emissions vans (light goods vehicles) (Tax Class 36) (weighing no more than 3,500kg revenue weight) (*Sch 1, para 1J*)	135	125	125	125
Private or light goods vehicles (PLG) registered before 1 March 2001 (Tax Class 11) (*Sch 1, para 1*)				
• Not over 1549 cc	135	130	125	125
• Over 1549 cc	220	215	205	190
Motorcycles (with or without a sidecar) (Tax Class 17) (*Sch 1, para 2*)				
• Not over 150cc	16	15	15	15
• 151 to 400cc	36	33	33	33
• 401 to 600cc	55	50	50	48
• Over 600cc	76	70	70	66
Motortricycles (weighing no more than 450kg) (Tax Class 50) (*Sch 1, para 2*)				
• Not over 150cc	16	15	15	15
• Any other case	76	70	70	66

Note

The lower rate of vehicle excise duty for lower emission vans applies to models which meet certain air quality pollutant emissions standards (see *VERA 1994, Sch 1, para 1K*) and were registered on or after 1 March 2003 and before 1 January 2007, or that meet the Euro 5 pollutant emissions standards and are registered on or after 1 January 2009 and before 1 January 2011 (*Sch 1, para 1M*).

13 Other taxes and duties

AIR PASSENGER DUTY

(FA 1994, ss 28–30, Sch 5A; FA 2010, s 14)

Band, and approximate distance in miles from London to the capital city of the destination country	'Standard class travel' rate			Rate for any other class		
	From 1 April 2012 £	From 1 Nov 2010 £	From 1 Nov 2009 £	From 1 April 2012 £	From 1 Nov 2010 £	From 1 Nov 2009 £
Band A (0–2,000)	13	12	11	26	24	22
Band B (2,001–4,000)	65	60	45	130	120	90
Band C (4,001–6,000)	81	75	50	162	150	100
Band D (over 6,000)	92	85	55	184	170	110

Notes

(1) Air passenger duty (APD) is chargeable on the carriage of each chargeable passenger at the specified rate *(FA 1994, s 30(1))*. A four destination band structure was introduced from 1 November 2009, based on geographical distance from London, each having two rates of duty depending upon the class of travel (hence eight different rates of duty). Prior to 1 November 2009, four rates of duty applied:

Standard rates

- £20 for specified European destinations; and
- £80 for all other destinations

Reduced rates

- £10 for specified European destinations; and
- £40 for all other destinations

(2) 'Standard class travel' means:
  (a) in the case of an aircraft on which only one class of travel is available, that class of travel
  (b) in any other case, the lowest class of travel available on the aircraft (FA 1994, s 30(10)).

(3) Where a seat pitch exceeds 1.016 metres (40 inches), whether the flight has a single class or more than one class, the standard rate (or "non-standard class travel" rate) of APD applies *(FA 1994, s 30(11); HMRC Notice 550, para 2.6.5)*.

(4) With effect from 1 November 2011, APD for passengers travelling on direct long-haul routes departing from airports in Northern Ireland is charged at the short-haul (Band A) rates (Written Ministerial Statement, 21 February 2012; Budget, 21 March 2012; *FB 2012, cl 189, Sch 23*).

(5) With effect from 1 April 2013, the scope of APD will be extended to business jets and smaller aircraft by reducing the de minimis weight limit for exemption from 10 tonnes to 5.7 tonnes, subject to certain exclusions (eg emergency flights). Business jets providing a premium service will pay APD at double the prevailing standard business/first class rates of APD. The definition of passenger is changed to ensure that passengers on private jets will be brought within the scope of APD *(FB 2012, cl 189, Sch 23)*. Legislation will be reviewed to ensure that certain pre-existing APD exemptions will continue (HMRC Consultation Response, 6 December 2011).

Air passenger duty

Band A *(FA 1994, Sch 5A, Part 1)*	Band B *(FA 1994, Sch 5A, Part 2)*	Band C *(FA 1994, Sch 5A, Part 3)*	Band D *(FA 1994, s 30(4A))*
Albania	Afghanistan	Angola	Any other place (Countries not listed in Bands A–C)
Algeria	Armenia	Anguilla	
Andorra	Azerbaijan	Antigua and Barbuda	
Austria	Bahrain		
Azores	Benin	Aruba	
Belarus	Bermuda	Ascension Island	
Belgium	Burkina Faso	Bahamas	
Bosnia and Herzegovina	Cameroon	Bangladesh	
	Canada	Barbados	
Bulgaria	Cape Verde	Belize	
Croatia	Central African Republic	Bhutan	
Cyprus		Botswana	
Czech Republic	Chad	Brazil	
Denmark (including the Faroe Islands)	Democratic Republic of Congo	British Indian Ocean Territory	
Estonia	Republic of Congo	British Virgin Islands	
Finland	Djibouti		
France (including Corsica)	Egypt	Burma	
	Equatorial Guinea	Burundi	
Germany	Eritrea	Cayman Islands	
Gibraltar	Ethiopia	China	
Greece	Gabon	Colombia	
Greenland	Gambia	Comoros	
Guernsey	Georgia	Costa Rica	
Hungary	Ghana	Cuba	
Iceland	Guinea	Dominica	
Republic of Ireland	Guinea-Bissau	Dominican Republic	
Isle of Man	Iran		
Italy (including Sicily and Sardinia)	Iraq	Ecuador	
	Israel and the Occupied Palestinian Territories	El Salvador	
Jersey		French Guiana	
Republic of Kosovo		Grenada	
Latvia		Guadeloupe	
Libya	Ivory Coast	Guatemala	
Liechtenstein	Jordan	Guyana	
Lithuania	Kazakhstan	Haiti	
Luxembourg	Kuwait	Honduras	
	Kyrgyzstan		

continued

177

13 Other taxes and duties

Band A (*FA 1994, Sch 5A, Part 1*)	Band B (*FA 1994, Sch 5A, Part 2*)	Band C (*FA 1994, Sch 5A, Part 3*)	Band D (*FA 1994, s 30(4A)*)
Former Yugoslav Republic of Macedonia	Lebanon	Hong Kong SAR	
Malta	Liberia	India	
Moldova	Mali	Jamaica	
Monaco	Mauritania	Japan	
Montenegro	Niger	Kenya	
Morocco	Nigeria	North Korea	
Netherlands	Oman	South Korea	
Norway (including Svalbard)	Pakistan	Laos	
Poland	Qatar	Lesotho	
Portugal (including Madeira)	Russian Federation, east of the Urals	Macao SAR	
Romania	Saint Pierre & Miquelon	Madagascar	
Russian Federation, west of the Urals	Sao Tome and Principe	Malawi	
San Marino	Saudi Arabia	Maldives	
Serbia	Senegal	Martinique	
Slovak Republic	Sierra Leone	Mauritius	
Slovenia	Sudan	Mayotte	
Spain (including the Balearic Islands and the Canary Islands)	Syria	Mexico	
Sweden	Tajikistan	Mongolia	
Switzerland	Togo	Montserrat	
Tunisia	Turkmenistan	Mozambique	
Turkey	Uganda	Namibia	
Ukraine	United Arab Emirates	Nepal	
Vatican City	United States of America	Netherlands Antilles	
Western Sahara	Uzbekistan	Nicaragua	
	Yemen	Panama	
		Puerto Rico	
		Reunion	
		Rwanda	
		Saint Barthelemy	
		Saint Christopher and Nevis (St Kitts and Nevis)	
		Saint Helena	
		Saint Lucia	
		Saint Martin	
		Saint Vincent and the Grenadines	

Band A (FA 1994, Sch 5A, Part 1)	Band B (FA 1994, Sch 5A, Part 2)	Band C (FA 1994, Sch 5A, Part 3)	Band D (FA 1994, s 30(4A))
		Seychelles	
		Somalia	
		South Africa	
		Sri Lanka	
		Suriname	
		Swaziland	
		Tanzania	
		Thailand	
		Trinidad and Tobago	
		Turks and Caicos Islands	
		Venezuela	
		Vietnam	
		Virgin Islands	
		Zambia	
		Zimbabwe	

BANK LEVY

(FA 2011, s 73, Sch 19)

Period	Short-term chargeable liabilities	Long-term chargeable equity and liabilities
From 1 January 2013	0.105%	0.0525%
1 January 2012–31 December 2012	0.088%	0.044%
1 May 2011–31 December 2011	0.075%	0.0375%
1 March 2011–30 April 2011	0.1%	0.05%
1 January 2011–28 February 2011	0.05%	0.025%

Notes

(1) General – The bank levy was introduced in *Finance Act 2011*. It is a tax based on total chargeable equity and liabilities as reported in the relevant balance sheets of UK banks and banking groups, building societies and building society groups, foreign banks and foreign banking groups operating in the UK and UK banks in non-banking groups at the end of a chargeable period.

(2) Threshold – The bank levy is nil if the amount of chargeable equity and liabilities is £20 billion or less. If this limit is exceeded, the first £20 billion (on which no levy is charged) is apportioned between long term equities and liabilities and short term

13   Other taxes and duties

liabilities, in accordance with the proportion of chargeable equity and liabilities of each (*FA 2011, Sch 19, para 6*).

(3) Payment – Payment of the bank levy is treated as a payment of corporation tax (*Sch 19, Pt 6*). It is subject to corporation tax payment procedures, including the Quarterly Instalment Payments system.

(4) Commencement – The bank levy applies to periods of account ending on or after 1 January 2011 (*Sch 19, paras 4(8), 5(4)*). Periods falling wholly before 1 January 2011 are ignored for these purposes.

14

National Insurance Contributions (NICs)

CLASS 1 PRIMARY (EMPLOYEE) CONTRIBUTIONS

(*SSCBA 1992, ss 5(1), 8, 19(4)*; *SI 2001/1004, regs 10, 131*; *Pension Schemes Act 1993, ss 41, 42A*; *SI 2006/1009, art 3*)

Class 1 NIC rates and thresholds	2012–13	2011–12	2010–11	2009–10
Lower earnings limit (LEL)	£107 per week	£102 per week	£97 per week	£95 per week
Primary threshold (PT)	£146 per week	£139 per week	£110 per week	£110 per week
Upper accrual point (UAP)	£770 per week	£770 per week	£770 per week	£770 per week
Upper earnings limit (UEL)	£817 per week	£817 per week	£844 per week	£844 per week
Not contracted out	12% on earnings between PT and UEL	12% on earnings between PT and UEL	11% on earnings between PT and UEL	11% on earnings between PT and UEL
	2% on excess over UEL	2% on excess over UEL	1% on excess over UEL	1% on excess over UEL
Contracted out (see Note 3 below)	10.6% on earnings between PT and UAP	10.4% on earnings between PT and UAP	9.4% on earnings between PT and UAP	9.4% on earnings between PT and UAP
	12% on earnings between UAP and UEL	12% on earnings between UAP and UEL	11% on earnings between UAP and UEL	11% on earnings between UAP and UEL
	2% on excess over UEL	2% on excess over UEL	1% on excess over UEL	1% on excess over UEL
Contracted out rebate – flat rate (see Note 3 below)	1.4%	1.6%	1.6%	1.6%
Reduced rate (see Note 4 below)	5.85% on earnings between PT and UEL	5.85% on earnings between PT and UEL	4.85% on earnings between PT and UEL	4.85% on earnings between PT and UEL
	2% on excess over UEL	2% on excess over UEL	1% on excess over UEL	1% on excess over UEL

14 National Insurance Contributions (NICs)

CLASS 1 PRIMARY (EMPLOYEE) CONTRIBUTIONS (CONTINUED)

(SSCBA 1992, ss 5(1), 8, 19(4); SI 2001/1004, regs 10, 131; Pension Schemes Act 1993, ss 41, 42A; SI 2006/1009, art 3)

Class 1 NIC rates and thresholds	2008–09	2007–08	2006–07
Lower earnings limit (LEL)	£90 per week	£87 per week	£84 per week
Primary threshold (PT)	£105 per week	£100 per week	£97 per week
Upper earnings limit (UEL)	£770 per week	£670 per week	£645 per week
Not contracted out	11% on earnings between PT and UEL	11% on earnings between PT and UEL	11% on earnings between PT and UEL
	1% on excess over UEL	1% on excess over UEL	1% on excess over UEL
Contracted out	9.4% on earnings between PT and UEL	9.4% on earnings between PT and UEL	9.4% on earnings between PT and UEL
	1% on excess over UEL	1% on excess over UEL	1% on excess over UEL
Contracted out rebate – flat rate	1.6%	1.6%	1.6%
Reduced rate (see Note 4 below)	4.85% on earnings between PT and UEL	4.85% on earnings between PT and UEL	4.85% on earnings between PT and UEL
	1% on excess over UEL	1% on excess over UEL	1% on excess over UEL

Notes

(1) No Class 1 contributions are payable on earnings between the lower earnings limit and primary threshold, but the employee is treated as having paid such contributions for the purposes of establishing or protecting entitlement to certain state benefits (*SSCBA 1992, s 6A*).

(2) The 'Upper Accrual Point' (UAP) was introduced from 6 April 2009 (*NICA 2008, s 3*). The UAP broadly represents the point at which entitlement to contributory related benefits ceases to accrue.

(3) With effect from 6 April 2012, it is no longer possible to contract out of the additional state pension on a defined contribution basis.

(4) The reduced rate applies to women married before 6 April 1977 who have elected to pay a reduced rate of Class 1 contributions.

(5) The *Finance Bill 2013* will provide that with effect from 6 April 2013 the Class 1 Upper Earnings Limit will continue to be aligned with the point at which the higher rate of income tax becomes payable (Budget, 21 March 2012).

CLASS 1 SECONDARY (EMPLOYER) CONTRIBUTIONS

(*SSCBA 1992, ss 6(1)(b), 9; SI 2001/1004, reg 10; Pension Schemes Act 1993, ss 41, 42A; SI 2006/1009, arts 2, 3*)

Class 1 NIC rates and thresholds	2012–13	2011–12	2010–11	2009–10
Secondary threshold (ST)	£144 per week	£136 per week	£110 per week	£110 per week
Not contracted out rate	13.8% on earnings above ST	13.8% on earnings above ST	12.8% on earnings above ST	12.8% on earnings above ST
Contracted out rates Salary related (COSR)	10.4%	10.1%	9.1%	9.1%
Money purchase (COMP) (see Note 2 below)	13.8%	12.4%	11.4%	11.4%
Contracted out rebate rates Salary related (COSR)	3.4%	3.7%	3.7%	3.7%
Money purchase (COMP) (see Note 2 below)	Abolished	1.4%	1.4%	1.4%

Class 1 NIC rates and thresholds	2008–09	2007–08	2006–07	2005–06
Secondary threshold (ST)	£105 per week	£100 per week	£97 per week	£94 per week
Not contracted out rate	12.8% on earnings above ST	12.8% on earnings above ST	12.8% on earnings above ST	12.8% on earnings above ST
Contracted out rates Salary related (COSR) Money purchase (COMP)	9.1% 11.4%	9.1% 11.4%	9.3% 11.8%	9.3% 11.8%
Contracted out rebate rates Salary related (COSR)	3.7%	3.7%	3.5%	3.5%
Money purchase (COMP)	1.4%	1.4%	1.0%	1.0%

Notes

(1) *General* – Class 1 contributions are not payable in respect of individuals under the age of 16 at the time of payment of the earnings. An employee who is at or over state pension age at the time of payment is not liable to pay primary Class 1 contributions, but employers must continue to pay secondary Class 1 contributions for employees over that age (*SSCBA 1992, s 6(3)*) (see *NIM1001*).

(2) *Contracting out* – With effect from 6 April 2012, it is no longer possible to contract out of the additional state pension on a defined contribution basis.

(3) *Regional employer NIC holiday for new businesses* – This voluntary scheme is available (on application) to new businesses that start up during the period from 22 June 2010 to 5 September 2012 in certain areas of the UK. During a 3-year qualifying period, from 6 September 2010 to 5 September 2013, such businesses will not have to pay the first £5,000 of employer's Class 1 contributions in the first 12 months of employment. The scheme applies to each of the first 10 employees engaged in the first year of business, and operates in selected countries (Scotland, Wales and Northern Ireland) and certain regions of England (the North East, Yorkshire and the Humber, the North West, the East Midlands, the West Midlands and the South West). Certain business sectors are excluded from the scheme (*National Insurance Contributions Act 2011, ss 4–11*).

(4) *Disguised remuneration* – Class 1 employee and employer contributions can arise on certain 'disguised remuneration' from Employee Benefit Trusts (EBTs), unapproved pension schemes (EFRBS) and other third party intermediaries where such income would not otherwise be within the charge to NICs (see *ITEPA 2003, ss 554A–554Z20; Social Security (Contributions) Regulations, SI 2001/1004 as amended by SI 2011/2700*)

(5) Under *The Social Security (Categorisation of Earners) 1978 (SI 1978/1689)*, lecturers, teachers, instructors and certain related workers at educational establishments were treated as employed for National Insurance purposes, whether or not they were employed or self-employed. These provisions are revoked with effect from 6 April 2012, and those in this category who are self-employed will be treated as such.

CLASS 1A CONTRIBUTIONS

(*SSCBA 1992, s 10*)

- Class 1A contributions are payable by employers (and certain third parties) on taxable benefits provided to employees. The Class 1A NIC charge is calculated as a percentage of the cash equivalent of the benefits.
- The Class 1A percentage is the same as the rate of secondary Class 1 contributions for the tax year in question (13.8% for 2012–13).
- No Class 1A NICs are due in some cases (see Booklet CWG5, Pt 2):
    - Benefits which are exempt from income tax (*SSCBA 1992, s 10(1)(a)*);
    - Benefits returned on form P9D (*SSCBA 1992, s 10(1)(b)*);
    - Benefits which are exempt from Class 1A NICs (*SI 2001/1004, Pt 3*) (see Booklet CWG5, pt 5);
    - Benefits covered by a dispensation (*ITEPA 2003, ss 65, 96*);
    - Benefits covered by an Extra-Statutory Concession (as listed in *SI 2001/1004, reg 40(7)*);
    - Benefits included in a PAYE Settlement Agreement (see Class 1B contributions below) (*SSCBA 1992, s 10(6)*);

- o Benefits provided for employment duties, where any use for private purposes is not significant (see *ITEPA 2003, s 316*);

- o Benefits which are already liable to Class 1 NICs (*SSCBA 1992, s 10(1)(c)*); and

- o Benefits which are exempt from Class 1 NICs (*SI 2001/1004, reg 40*)

CLASS 1B CONTRIBUTIONS

(*SSCBA 1992, s 10A*)

- Class 1B contributions are payable by employers who enter into a PAYE Settlement Agreement (PSA) with HMRC. A PSA is a formal agreement between HMRC and an employer, which allows the employer to account for tax on certain expense payments and benefits in a lump sum after the end of the tax year.

- The Class 1B NIC charge applies to items contained within a PSA that would normally attract a liability for Class 1 or Class 1A NICs, and to the total tax payable under the PSA. The Class 1B charge is calculated as a percentage of the total amount chargeable.

- The Class 1B percentage is the same as the rate of secondary Class 1 contributions for the tax year in question (13.8% for 2012–13).

- Payment of Class 1B NIC is due by 19 October in the tax year following the tax year to which the PSA applies (22 October for electronic payments) (*SI 2003/2682, reg 109(2)*).

CLASS 2 CONTRIBUTIONS

(*SSCBA 1992, ss 11, 12*)

Rates (weekly)

(*SSCBA 1992, ss 11(1), 117(1); SI 2001/1004, regs 125(c), 152(b)*)

Tax year	Flat rate £	Share fishermen £	Volunteer development workers £
2012–13	2.65	3.30	5.35
2011–12	2.50	3.15	5.10
2010–11	2.40	3.05	4.85
2009–10	2.40	3.05	4.75
2008–09	2.30	2.95	4.50
2007–08	2.20	2.85	4.35
2006–07	2.10	2.75	4.20

14   National Insurance Contributions (NICs)

Notes

(1) *General* – Class 2 contributions are generally payable by self-employed persons over the age of 16, but are not payable in respect of any period after the earner has reached pensionable age, are excepted in certain prescribed circumstances (*SI 2001/1004, reg 43*), and are subject to a residence test (*SI 2001/1004, reg 145(1)(c), (d)*) and a small earnings exception (see below).

(2) From April 2011, payments of Class 2 contributions are due on 31 July and 31 January under the normal self assessment rules (previously they were generally paid quarterly by direct debit, where appropriate).

(3) *Deferment* – A person who is both employed and self-employed is liable for both Class 1 and Class 2 (and Class 4) contributions, subject to an annual maximum. If the individual expects to pay more than the annual maximum, an application can be made to defer payment of Class 2 (and Class 4) contributions (*SI 2001/1004, regs 21, 90*) (see NIM20725).

Small earnings exception

(*SSCBA 1992, s 11(4); SI 2001/1004, reg 46(a)*)

Tax year	Limit £
2012–13	5,595
2011–12	5,315
2010–11	5,075
2009–10	5,075
2008–09	4,825
2007–08	4,635
2006–07	4,465

Notes

(1) *Application for exception* – A person whose net profits from self-employment are less than the small earnings exception limit for the relevant tax year may claim exception from liability to pay Class 2 NICs. An application for exception from liability for Class 2 contributions (form CF10) is available via HMRC's website: www.hmrc.gov.uk/forms/cf10.pdf.

(2) *Voluntary contributions* – Class 2 contributions can be paid voluntarily for weeks of self-employment covered by the small earnings exception (SI 2001/1004, reg 46(b)). Alternatively, an individual may pay Class 3 contributions (see below) if entitled to do so (*NIM21044*).

CLASS 3 CONTRIBUTIONS

(*SSCBA 1992, s 13*)

Tax Year	Weekly Rate £
2012–13	13.25
2011–12	12.60
2010–11	12.05
2009–10	12.05
2008–09	8.10
2007–08	7.80
2006–07	7.55

Notes

(1) *Eligibility* – Individuals wishing to pay Class 3 contributions in order to meet the conditions for entitlement to certain benefits must be over the age of 16 and satisfy conditions as to residence in Great Britain or Northern Ireland in the relevant tax year (*SSCBA 1992, s 1(6)(b)*; *SI 2001/1004, regs 48(1), 145(1)(e)*).

(2) *Earnings factor* – An individual is entitled to pay Class 3 contributions if his or her earnings factor (EF) derived from Class 1, 2 and/or 3 NICs is less than the qualifying earnings factor for the relevant tax year, subject to certain restrictions on the right to pay. A qualifying earnings factor is an amount equal to 52 times that year's lower earnings limit for Class 1 contributions (*SSCBA 1992, s 14*; *SI 1979/676, Sch 1, Pt 2*) (see NIM25001).

CLASS 4 CONTRIBUTIONS

(*SSCBA 1992, s 15*)

Class 4 NIC rates

(*SSCBA 1992, s 15(3ZA)*)

Tax Year	Main Class 4 percentage %	Additional Class 4 percentage %
2012–13	9	2
2011–12	9	2
2010–11	8	1
2009–10	8	1
2008–09	8	1
2007–08	8	1
2006–07	8	1

National Insurance Contributions (NICs)

Notes

(1) *General* – Class 4 contributions are payable on profits from trades, professions or vocations, which are chargeable to income tax under *ITTOIA 2005, Pt 2, Ch 2*, and are not profits from a trade, profession or vocation carried on wholly outside the UK.

(2) *Exceptions* – The liability to pay Class 4 contributions is subject to certain exceptions in *SI 2001/1004, Pt 8*. These include individuals who are over pensionable age at the beginning of the relevant tax year. Individuals who are under the age of 16 at the beginning of the tax year are also exempt if they obtain a certificate of exception from HMRC (*SI 2001/1004, regs 91, 93*).

CLASS 4 NIC PROFIT LIMITS

(*SSCBA 1992, s 15(3)*)

Tax Year	Lower profits limit £	Upper profits limit £
2012–13	7,605	42,475
2011–12	7,225	42,475
2010–11	5,715	43,875
2009–10	5,715	43,875
2008–09	5,435	40,040
2007–08	5,225	34,840
2006–07	5,035	33,540

Notes

(1) *General* – Class 4 contributions are payable at the main rate on profits between the lower and upper profits limits, and at the additional rate on profits above the upper profits limit.

(2) The *Finance Bill 2013* will provide that with effect from 6 April 2013 the Class 4 Upper Profits Limit will continue to be aligned with the point at which the higher rate of income tax becomes payable (Budget, 21 March 2012).

(3) *Deferment* – An individual can apply to defer payment of Class 4 NIC if appropriate, in order to avoid an overpayment of contributions (eg if there are earnings from both employment and self-employment in the same tax year). However, contributions remain payable at the additional rate. An application to HMRC for deferment of payment of Class 4 (and/or Class 2) NICs is made on form CA72B, which is available via HMRC's website (www.hmrc.gov.uk/forms/ca72b.pdf).

(4) *Annual maximum* – Class 4 contributions are subject to an annual maximum, calculated in accordance with *SI 2001/1004, reg 100*. The liability for contributions at the main rate is broadly limited to a maximum of 53 times the appropriate weekly amount of Class 2 NICs, plus the maximum amount of Class 4 contributions payable at the main rate, less any Class 2 NICs and any Class 1 NICs paid at the main rate. However, Class 4 NICs remain payable at the additional rate. An

application to HMRC for a refund of Class 4 NICs (if appropriate) can be made on form CA5610, which is available via HMRC's website (www.hmrc.gov.uk/forms/ca5610.pdf).

INCOME TAX AND NICS REFORM

The Government announced in Budget 2011 that it would consult on the options, stages and timing of reforms to integrate the operation of income tax and NICs. Since then consultations have taken place. The Government has announced that it will consult further on a broad range of options for employee, employer and self employed NICs (Budget, 21 March 2012).

15

Tax Credits

CHILD TAX CREDIT (CTC)

(*Child Tax Credit Regulations 2002, SI 2002/2007, reg 7, as amended*)

Maximum amounts per year:

Rates and Thresholds	2012–13	2011–12	2010–11
Child Tax Credit Family element (Basic)	£545	£545	£545
Family element, baby addition (single payment paid to families for all children under the age of one)	–	–	£545
Child element (for each child or qualifying young person)	£2,690	£2,555	£2,300
Disabled child element (additional payment for each disabled child or qualifying young person)	£2,950	£2,800	£2,715
Severely disabled child element (further additional payment for each severely disabled child or qualifying young person)	£1,190	£1,130	£1,095

Notes

(1) *Family element, baby addition* – This payment was removed from 6 April 2011.

(2) *Child element* – From April 2011 the CPI is used for the indexation of all benefits, tax credits and public service pensions, instead of the RPI.

(3) *Qualifying young person* – For the meaning of 'qualifying young person', see *SI 2002/2007, regs 4 and 5*.

(4) *Disabled or severely disabled* – As to what constitutes disability or severe disability for these purposes, see *SI 2002/2007, reg 8*.

WORKING TAX CREDIT (WTC)

(*Working Tax Credit (Entitlement and Maximum Rate) Regulations 2002, SI 2002/2005*)

Maximum amounts per year (SI 2002/2005, reg 20(1), Sch 2, para 1):

Rates and Thresholds	2012–13	2011–12	2010–11
Basic element (*reg 4*)	£1,920	£1,920	£1,920
Second adult and lone parent element (*regs 11, 12*)	£1,950	£1,950	£1,890
30 hour element (*reg 10*)	£790	£790	£790
Disability element (*reg 9*)	£2,790	£2,650	£2,570
Severe disability element (*reg 17*)	£1,190	£1,130	£1,095
50+ Return to work payment (16–29 hours) (*reg 18*)	–	£1,365	£1,320
50+ Return to work payment (30+ hours) (*reg 18*)	–	£2,030	£1,965

Notes

(1) *Indexation of Tax Credits* – From April 2011 the Consumer Prices Index (CPI) is used for the price indexation of tax credits (and benefits) (PN02, 22 June 2010).

(2) *50+ Tax Credits* – It was announced in the Budget on 22 June 2010 that a number of elements would be removed from the Tax Credits system, including the age 50+ element with effect from 6 April 2012 (www.hmrc.gov.uk/budget2010/individuals.htm).

(3) *Online tools* – An online questionnaire to assist in determining entitlement to Tax Credits is available on HMRC's website (www.hmrc.gov.uk/taxcredits/start/who-qualifies/quick-questionnaire.htm). An online Tax Credits calculator is also available via the Tax Credits section of the HMRC website (www.hmrc.gov.uk/taxcredits/payments-entitlement/entitlement/question-how-much.htm).

CHILDCARE ELEMENT OF THE WORKING TAX CREDIT

(*Working Tax Credit (Entitlement and Maximum Rate) Regulations 2002, SI 2002/2005*)

Maximum rates per year (SI 2002/2005, reg 20(2), (3)):

Rates and Thresholds	2012–13	2011–12	2010–11
Maximum eligible cost for one child (per week)	£175	£175	£175
Maximum eligible cost for two or more children (per week)	£300	£300	£300
Percentage of eligible costs covered	70%	70%	80%

15 Tax Credits

Notes

(1) *Entitlement* – The childcare element applies where the claimant pays for registered or approved childcare (*SI 2001/2005, regs 13, 14*).

(2) Childcare help from employers – There is guidance on the HMRC website on getting help from an employer to pay for childcare (www.hmrc.gov.uk/leaflets/ir115.pdf). An online calculator is available for cases in which the claimant's employer offers childcare vouchers, to help the claimant decide whether it would be beneficial to accept the childcare vouchers, eg in terms of the effect on Tax Credit entitlement (www.hmrc.gov.uk/calcs/ccin.htm).

INCOME THRESHOLDS AND WITHDRAWAL RATES*

(*Tax Credits Act 2002, ss 7, 13(2); Tax Credits (Income Thresholds and Determination of Rates) Regulations 2002, SI 2002/2008, regs 3, 7, 8*)

Rates and Thresholds	2012–13	2011–12	2010–11
First income threshold	£6,420	£6,420	£6,420
First withdrawal (or taper) rate	41%	41%	39%
Second income threshold	–	£40,000	£50,000
Second withdrawal rate	–	41%	6.67%
First threshold for those entitled to Child Tax Credit only	£15,860	£15,860	£16,190
Income rise disregard	£10,000	£10,000	£25,000
Income fall disregard	£2,500	–	–

*Amounts per year.

Notes

(1) *First withdrawal rate* – Entitlement of a claimant of both WTC and CTC (or WTC only) is reduced at the first withdrawal rate on each £1 by which their income exceeds £6,420 a year (£15,860 a year for claimants of CTC only) in 2012–13. Examples of how income can affect tax credits payments are available on the Directgov website (www.direct.gov.uk/en/MoneyTaxAndBenefits/TaxCreditsandChildBenefit/TaxCredits/Paymentsandentitlement/entitlement/DG_186815).

(2) *Second withdrawal rate* – Up to and including 2011–12, CTC claimants receive the full family element until their income reaches the second income threshold, after which that element is reduced at the second withdrawal rate on each £1 by which their income exceeds that threshold (*SI 2002/2008, reg 8(3)*). With effect from 2012–13 there is no second income threshold, and the family element starts to be reduced (still at the first withdrawal rate on each further £1 of income) as soon as all of the other credits have been withdrawn.

(3) *Income disregards* – Claimants' awards are initially based on their previous year's income. Once they report their current year's income, the award can be finalised. For 2012–13 the first £10,000 of any excess of their current year's income over that of the previous year, or the first £2,500 of any shortfall, is disregarded when calculating their final award (see *TCTM05200*).

16

National Minimum Wage (NMW)

NMW RATES
(NMWA 1998, s 2; SI 1999/584, Pt 2 (as amended))

Hourly rate from	Adult rate (Aged 21 and over)	Development rate (Aged 18 to 20)	Under 18 rate	Apprentice rate
	£	£	£	£
1 October 2012	6.19	4.98	3.68	2.65
1 October 2011	6.08	4.98	3.68	2.60
1 October 2010	5.93	4.92	3.64	2.50
1 October 2009	5.80	4.83	3.57	–
1 October 2008	5.73	4.77	3.53	–
1 October 2007	5.52	4.60	3.40	–
1 October 2006	5.35	4.45	3.30	–
1 October 2005	5.05	4.25	3.00	–

Notes

(1) *Adult rate (SI 1999/584, reg 11)* – The adult NMW rate was extended to workers aged 21 or over from 1 October 2010 *(reg 13(1), as amended)*. Previously, this rate applied to workers aged 22 or over.

(2) *Development rate (SI 1999/584, reg 13(1))* – From 1 October 2010, the rate applies to workers who have reached the age of 18, but not 21. Previously, this rate applied to workers who had not reached the age of 22.

(3) *Apprentice minimum wage (SI 1999/584, reg 13(3))* – The apprentice rate applies to apprentices who are either under 19 or in the first year of their apprenticeship.

NMW: ACCOMMODATION OFFSET RATE
(SI 1999/584, regs 30(d), 36)

Period	Daily offset £	Period	Daily offset £
1 October 2012	4.82	1 October 2008	4.46
1 October 2011	4.73	1 October 2007	4.30
1 October 2010	4.61	1 October 2006	4.15
1 October 2009	4.51	1 October 2005	3.90

16 National Minimum Wage (NMW)

Notes

(1) The above rates represent the maximum permitted daily rate of accommodation offset by the employer in relation to the NMW.

(2) Information on calculating the NMW when accommodation is provided by the employer is available on the Directgov website: www.direct.gov.uk/en/Employment/Employees/TheNationalMinimumWage/DG_175108.

17

HMRC Powers, Deterrents and Safeguards

IMPLEMENTATION OF LEGISLATION, ETC

Legislation etc	Statutory ref.	Implementation date	Commencement Order
Compliance *(Information and inspection powers, record keeping, time limits etc)*			
• Compliance checks etc: Excise Duties (legislation updating compliance checks, including information and inspection powers, record keeping and time limits)	*F(No.3)A 2010, s 29, Sch 13*	**Note 2**	*SI 2011/777*
• Data gathering powers	*FA 2011 (s 86, Sch 23)*	1 April 2012	*SI 2012/847*
• Information and inspection powers: Main taxes (**Note 3**)	*FA 2008, s 113, Sch 36*	1 April 2009	*SI 2009/404*
• Information and inspection powers: amendments	*FA 2009, s 95, Sch 47*	13 August 2009	*SI 2009/2035*
	FA 2011, s 86(2), Sch 24	19 July 2011	N/A
• Information and inspection powers: extension to other taxes (**Note 3**)	*FA 2009, s 96, Sch 48*	1 April 2010	*SI 2009/3054*
• Computer records	*FA 2008, s 114*	21 July 2008	
• Record keeping (**Note 4**)	*FA 2008, s 115, Sch 37*	1 April 2009	*SI 2009/402*
• Record keeping: other taxes (**Note 4**)	*FA 2009, s 98, Sch 50*	1 April 2010	*SI 2010/815*

continued

17   HMRC Powers, Deterrents and Safeguards

Legislation etc	Statutory ref.	Implementation date	Commencement Order
• Assessment time limits (**Note 5**)	*FA 2008, s 118, Sch 39*	1 April 2009 1 April 2010	*SI 2009/403 (General)* *SI 2009/586 (VAT)* *SI 2009/470 (Student loans)* *SI 2009/588 (PAYE)* *SI 2009/600 (NIC)*
• Assessment time limits: other taxes (**Note 5**)	*FA 2009, s 99, Sch 51*	1 April 2010 (Environmental taxes, IPT) 1 April 2011 (Other taxes) 1 April 2011 (SDRT)	*SI 2010/867* *SI 2010/664* (nb also amends SDRT inspection powers from 1 April 2010)
• Assessment time limits etc: Consequential amendments to the Aggregates Levy (General) Regulations 2002		1 April 2010	*SI 2010/642*
• Assessment time limits etc: Consequential amendments to the Climate Change Levy (General) Regulations 2001		1 April 2010	*SI 2010/643*
• Correction and amendment of tax returns	*FA 2008, s 119*	1 April 2010	*SI 2009/405*
Criminal investigation powers			
• Provisions dealing with search warrants, production orders and powers of arrest	*FA 2007, ss 82–86, Sch 23*	8 Nov 2007 1 Dec 2007 (*s 84(4), Sch 23*)	*SI 2007/3166*
• Provisions that allow HMRC to use its most potent powers in all its investigations into serious crime	*SCA 2007, s 88, Sch 12*		

Implementation of legislation, etc

Legislation etc	Statutory ref.	Implementation date	Commencement Order
HMRC Charter			
• Legislation requiring HMRC to prepare and maintain a Charter	FA 2009, s 92	21 July 2009	N/A
Payments, repayments and debt (Note 11)			
• Managed payment plans	FA 2009, s 111 (now TMA 1970, ss 59G–59H)	Deferred (announced at Budget 2010)	N/A
• Payment and enforcement: County Court proceedings etc	FA 2008, ss 137–139	21 July 2008	N/A
• Payment and enforcement: Taking control of goods etc.			
○ England and Wales	FA 2008, ss 127–129, Schs 43, 44	TBA	**Note 6**
○ Scotland	FA 2008, s 128, Sch 43, Pt 2	23 Nov 2009	SI 2009/3024, art 3
• Payment methods: Fee for payment (nb enables HMRC to accept payment by credit card and pass on the associated fees)	FA 2008, s 136	9 Dec 2008 1 April 2011 (Payment by internet) 13 Aug 2008 2 April 2012 (Payment by telephone)	SI 2008/2991 (*revoked*) SI 2011/711 (Payment by internet); SI 2008/1948 (*revoked*) SI 2012/68 (Payment by telephone)
• Powers to obtain contact details for debtors	FA 2009, s 97, Sch 49	21 July 2009	N/A
• Recovery of debts using PAYE regulations	FA 2009, s 110, Sch 58	20 July 2011 6 April 2012 20 July 2011	SI 2011/1583 SI 2011/1584 SI 2011/1585
• Security for payment of PAYE & NIC	FA 2011, s 85	6 April 2012	SI 2012/822
• Set off (Overpayments against amounts owed)	FA 2008, ss 130–132	21 July 2008	N/A
• Mutual assistance for the recovery of taxes etc	FA 2011, s 87	19 July 2011	N/A
Penalties for inaccuracies			
• Main taxes (**Note 7**)	FA 2007, s 97, Sch 24	1 April 2008	SI 2008/568

continued

17 HMRC Powers, Deterrents and Safeguards

Legislation etc	Statutory ref.	Implementation date	Commencement Order
• Other taxes (**Note 7**)	FA 2008, s 122, Sch 40	1 April 2009	SI 2009/571
• Failure to notify and certain VAT and Excise wrongdoing	FA 2008, s 123, Sch 41	1 April 2010	SI 2009/511
Penalties for late returns, late payment and interest			
• Penalties for failure to make returns	FA 2009, s 106, Sch 55; F(No.3)A 2010, s 26, Sch 10	See below	See below
• Penalties for failure to pay tax	FA 2009, s 107, Sch 56; F(No.3)A 2010, s 27, Sch 11	Note 8	Note 8
• Interest (**Note 9**)	FA 2009, ss 101–105, Schs 53, 54; F(No.3)A 2010, s 25, Sch 9; SI 2009/2032	Note 10	SI 2010/1878 SI 2011/701 SI 2011/2391 SI 2011/2401
Penalties for late returns, late payment and interest: Implementation		HMRC are implementing these provisions over a number of years	
• Bank Payroll Tax	See above		
○ Interest charged and paid		31 August 2010	SI 2010/1878
○ Late payment and filing penalties		31 August 2010	SI 2010/1878
• Construction Industry Scheme	See above		
○ Late return penalties		6 October 2011	SI 2011/2391
○ Late payment interest on late return penalties not paid by the due and payable date		6 October 2011	SI 2011/2391
• PAYE (including income tax (IT), NIC, CIS and student loan deductions	See above	6 April 2010	SI 2010/466 (IT & CIS); SI 2010/661 (Student loans); SI 2010/721 (NIC)
• Pension scheme returns	See above		
○ Late payment penalties		6 April 2010	SI 2010/466
○ Late filing penalties		1 & 6 April 2011	SI 2011/702 SI 2011/703

Implementation of legislation, etc

Legislation etc	Statutory ref.	Implementation date	Commencement Order
• Self Assessment (Income tax)	See above		
○ Late payment penalties		1 & 6 April 2011	SI 2011/702
○ Late filing penalties		1 & 6 April 2011	SI 2011/703
○ Interest charged and paid		6 April 2011 & 31 Oct 2011	SI 2011/784 *(Student loans)* SI 2011/701 *(Student loans)*
Penalties: Offshore income etc			
• Penalty framework for offshore non-compliance, applicable to income tax and CGT	*FA 2010, s 35, Sch 10*	6 April 2011 6 April 2011	SI 2011/975 SI 2011/976
Publishing details of deliberate tax defaulters			
• Allows HMRC to publish details of persons who are penalised for deliberate tax defaults	*FA 2009, s 94*	1 April 2010	SI 2010/574

Notes

(1) *Acknowledgement* – The above tables are adapted from the 'Review of HMRC's Powers, Deterrents and Safeguards: Implementation of legislation and related work' (version January 2012) (www.hmrc.gov.uk/about/road-map.pdf).

(2) *Compliance checks etc: Excise duties* – The implementation date of 1 April 2011 is subject to transitional provisions in certain circumstances (*SI 2011/777, arts 3–8*).

(3) *Information and inspection powers*

- *Main taxes* – Income tax (including PAYE and CIS), corporation tax, CGT and VAT, as well as NIC and student loan repayments.

- *Other taxes* – IPT, IHT, SDLT, SDRT, PRT, aggregates levy, climate change levy, landfill tax. In addition, from 31 August 2010 HMRC's information and inspection powers can be used to check bank payroll tax (CH21050).

(4) *Record keeping*

- *Main taxes* – The rules apply from 1 April 2009 in respect of income tax, CGT, corporation tax, direct tax claims not included in a return and VAT.

- *Other taxes* (from 1 April 2010) – IPT, SDLT, aggregates levy, climate change levy and landfill tax. In addition, record keeping requirements apply to bank payroll tax from 8 April 2010, and excise duties from 1 April 2011 (CH10100).

(5) *Time limits (for assessments, claims etc)* – The changes in *FA 2008, Sch 39* relate to assessments and claims for income tax, CGT, corporation tax and VAT. The time limits entered into force from 1 April 2009 (VAT), 1 April 2010 (direct taxes, and IPT, aggregates levy, climate change levy and landfill tax) and 1 April 2011 (SDLT, SDRT, PRT, excise duty and IHT), subject to transitional provisions (in *SI 2009/403, art 10*) whereby in some cases the change in time limits does not apply until 1 April 2012.

17 HMRC Powers, Deterrents and Safeguards

(6) *Payment and enforcement: Taking control of goods etc* – *FA 2008, s 127, Sch 43* to be brought into force (England and Wales) by Statutory Instrument alongside the commencement of TCEA 2007, Part 3.

(7) *Penalties for errors*

- *Main taxes* – Income tax (including PAYE and CIS), CGT, corporation tax, VAT, NICs.
- *Other taxes* – Including IPT, IHT, SDLT, SDRT, PRT and environmental taxes (aggregates levy, climate change levy, landfill tax); see CH81013 and CH81020.

(8) *Penalties for failure to pay tax* – The *Finance Act 2009, Schedule 56 (Appointed Day and Consequential Provisions) Order, SI 2010/466* appoints 6 April 2010 as the day on which the penalty provisions apply in respect of PAYE and CIS payments, and tax charges payable by scheme administrators under *FA 2004, Pt 4*.

(9) *Penalties for late returns, late payment and interest: Interest* – The *Taxes and Duties (Interest Rate) (Amendment) Regulations, SI 2009/2032*, which align rates for those taxes where HMRC charged and paid interest, came into force on 12 August 2009.

(10) *Interest* – The interest regime in FA 2009, s 103 comes into force on 31 August 2010 for bank payroll tax (SI 2010/1878), 31 October 2011 for *income tax self assessment (SI 2011/701)* and CIS *(SI 2011/2391)*, and on 6 October 2011 for other taxes generally *(SI 2011/2401)*.

(11) *Cost awards* – With effect from April 2012, where HMRC enters a case in county court in England and Wales to pursue amounts owing to them and judgment is awarded in HMRC's favour, fixed costs will be charged based on a sliding scale set by the Ministry of Justice (*Civil Procedure Rules 1998*, as amended by *Civil Procedure (Amendment) Rules 2011 (SI 2011/88)*; see also www.hmrc.gov.uk/news/courtcosts.htm). HMRC are not proposing any changes to their existing practice for seeking awards of costs in sheriff court proceedings in Scotland.

TAX AGENTS: DISHONEST CONDUCT

(FB 2012, cl 221, Sch 37)

The *Finance Bill 2012* proposes new powers allowing HMRC to obtain working papers from tax agents who engage in dishonest conduct, impose penalties on them and allow the Commissioners of HMRC to publish their details. These powers will come into force by means of a Treasury order, made by statutory instrument.

For this purpose a tax agent is an individual who, in the course of business, assists other persons (ie clients) with their tax affairs, and these terms are defined widely (*FB 2012, Sch 37, para 2*).

An individual engages in dishonest conduct if, in the course of acting as a tax agent, the individual does something dishonest with a view to bringing about a loss of tax revenue (*FB 2012, Sch 37, para 3*).

Further provisions deal with establishing dishonest conduct, the tax agent's right of appeal against a 'conduct notice, HMRC's power to obtain tax agent's files etc, sanctions for dishonest conduct, and penalties (*FB 2012, Sch 37, Pts 2–7*).

DATA-GATHERING POWERS

(FA 2011, s 86, Schs 23, 24)

Penalties

(FA 2011, Sch 23, Pt 4)

Offence	Penalty
Failure to comply with a data-holder notice *(FA 2011, Sch 23, paras 30, 31)*	
Initial penalty	£300
Continued failure	Up to £60 per day on which the failure continues
Provision of inaccurate data (ie where condition A, B or C is met in *FA 2011, Sch 23, para 32*)	Up to £3,000 per inaccuracy

Notes

(1) *General* – An HMRC officer may require a 'relevant data-holder' to provide 'relevant data' (both as defined). Penalties apply to a failure by the data-holder to comply with a data-holder notice. The above penalty regime generally applies with effect from 1 April 2012, to relevant data with a bearing on any period (ie before, on or after that date) *(FA 2011, Sch 23, para 65)*. There is a right of appeal against the liability to, or amount of, the penalties listed in the table above *(para 36)*.

(2) *Daily penalties* – If daily penalties have been assessed as above and the failure continues for more than 30 days, an HMRC officer may apply to the tribunal for penalties of up to £1,000 per day to be applied instead *(FA 2011, Sch 23, para 38)*.

(3) *Reasonable excuse* – The £300 fixed penalty, and the penalties of up to £60 per day, do not apply if there is a 'reasonable excuse' for the failure *(FA 2011, Sch 23, para 34)*.

RECOVERY OF HMRC DEBTS THROUGH PAYE

(ITEPA 2003, s 684(2), (3A); SI 2011/1585)

- PAYE regulations may provide (among other things) for deductions to be made in respect of 'relevant debts' (see below) of a payee. Deductions up to £3,000 may be made from a payee's income for a tax year, without the payee's consent.

- The £3,000 limit was increased with effect from 20 July 2011. The previous limit was £2,000.

- 'Relevant debts' are defined as including any debt payable to the Commissioners for HMRC, excluding tax credits *(ITEPA 2003, s 684(7AA))*.

- HMRC may determine an employee's PAYE code, to recover all or part of a relevant debt up to the above limit *(SI 2003/2682, reg 14A(1))*, with effect from 6 April 2012 *(SI 2011/1584, reg 2(2))*.

18

Social security benefit rates

(ITEPA 2003, Pts 9, 10)

Benefit (weekly rates)	April 2012 £	April 2011 £	April 2010 £
Attendance allowance			
• Higher rate	77.45	73.60	71.40
• Lower rate	51.85	49.30	47.80
Bereavement Benefit			
• Bereavement Payment (lump sum)	2,000.00	2,000.00	2,000.00
• Widowed Parent's Allowance	105.95	100.70	97.65
• Bereavement Allowance (Standard rate)	105.95	100.70	97.65
Carer's Allowance	58.45	55.55	53.90
Disability Living Allowance			
Care component			
• Highest	77.45	73.60	71.40
• Middle	51.85	49.30	47.80
• Lowest	20.55	19.55	18.95
Mobility component			
• Higher	54.05	51.40	49.85
• Lower	20.55	19.55	18.95
Incapacity Benefit			
Long-term	99.15	94.25	91.40
Short-term (under state pension age)			
• Lower rate	74.80	71.10	68.95
• Higher rate	88.55	84.15	81.60
Short-term (over state pension age)			
• Lower rate	95.15	90.45	87.75
• Higher rate	99.15	94.25	91.40
Increase of Long-term Incapacity Benefit for age			
• Higher rate	11.70	13.80	15.00
• Lower rate	5.90	5.60	5.80
Invalidity Allowance (Transitional)			
• Higher rate	11.70	13.80	15.00
• Middle rate	5.90	7.10	8.40
• Lower rate	5.90	5.60	5.45

Social security benefit rates

Benefit (weekly rates)	April 2012 £	April 2011 £	April 2010 £
Income support			
Personal Allowances			
Single			
• Under 25	56.25	53.45	51.85
• 25 or over	71.00	67.50	65.45
Lone parent			
• Under 18	56.25	53.45	51.85
• 18 or over	71.00	67.50	65.45
Couple			
• Both under 18	56.25	53.45	51.85
• Both under 18 – higher rate	84.95	80.75	78.30
• One under 18, one under 25	56.25	53.45	51.85
• One under 18, one 25 and over	71.00	67.50	65.45
• Both 18 or over	111.45	105.95	102.75
• Dependent children	64.99	62.33	57.57
Premiums			
Family / lone parent	17.40	17.40	17.40
Pensioner (applies to couples only)	106.45	103.75	99.65
Disability			
• Single	30.35	28.85	28.00
• Couple	43.25	41.10	39.85
Enhanced disability			
• Single	14.80	14.05	13.65
• Disabled child	22.89	21.63	21.00
• Couple	21.30	20.25	19.65
Severe disability			
• Single	58.20	55.30	53.65
• Couple (lower rate)	58.20	55.30	53.65
• Couple (higher rate)	116.40	110.60	107.30
Disabled child	56.63	53.62	52.08
Carer	32.60	31.00	30.05
Relevant sum for strikers	38.00	36.00	35.00
Industrial Death Benefit			
Widow's pension			
• Higher rate	107.45	102.15	97.65
• Lower rate	32.24	30.65	29.30
Widower's pension	107.45	102.15	97.65

continued

18 Social security benefit rates

Benefit (weekly rates)	April 2012 £	April 2011 £	April 2010 £
Jobseeker's Allowance (JSA)			
Contribution-based JSA – Personal rates			
• Under 25	56.25	53.45	51.85
• 25 or over	71.00	67.50	65.45
Income-based JSA – personal allowances			
• Under 25	56.25	53.45	51.85
• 25 or over	71.00	67.50	65.45
Lone parent			
• Under 18	56.25	53.45	51.85
• 18 or over	71.00	67.50	65.45
Couple			
• Both under 18	56.25	53.45	51.85
• Both under 18 – higher rate	84.95	80.75	78.30
• One under 18, one under 25	56.25	53.45	51.85
• One under 18, one 25 and over	71.00	67.50	65.45
• Both 18 or over	111.45	105.95	102.75
Dependent children	64.99	62.33	57.57
Premiums			
Family / lone parent	17.40	17.40	17.40
Pensioner			
• Single	71.70	69.85	67.15
• Couple	106.45	103.75	99.65
Disability			
• Single	30.35	28.85	28.00
• Couple	43.25	41.10	39.85
Enhanced Disability			
• Single	14.80	14.05	13.65
• Disabled child	22.89	21.63	21.00
• Couple	21.30	20.25	19.65
Severe Disability			
• Single	58.20	55.30	53.65
• Couple (lower rate)	58.20	55.30	53.65
• Couple (higher rate)	116.40	110.60	107.30
Disabled child	56.63	53.62	52.08
Carer	32.60	31.00	30.05
Prescribed sum for strikers	38.00	36.00	35.00
Maternity Allowance			
• Standard rate	135.45	128.73	124.88
• Maternity Allowance threshold	30.00	30.00	30.00

Social security benefit rates

Benefit (weekly rates)	April 2012 £	April 2011 £	April 2010 £
Pension Credit			
Standard minimum guarantee			
• Single	142.70	137.35	132.60
• Couple	217.90	209.70	202.40
Additional amount for severe disability			
• Single	58.20	55.30	53.65
• Couple (one qualifies)	58.20	55.30	53.65
• Couple (both qualify)	116.40	110.60	107.30
Additional amount for carers	32.60	31.00	30.05
Savings credit			
• Threshold – single	111.80	103.15	98.40
• Threshold – couple	178.35	164.55	157.25
• Maximum – single	18.54	20.52	20.52
• Maximum – couple	23.73	27.09	27.09
Amount for claimant and first spouse in polygamous marriage	217.90	209.70	202.40
Additional amount for additional spouse	75.20	72.35	69.80
Severe Disablement Allowance			
Basic rate	69.00	62.95	59.45
Age-related addition (from Dec 1990)			
• Higher rate	11.70	13.80	15.00
• Middle rate	5.90	7.10	8.40
• Lower rate	5.90	5.60	5.45
State Pension			
Basic			
• Single man or woman	107.45	102.15	97.65
• Married man, married woman or civil partner (who qualify with their own National Insurance contributions)	107.45	102.15	97.65
• Married man, married woman or civil partner (using spouse's or civil partner's National Insurance contributions record)	64.40	61.20	58.50
• Non-contributory	64.40	61.20	58.50
Age addition (at age 80)	0.25	0.25	0.25
Statutory Adoption Pay			
• Earnings threshold	107.00	102.00	97.00
• Standard rate	135.45	128.73	124.88
Statutory Maternity Pay			
• Earnings threshold	107.00	102.00	97.00
• Standard rate	135.45	128.73	124.88

continued

18 Social security benefit rates

Benefit (weekly rates)	April 2012 £	April 2011 £	April 2010 £
Statutory Paternity Pay			
• Earnings threshold	107.00	102.00	97.00
• Standard rate	135.45	128.73	124.88
Statutory Sick Pay			
• Earnings threshold	107.00	102.00	97.00
• Standard rate	85.85	81.60	79.15
Widow's Benefit			
Widowed Mother's Allowance	105.95	100.70	97.65
Widow's Pension (Standard rate)	105.95	100.70	97.65

(*Source – Directgov (www.direct.gov.uk)*)

Notes

(1) *General* – The above represents a selection of state benefit rates. A more comprehensive list of rates can be downloaded from the Directgov website.

(2) *Commencement* – The proposed benefit rates from April 2012 above are as announced in December 2011.

Benefit rates for 2011 were uprated by The Social Security Benefits Up-rating Regulations, SI 2011/830 (http://www.legislation.gov.uk/uksi/2011/830/made/data.pdf).

(3) *Uprating of benefits* – The annual uprating of benefits take place for State Pensions and most other benefits in the first full week of the tax year.

NON-TAXABLE SOCIAL SECURITY BENEFITS

(ITEPA 2003, Pt 10)

Summary

- Attendance Allowance
- Back to Work Bonus
- Bereavement Payment
- Child Benefit
- Child's Special Allowance
- Child Tax Credit
- Cold Weather Payments (see also Winter Fuel payment)
- Council Tax Benefit
- Constant Attendance Allowance (see Industrial Injuries Benefits)
- Disability Living Allowance
- Income-related Employment and Support Allowance

Non-taxable social security benefits

- Employment and Support Allowance (income related)
- Exceptionally Severe Disablement Allowance (see Industrial Injuries Benefits)
- Guardian's Allowance
- Health in pregnancy grant
- Housing Benefit
- Incapacity Benefit (for first 28 weeks of entitlement, taxable thereafter)
- Income Support (certain payments)
- Income-related employment and support allowance
- Industrial Injuries Benefits (ie industrial injuries pension, reduced earnings allowance, retirement allowance, constant attendance allowance and exceptionally severe disablement allowance)
- Invalidity Benefit
- In-work credit
- In-work emergency discretion fund payment
- In-work emergency fund payment
- Maternity Allowance
- Payments to reduce under-occupation by housing benefit claimants
- Pensioner's Christmas Bonus
- Reduced Earnings Allowance (see Industrial Injuries Benefits)
- Retirement Allowance (see Industrial Injuries Benefits)
- Return to work credit
- Severe Disablement Allowance
- Social Fund Payments
- State Pension credit
- War Widow's pension
- Winter Fuel payment
- Working Tax Credit

(*Sources – ITEPA 2003, s 677 (Table B); EIM76100; Directgov (www.direct.gov.uk)*)

Notes

(1) *Bereavement Payment* – replaced Widow's Payment from 9 April 2001.

(2) *Incapacity benefit* – From 27 October 2008, Employment and Support Allowance replaced Incapacity Benefit and Income Support paid on incapacity grounds for anyone starting a claim. However, existing recipients of Incapacity Benefit or Income Support will initially continue to receive their existing benefits, so long as they continue to satisfy the entitlement conditions (EIM76180).

18 Social security benefit rates

(3) *Industrial injuries benefits* – The above excludes industrial death benefit, which is taxable (*ITEPA 2003, ss 577(1), 677(2)*).

(4) *Income support* – For further information on taxable and non-taxable income support, see EIM76190.

(5) *Invalidity benefit* – Replaced by Incapacity benefit from April 1995, but still payable where invalidity commenced before April 1995.

(6) *Payments out of the Social Fund* – Payments are made to people on low incomes to help with maternity expenses, funeral costs, financial crises and as community care grants. The fund also makes interest-free loans.

(7) *Return to work credit* – Includes the self-employment credit.

(8) *War Widow's pension* – Where a pension or allowance is not paid or only a reduced amount is paid because the claimant gets a different benefit (eg widowed mother's allowance or widow's pension), the amount of that other benefit that equals the amount of pension withheld, is exempt from income tax (*ITEPA 2003, s 640*; see EIM76103).

With regard to wounds and disability pensions for service with the forces, see EIM74302. For allowances payable to civilians in respect of war injuries, see EIM74700.

(9) *Foreign benefits* – Certain foreign social security payments are exempt from UK tax (see *ITEPA 2003, Pt 10, Ch 7*).

(10) *High income child benefit charge* – An income tax charge will be applied to 'high income' taxpayers, i.e. whose adjusted net income exceeds £50,000 in a tax year and who is in receipt of child benefit, and to taxpayers whose adjusted net income exceeds £50,000 and whose 'partner' (as defined) is in receipt of child benefit. If the income of both partners exceeds £50,000, the charge applies to the partner with the highest income. For taxpayers with income between £50,000 and £60,000, the tax charge is 1% of child benefit for every £100 of income in excess of £50,000. For taxpayers with income above £60,000, the tax charge is 100% of the child benefit received. The amount of child benefit payable is unaffected by the charge, which comes into effect from 7 January 2013 (*ITEPA 2003, ss 681B–681H, as inserted by FB 2012, cl 8, Sch 1*).

TAXABLE SOCIAL SECURITY BENEFITS

(*ITEPA 2003, Pts 9, 10*)

Summary

- Additional Statutory Paternity Pay
- Bereavement Allowance
- Carer's Allowance
- Employment and Support Allowance (contribution-based)
- Graduated retirement benefit
- Incapacity Benefit (certain payments)

Taxable social security benefits

- Income Support (certain payments)
- Industrial Death Benefit scheme pensions
- Jobseeker's Allowance
- Ordinary Statutory Paternity Pay
- State pension
- Statutory Sick Pay
- Statutory Maternity Pay
- Statutory Adoption Pay
- Widowed Parent's Allowance
- Widow's pension

(Sources – ITEPA 2003, s 660(1) (Table A); EIM76101; Directgov (www.direct.gov.uk))

Notes

(1) *General* – Only those UK social security benefits that are specified in Table A at *ITEPA 2003, s 660(1)* are taxable as social security income under *ITEPA 2003, Pt 10*. Some other social security benefits, specified at *ITEPA 2003, s 577*, are taxable as pension income under *ITEPA 2003, Pt 9*.

(2) *Bereavement Allowance* – Replaced widow's pension from 9 April 2001 (see EIM76173).

(3) *Carer's Allowance* – Formerly invalid care allowance until 1 April 2003 (see EIM76210).

(4) *Incapacity Benefit* – From 27 October 2008, Employment and Support Allowance replaced Incapacity Benefit and Income Support paid on incapacity grounds for anyone starting a claim. However, existing recipients of Incapacity Benefit or Income Support initially continue to receive their existing benefits, so long as they continue to satisfy the entitlement conditions (EIM76180).

(5) *Income Support* – If paid during strikes to some strikers or people interested in a trade dispute, income support is taxable (see EIM76190).

(6) *Industrial Death Benefit scheme pensions* – Industrial death benefit is not payable in respect of deaths occurring on or after 11 April 1988 (see EIM76200).

(7) *State pension* – An individual who qualifies for the State pension may choose to defer claiming the State pension. If the person defers for a period of more than 12 months (from 6 April 2005), that person may opt to receive either the pension foregone as a lump sum or a higher pension. The State pension lump sum is taxable (*F(No.2)A 2005, ss 7–10*; see EIM74650).

(8) *Widowed Parent's Allowance* – Replaced Widowed Mother's Allowance (WMA) from 9 April 2001, although WMA is still paid to widows whose entitlement arose before 9 April 2001 (see EIM76172, EIM76177).

(9) *Widow's Pension* – Replaced by Bereavement Allowance (see EIM76173) for new claimants on or after 9 April 2001. However, widows in receipt of widow's pension before that date continue to receive widow's pension (see EIM76178).

19

General

RETAIL PRICES INDEX (RPI)

(1) RPI is the most familiar general purpose domestic measure of inflation in the UK. Historically, the Government has used it for the uprating of pensions, benefits and index-linked gilts, and for certain tax purposes (see below). However, it was announced in the 2011 Budget that from 2012–13 the Consumer Prices Index (CPI) will instead be used as the measure of inflation for pensions and most tax and NIC purposes.

(2) An RPI table can be downloaded (in pdf format) from the Office for National Statistics website: www.ons.gov.uk

(3) RPI factors are used in the calculation of indexation allowance for companies within the charge to corporation tax (*TCGA 1992, s 52A*). Indexation allowance tables are published on the HMRC website:

www.hmrc.gov.uk/rates/cg-indexation-allowance/index.htm

(4) For individuals, trustees and personal representatives, indexation allowance was abolished for disposals from 6 April 2008. The allowance was frozen for disposals between 6 April 1998 and 5 April 2008.

(5) For indexation allowance tables, and as to the calculation of the allowance (*TCGA 1992, s 54(1)*), see **Capital gains tax: Indexation allowance**.

BANK BASE RATES

Date changed	Rate %	Date changed	Rate %
Thu, 05 Mar 2009	0.50	Thu, 05 Jul 2007	5.75
Thu, 05 Feb 2009	1.00	Thu, 10 May 2007	5.50
Thu, 08 Jan 2009	1.50	Thu, 11 Jan 2007	5.25
Thu, 04 Dec 2008	2.00	Thu, 09 Nov 2006	5.00
Thu, 06 Nov 2008	3.00	Thu, 03 Aug 2006	4.75
Wed, 08 Oct 2008	4.50	Thu, 04 Aug 2005	4.50
Thu, 10 Apr 2008	5.00	Thu, 05 Aug 2004	4.75
Thu, 07 Feb 2008	5.25	Thu, 10 Jun 2004	4.50
Thu, 06 Dec 2007	5.50	Thu, 06 May 2004	4.25

Date changed	Rate %	Date changed	Rate %
Thu, 05 Feb 2004	4.00	Thu, 02 Aug 2001	5.00
Thu, 06 Nov 2003	3.75	Thu, 10 May 2001	5.25
Thu, 10 Jul 2003	3.50	Thu, 05 Apr 2001	5.50
Thu, 06 Feb 2003	3.75	Thu, 08 Feb 2001	5.75
Thu, 08 Nov 2001	4.00	Thu, 10 Feb 2000	6.00
Thu, 04 Oct 2001	4.50	Thu, 13 Jan 2000	5.75
Tue, 18 Sep 2001	4.75	Thu, 04 Nov 1999	5.50

Note

Source: Bank of England Statistical Interactive Database – official Bank Rate history (www.bankofengland.co.uk/mfsd/iadb/Repo.asp).

CERTIFICATES OF TAX DEPOSIT

Notes to the table on pages 212–213

(1) The certificate of tax deposit scheme is open to individuals, partnerships (to pay liabilities of the partnership), individual partners (to pay liabilities that apply solely to them), companies, personal representatives (to pay liabilities of a deceased individual's estate) and trustees (to pay liabilities of the trust). Tax deposits can be used to pay liabilities relating to income tax, Class 4 NICs, capital gains tax, petroleum revenue tax, petroleum royalty and inheritance tax, but cannot be used to pay corporation tax liabilities.

(2) The first tax deposit must be for a minimum of £500. The minimum for subsequent deposits is the lower of £250 and the amount needed to bring total deposits with HMRC back to £500 if it has dropped below that level. There is no maximum amount for a tax deposit.

(3) For further information about the scheme, visit www.hmrc.gov.uk/payinghmrc/cert-tax-deposit.htm.

19 General

Deposits From	Deposits held for under 1 month		Deposits of £100,000 or more								Deposits under £100,000	
			Deposits held for 1 to under 3 months		Deposits held for 3 to under 6 months		Deposits held for 6 to under 9 months		Deposits held for 9 to 12 months			
	Applied in payment of tax %	Cash value %	Applied in payment of tax %	Cash value %	Applied in payment of tax %	Cash value %	Applied in payment of tax %	Cash value %	Applied in payment of tax %	Cash value %	Applied in payment of tax %	Cash value %
6 Mar. 2009	0.00	0.00	0.75	0.25	0.75	0.25	0.75	0.25	0.75	0.25	0.00	0.00
6 Feb. 2009	0.00	0.00	1.00	0.50	1.00	0.50	1.00	0.50	0.75	0.25	0.00	0.00
9 Jan. 2009	0.00	0.00	1.50	0.75	1.25	0.50	1.25	0.50	1.25	0.50	0.00	0.00
5 Dec. 2008	0.00	0.00	2.50	1.25	2.50	1.25	2.50	1.25	2.25	1.00	0.00	0.00
7 Nov. 2008	1.75	0.75	4.50	2.25	4.25	2.00	4.25	2.00	4.00	2.00	1.75	0.75
9 Oct. 2008	2.50	1.25	5.25	2.50	5.00	2.50	5.00	2.50	4.75	2.25	2.50	1.25
11 Apr. 2008	2.00	1.00	4.75	2.25	4.50	2.25	4.25	2.00	4.25	2.00	2.00	1.00
8 Feb. 2008	2.00	1.00	4.50	2.25	4.25	2.25	4.00	2.00	3.75	1.50	2.00	1.00
7 Dec. 2007	3.00	1.50	5.50	2.75	5.00	2.50	4.75	2.25	4.50	2.25	3.00	1.50
06 Jul. 2007	2.25	1.10	5.00	2.50	4.75	2.25	4.75	2.25	4.75	2.25	2.25	1.10
11 May 2007	2.00	1.00	4.75	2.25	4.50	2.25	4.50	2.25	4.50	2.25	2.00	1.00
12 Jan. 2007	1.50	0.75	4.25	2.00	4.00	2.00	4.00	2.00	4.00	2.00	1.50	0.75
10 Nov. 2006	1.50	0.75	4.00	2.00	4.00	2.00	3.75	1.75	3.75	1.75	1.50	0.75
4 Aug. 2006	1.75	0.75	4.25	2.00	4.25	2.00	4.00	2.00	4.00	2.00	1.75	0.75
5 Aug. 2005	1.00	0.50	3.50	1.75	3.25	1.50	3.00	1.50	3.00	1.50	1.00	0.50
6 Aug. 2004	1.25	0.50	3.75	1.75	3.75	1.75	3.75	1.75	3.75	1.75	1.25	0.50
11 Jun. 2004	1.00	0.50	3.75	1.75	3.50	1.75	3.75	1.75	3.75	1.75	1.00	0.50
07 May 2004	0.75	0.25	3.25	1.50	3.25	1.50	3.25	1.50	3.25	1.50	0.75	0.25
6 Feb. 2004	0.50	0.25	3.00	1.50	3.00	1.50	3.00	1.50	3.00	1.50	0.50	0.25

Certificates of tax deposit

Date										
7 Nov.	2003	0.25	0.00	3.00	1.50	3.00	1.50	3.00	1.50	0.25	0.00
11 Jul.	2003	Nil	Nil	2.50	1.25	2.25	1.00	2.00	1.00	0.00	0.00
7 Feb.	2003	0.25	Nil	2.75	1.25	2.25	1.00	2.00	1.00	0.25	0.00
9 Nov.	2001	0.50	0.25	2.75	1.50	2.50	1.25	2.25	1.25	0.50	0.25
5 Oct.	2001	1.00	0.50	3.25	1.75	3.00	1.50	3.00	1.50	1.00	0.75
19 Sep.	2001	1.25	0.75	3.50	1.75	3.25	1.75	3.00	1.50	1.25	0.75
3 Aug.	2001	1.50	0.75	4.00	2.00	3.75	2.00	3.75	2.00	1.50	0.75
11 May	2001	2.00	1.00	4.00	2.00	3.75	2.00	3.75	2.00	2.00	1.00
6 Apr.	2001	2.00	1.00	4.25	2.25	3.75	2.00	3.50	1.75	2.00	1.00
9 Feb.	2001	2.25	1.25	4.75	2.50	4.25	2.25	4.00	2.00	2.25	1.25
11 Feb.	2000	2.50	1.25	5.25	2.75	5.25	2.75	5.25	2.75	2.50	1.25
14 Jan.	2000	2.25	1.25	5.00	2.50	5.00	2.50	5.25	2.75	2.25	1.25
4 Nov.	1999	2.00	1.00	5.00	2.50	4.75	2.50	4.75	2.50	2.00	1.00
9 Sept.	1999	1.75	1.00	4.50	2.25	4.50	2.25	4.50	2.25	1.75	1.00
11 Jun.	1999	1.50	0.75	4.00	2.00	4.00	2.00	4.00	2.00	1.50	0.75
9 Apr.	1999	1.75	1.00	4.25	2.25	4.00	2.00	3.75	2.00	1.75	1.00
5 Feb.	1999	1.75	1.00	4.50	2.25	4.00	2.00	3.75	2.00	1.75	1.00
8 Jan.	1999	2.50	1.25	5.00	2.50	4.50	2.25	4.00	2.00	2.50	1.25
11 Dec.	1998	3.00	1.50	5.25	2.75	4.75	2.50	4.25	2.25	3.25	1.75
6 Nov.	1998	3.25	1.75	5.75	3.00	5.25	2.75	4.75	2.50	3.25	1.75
9 Oct.	1998	3.75	2.00	6.25	3.25	5.75	3.00	5.25	2.75	3.75	2.00
05 Jun.	1998	4.00	2.00	6.50	3.25	6.25	3.25	6.00	3.00	4.00	2.00
7 Nov.	1997	4.00	2.00	6.50	3.25	6.25	3.25	6.25	3.25	4.00	2.00
8 Aug.	1997	4.50	2.25	6.00	3.00	6.00	3.00	5.75	3.00	4.50	2.25
11 Jul.	1997	3.25	1.75	6.00	3.00	5.75	3.00	6.00	3.00	3.25	1.75
09 Jun.	1997	3.00	1.50	5.50	2.75	5.50	2.75	5.50	2.75	3.00	1.50
07 May	1997	2.75	1.50	5.50	2.75	5.50	2.75	5.25	2.75	2.75	1.50

19 General

FOREIGN EXCHANGE RATES

Average for the year to 31 December 2011		Country/Currency			Average for the year to 31 March 2012	
Sterling value (£) of 1 currency unit	Currency units per £1	Country	Unit of Currency		Sterling value (£) of 1 currency unit	Currency units per £1
0.8683	1.151701	European Community	Euro		0.8716	1.147268
0.1698	5.888749	Abu Dhabi	Dirham		0.1695	5.900621
0.0145	69.078780	Afghanistan	Afghani		0.0144	69.248197
0.0062	161.708470	Albania	Lek		0.0062	161.044526
0.0085	117.053862	Algeria	Dinar		0.0085	117.228973
0.0067	150.193725	Angola	Readj Kwanza		0.0066	150.838631
0.231	4.328835	Antigua	E Caribbean Dollar		0.2305	4.337571
0.1513	6.611286	Argentina	Peso		0.1497	6.679004
0.0017	595.023235	Armenia	Dram		0.0017	601.119973
0.3484	2.869862	Aruba	Florin		0.3477	2.87565
0.6438	1.553232	Australia	Dollar		0.6498	1.538865
0.8683	1.151701	Austria	Euro		0.8716	1.147268
0.7895	1.266621	Azerbaijan	New Manat		0.7902	1.265468
0.6235	1.603844	Bahamas	Dollar		0.6238	1.602980
1.6017	0.624317	Bahrain	Dinar		1.5815	0.632318
0.0085	118.157254	Bangladesh	Taka		0.0083	119.814657
0.3119	3.206519	Barbados	Dollar		0.3112	3.212989
0.0001	8126.321960	Belarus	Rouble		0.0001	9262.538421
0.8683	1.1517019	Belgium	Euro		0.8716	1.147268
0.3159	3.165149	Belize	Dollar		0.314	3.184721

214

Foreign exchange rates

Average for the year to 31 December 2011		Country/Currency		Average for the year to 31 March 2012	
Sterling value (£) of 1 currency unit	Currency units per £1	Country	Unit of Currency	Sterling value (£) of 1 currency unit	Currency units per £1
0.0013	755.748666	Benin	CFA Franc	0.0013	750.873473
0.6235	1.603844	Bermuda	Dollar (US)	0.6238	1.602980
0.0134	74.557648	Bhutan	Ngultrum	0.0132	75.633995
0.0899	11.126	Bolivia	Boliviano	0.0899	11.126486
0.4438	2.2534	Bosnia-Herzegovinia	Marka	0.4467	2.238865
0.0916	10.915992	Botswana	Pula	0.0908	11.018805
0.3735	2.67755	Brazil	Real	0.3716	2.690953
0.4965	2.013958	Brunei	Dollar	0.4988	2.004905
0.4438	2.253421	Bulgaria	Lev	0.4467	2.238884
0.0013	755.748666	Burkina Faso	CFA Franc	0.0013	750.873473
0.0005	2015.156274	Burundi	Franc	0.0005	2031.513421
0.0002	6475.575490	Cambodia	Riel	0.0002	6521.079473
0.0013	755.748666	Cameroon Republic	CFA Franc	0.0013	750.873473
0.6312	1.584378	Canada	Dollar	0.6306	1.585670
0.0081	124.081607	Cape Verde Islands	Escudo	0.0081	123.244789
0.0615	16.269574	Cayman Islands	Dollar	0.0468	21.388360
0.0013	755.748666	Central African	CFA Franc	0.0013	750.873473
0.0013	755.748666	Chad	CFA Franc	0.0013	750.873473
0.0013	771.550411	Chile	Peso	0.0013	774.093184
0.0964	10.374478	China	Yuan (Renminbi)	0.0968	10.331410
0.0003	2959.414509	Colombia	Peso	0.0003	2947.012631
0.0018	566.812980	Comoros	Franc	0.0018	563.157078

continued

215

19 General

| Average for the year to 31 December 2011 || Country/Currency || Average for the year to 31 March 2012 ||
Sterling value (£) of 1 currency unit	Currency units per £1	Country	Unit of Currency	Sterling value (£) of 1 currency unit	Currency units per £1
0.0013	755.748666	Congo (Brazaville)	CFA Franc	0.0013	750.873473
0.0007	1458.637352	Congo (DemRep)	Congo Fr	0.0007	1455.135657
0.0012	810.964078	Costa Rica	Colon	0.0012	813.537868
0.0013	755.748666	Cote d'Ivoire	CFA Franc	0.0013	750.873473
0.1168	8.560872	Croatia	Kuna	0.1174	8.517565
0.6237	1.603278	Cuba	Peso	0.6225	1.606513
0.8683	1.151701	Cyprus	Euro	0.8716	1.147268
0.0353	28.314162	Czech Republic	Koruna	0.0355	28.175426
0.1166	8.576243	Denmark	Krone	0.117	8.545717
0.0036	280.387372	Djibouti	Franc	0.0036	280.852157
0.231	4.328835	Dominica	E Caribbean Dollar	0.2305	4.337571
0.0164	60.816127	Dominican Republic	Peso	0.0163	61.193413
0.1698	5.888749	Dubai	Dirham	0.1695	5.900621
0.6235	1.603844	Ecuador	Dollar	0.6238	1.602980
0.105	9.519580	Egypt	Pound	0.1044	9.583036
0.0713	14.0245470	El Salvador	Colon	0.0712	14.0528447
0.0013	755.748666	Equatorial Guinea	CFA Franc	0.0013	750.873473
0.0416	24.0489156	Eritrea	Nakfa	0.0415	24.097439
0.5554	1.8004	Estonia	Euro	0.8716	1.147268
0.0368	27.194339	Ethiopia	Birr	0.0365	27.394936
0.3479	2.874145	Fiji Islands	Dollar	0.35	2.857002
0.8683	1.151701	Finland	Euro	0.8716	1.147268

Foreign exchange rates

Average for the year to 31 December 2011		Country/Currency		Average for the year to 31 March 2012	
Sterling value (£) of 1 currency unit	Currency units per £1	Country	Unit of Currency	Sterling value (£) of1 currency unit	Currency units per £1
0.0073	137.471117	Fr. Polynesia	CFP Franc	0.0073	136.599473
0.8683	1.1517019	France	Euro	0.8716	1.147268
0.0013	755.748666	Gabon	CFA Franc	0.0013	750.873473
0.022	45.487305	Gambia	Dalasi	0.0219	45.660571
0.0213	47.057882	Georgia	Lari	0.0212	47.071768
0.8683	1.151701	Germany	Euro	0.8716	1.147268
0.4046	2.471605	Ghana	Cedi	0.4011	2.493189
0.8683	1.151701	Greece	Euro	0.8716	1.147268
0.231	4.328835	Grenada	E Caribbean Dollar	0.2305	4.337571
0.08	12.498837	Guatemala	Quetzal	0.0801	12.491665
0.0013	755.748666	Guinea Bissau	CFA Franc	0.0013	750.873473
0.0001	11127.678431	Guinea Republic	Franc	0.0001	10987.394736
0.0031	325.050529	Guyana	Dollar	0.0031	325.518105
0.0155	64.599154	Haiti	Gourde	0.0154	64.822092
0.033	30.287207	Honduras	Lempira	0.033	30.346134
0.0801	12.484348	Hong Kong	Dollar	0.0802	12.475751
0.0031	321.140764	Hungary	Forint	0.0031	321.176289
0.0054	185.767450	Iceland	Krona	0.0054	185.886342
0.0134	74.557648	India	Rupee	0.0132	75.633995
0.0001	14037.286274	Indonesia	Rupiah	0.0001	13966.952631
0.0001	16977.892156	Iran	Rial	0.0001	17142.244736
0.0005	1872.536274	Iraq	Dinar	0.0005	1874.359210

continued

217

19 *General*

Average for the year to 31 December 2011		Country/Currency			Average for the year to 31 March 2012	
Sterling value (£) of 1 currency unit	Currency units per £1	Country	Unit of Currency	Sterling value (£) of 1 currency unit	Currency units per £1
0.8683	1.151701	Ireland	Euro	0.8716	1.147268
0.1747	5.724734	Israel	Shekel	0.1745	5.729460
0.8683	1.151701	Italy	Euro	0.8716	1.147268
0.0073	137.120411	Jamaica	Dollar	0.0073	137.520789
0.0078	128.003692	Japan	Yen	0.0079	126.522975
0.8804	1.135860	Jordan	Dinar	0.8785	1.138360
0.0043	235.107098	Kazakhstan	Tenge	0.0042	235.628578
0.007	142.140686	Kenya	Schilling	0.0068	146.097868
0.1634	6.119613	Korea (North)	Won	0.4788	2.088444
2.2557	0.443325	Kuwait	Dinar	2.261	0.442289
0.0213	47.0578823	Kyrgyz Republic	Som	0.0212	47.071768
0.0001	12823.652941	Lao People's Dem Rep	Kip	0.0001	12837.960526
1.2284	0.814049	Latvia	Lat	1.2354	0.809481
0.0004	2413.901568	Lebanon	Pound	0.0004	2421.354210
0.0865	11.560037	Lesotho	Loti	0.0854	11.704389
0.6235	1.603844	Liberia	Dollar (US)	0.6238	1.602980
0.5137	1.946633	Libya	Dinar	0.5156	1.939334
0.2514	3.978150	Lithuania	Litas	0.253	3.952473
0.8683	1.151701	Luxembourg	Euro	0.8716	1.147268
0.0778	12.854964	Macao	Pataca	0.0776	12.880076
0.0141	70.877366	Macedonia	Denar	0.0142	70.350684
0.0003	3246.625294	Madagascar	Malagasy Ariary	0.0003	3237.225526

Foreign exchange rates

Average for the year to 31 December 2011		Country/Currency		Average for the year to 31 March 2012	
Sterling value (£) of 1 currency unit	Currency units per £1	Country	Unit of Currency	Sterling value (£) of 1 currency unit	Currency units per £1
0.004	250.396784	Malawi	Kwacha	0.0039	253.849868
0.2041	4.899313	Malaysia	Ringgit	0.2038	4.906721
0.0433	23.093664	Maldive Islands	Rufiyaa	0.0416	24.014931
0.0013	755.748666	Mali Republic	CFA Franc	0.0013	750.873473
0.8683	1.151701	Malta	Euro	0.8716	1.147268
0.0022	451.256274	Mauritania	Ouguiya	0.0022	451.345473
0.0217	46.046884	Mauritius	Rupee	0.0219	45.642373
0.0503	19.867946	Mexico	Mexican Peso	0.0497	20.118153
0.0532	18.811905	Moldova	Leu	0.0536	18.670242
0.0005	2021.839215	Mongolia	Tugrik	0.0005	2032.758157
0.231	4.328835	Montserrat	E Caribbean Dollar	0.2305	4.337571
0.0785	12.740574	Morocco	Dirham	0.0794	12.597028
0.0214	46.630631	Mozambique	Metical	0.0221	45.182634
0.0973	10.276898	Myanmar	Kyat	0.0971	10.297636
0.0084	119.028039	Nepal	Rupee	0.0083	120.210473
0.8683	1.151701	Netherland	Euro	0.8716	1.147268
0.0073	137.471117	New Caledonia	CFP Franc	0.0073	136.599473
0.4927	2.029523	New Zealand	Dollar	0.4999	2.000387
0.0279	35.904198	Nicaragua	Gold Cordoba	0.0276	36.199213
0.0013	755.748666	Niger Republic	CFA Franc	0.0013	750.873473
0.004	249.169352	Nigeria	Naira	0.004	250.839657
0.1114	8.977276	Norway	Norwegian Krone	0.112	8.930839

continued

219

19 General

| Average for the year to 31 December 2011 ||| Country/Currency ||| Average for the year to 31 March 2012 ||
Sterling value (£) of 1 currency unit	Currency units per £1	Country	Unit of Currency	Sterling value (£) of 1 currency unit	Currency units per £1
1.6199	0.617333	Oman	Rial	1.6167	0.618560
0.0072	138.291588	Pakistan	Rupee	0.0072	138.962552
0.6237	1.603278	Panama	Balboa	0.6225	1.606513
0.2637	3.792364	Papua New Guinea	Kina	0.2728	3.665605
0.0001	6744.826274	Paraguay	Guarani	0.0002	6565.489473
0.2264	4.416507	Peru	New Sol	0.2266	4.412378
0.0144	69.410809	Philippines	Peso	0.0145	69.168153
0.2114	4.731154	Poland	Zloty	0.2098	4.766465
0.8683	1.151701	Portugal	Euro	0.8716	1.147268
0.1713	5.837937	Qatar	Riyal	0.1709	5.849957
0.2046	4.887498	Romania	New Leu	0.2059	4.856684
0.0213	47.057882	Russia	Rouble	0.0212	47.071768
0.001	961.775333	Rwanda	Franc	0.001	964.767289
0	28235.141176	Saotome & Principe	Dobra	0	28064.623684
0.1663	6.014736	Saudi Arabia	Riyal	0.1663	6.011490
0.0013	755.748666	Senegal	CFA Franc	0.0013	750.873473
0.0085	117.515235	Serbia	Dinar	0.0086	115.877184
0.0504	19.832025	Seychelles	Rupee	0.0501	19.940507
0.0001	6965.582156	Sierra Leone	Leone	0.0001	7033.207894
0.4962	2.015259	Singapore	Dollar	0.4986	2.005682
0.8683	1.151701	Slovakia	Euro	0.8716	1.147268
0.8683	1.151701	Slovenia	Euro	0.8716	1.147268

Foreign exchange rates

| Average for the year to 31 December 2011 || Country/Currency || Average for the year to 31 March 2012 ||
Sterling value (£) of 1 currency unit	Currency units per £1	Country	Unit of Currency	Sterling value (£) of 1 currency unit	Currency units per £1
0.0825	12.114521	Soloman Islands	Dollar	0.0832	12.0155473
0.0004	2510.116862	Somali Republic	Schilling	0.0004	2523.075789
0.0864	11.578746	South Africa	Rand	0.085	11.768892
0.0006	1774.787692	South Korea	Won	0.0006	1769.470487
0.8683	1.151701	Spain	Euro	0.8716	1.147268
0.0056	177.075039	Sri Lanka	Rupee	0.0056	177.253
0.231	4.328835	St Christopher &	E Caribbean Dollar	0.2305	4.337571
0.231	4.328835	St Lucia	E Caribbean Dollar	0.2305	4.337571
0.231	4.328835	St Vincent	E Caribbean Dollar	0.2305	4.337571
0.2364	4.230813	Sudan Republic	Pound	0.232	4.311092
0.1921	5.205325	Surinam	Dollar	0.1886	5.301478
0.0865	11.560037	Swaziland	Lilangeni	0.0854	11.704389
0.0962	10.395490	Sweden	Krona	0.0961	10.407814
0.7036	1.421359	Switzerland	Franc	0.7162	1.396221
0.013	76.863907	Syria	Pound	0.0129	77.691921
0.0212	47.081596	Taiwan	Dollar	0.0212	47.163724
0.0213	47.057882	Tajikistan	Somoni	0.0212	47.071768
0.0004	2535.730980	Tanzania	Schilling	0.0004	2585.166315
0.0205	48.820230	Thailand	Baht	0.0205	48.846695
0.0013	755.748666	Togo Republic	CFA Franc	0.0013	750.873473
0.6438	1.553232	Tonga Islands	Pa'anga (AUS)	0.6498	1.538865
0.0974	10.261809	Trinidad/Tobago	Dollar	0.0972	10.286721

continued

19 General

| Average for the year to 31 December 2011 || Country/Currency || Average for the year to 31 March 2012 ||
Sterling value (£) of 1 currency unit	Currency units per £1	Country	Unit of Currency	Sterling value (£) of 1 currency unit	Currency units per £1
0.4437	2.253631	Tunisia	Dinar	0.4445	2.249884
0.3734	2.677966	Turkey	Turkish Lira	0.3657	2.734268
0.2193	4.560825	Turkmenistan	New Manat	0.2188	4.569584
0.1698	5.888749	UAE	Dirham	0.1695	5.900621
0.0002	4042.469215	Uganda	Schilling	0.0002	4145.065789
0.0781	12.797878	Ukraine	Hryvnia	0.0779	12.841105
0.0324	30.822629	Uruguay	Peso	0.0326	30.669321
0.6235	1.603844	USA	Dollar	0.6238	1.602980
0.0004	2741.073725	Uzbekistan	Sum	0.0004	2776.577368
0.0067	149.979921	Vanuatu	Vatu	0.0067	149.282368
0.1452	6.885468	Venezuela	Bolivar Fuerte	0.1449	6.899357
0	33063.927450	Vietnam	Dong	0	33398.544736
0.0073	137.471117	Wallis & Futuna Islands	CFP Franc	0.0073	136.599473
0.2688	3.720178	Western Samoa	Tala	0.2706	3.695884
0.0029	345.071235	Yemen (Rep of)	Rial	0.0029	346.547710
0.0001	7779.138823	Zambia	Kwacha	0.0001	7837.674736
0.0016	606.220352	Zimbabwe	Dollar	0.0016	607.415657

Note

This table is reproduced from information provided by HMRC (www.hmrc.gov.uk/exrate/exchangerates-1112.pdf) and is Crown copyright.

Appendix A Table of spot rates on 31 March 2011 and 31 December 2011

31 March 2011		Country/Currency		31 December 2011	
Sterling value (£) of 1 currency unit	Currency units per £1	Country	Unit of currency	Sterling value (£) of 1 currency unit	Currency units per £1
0.6452	1.55	Australia	AUD Dollar	0.6597	1.5159
0.6413	1.5593	Canada	CAD Dollar	0.6319	1.5825
0.1187	8.4221	Denmark	DKK Krone	0.1124	8.8978
0.8853	1.1296	European Community	EUR Euro	0.8353	1.1972
0.0802	12.4681	Hong Kong	HKD Dollar	0.0828	12.0701
0.0075	132.853	Japan	JPY Yen	0.0084	119.572
0.1128	8.8671	Norway	NOK Norwegian Krone	0.1078	9.2748
0.0923	10.8351	South Africa	ZAR Rand	0.0797	12.5469
0.0989	10.1121	Sweden	SEK Krona	0.0939	10.6539
0.6819	1.4665	Switzerland	CHF Franc	0.6881	1.4532
0.6238	1.603	USA	USD Dollar	0.6435	1.5541

Notes

(1) This table is reproduced from information provided by HMRC (www.hmrc.gov.uk/exrate/exchangerates-1112.pdf) and is Crown copyright.

(2) At the time of going to press, HMRC had not yet published their table of spot rates as at 31 March 2012.

RECOGNISED STOCK EXCHANGES

(*ITA 2007, s 1005*; *CTA 2010, s 1137*)

A 'recognised stock exchange' is one which is either:

- A recognised investment exchange designated as a recognised stock exchange by an order of the Commissioners for HMRC; or
- any designated market outside the UK.

A recognised stock exchange within *ITA 2007, s 1005* is also treated as such for corporation tax purposes (*CTA 2010, s 1137(1)*).

Stock exchanges designated as recognised stock exchanges

Stock exchange	Date of recognition
The Athens Stock Exchange	14 June 1993
The Australian Stock Exchange (and any of its stock exchange subsidiaries)	22 September 1988
Bahamas International Securities Exchange (BISX)	19 April 2010
The Bermuda Stock Exchange	4 December 2007
The Bond Exchange of South Africa	16 April 2008
The Cayman Islands Stock Exchange	4 March 2004
The Colombo Stock Exchange	21 February 1972
The Copenhagen Stock Exchange	22 October 1970
The Cyprus Stock Exchange	22 June 2009
The Helsinki Stock Exchange	22 October 1970

continued

19 General

Stock exchange	Date of recognition
The Iceland Stock Exchange	31 March 2006
The Johannesburg Stock Exchange	22 October 1970
The Korea Stock Exchange	10 October 1994
The Kuala Lumpur Stock Exchange	10 October 1994
The London International Financial Futures and Options Exchange Administration and Management (LIFFE A&M)	26 September 2011
The London Stock Exchange	19 July 2007
The Malta Stock Exchange	29 December 2005
The Stock Exchange of Mauritius	31 January 2011
The Mexico Stock Exchange	10 October 1994
The MICEX Stock Exchange	5 January 2011
NASDAQ OMX Tallinn (except its First North market)	5 May 2010
The New Zealand Stock Exchange	22 September 1988
NASDAQ OMX Vilnius (except securities quoted solely on its First North market)	12 March 2012
The Plus-listed Market	19 July 2007
The Rio De Janeiro Stock Exchange	17 August 1995
The Sao Paulo Stock Exchange	11 December 1995
The Singapore Stock Exchange	30 June 1977
The Stockholm Stock Exchange	16 July 1985
The Stock Exchange of Thailand	10 October 1994
The Swiss Stock Exchange	12 May 1997
The Warsaw Stock Exchange	25 February 2010

Recognised stock exchange countries

The following are countries where any stock exchange in that country that is a stock exchange within the law of that country is a recognised stock exchange.

Stock exchange	Date of recognition
Austria	22 October 1970
Belgium	22 October 1970
Canada	22 October 1970
France	22 October 1970
Germany	5 August 1971
Guernsey	10 December 2002
Hong Kong	26 February 1971
Ireland (Republic of)	22 October 1970
Italy	3 May 1972
Japan	22 October 1970
Luxembourg	21 February 1972
Netherlands	22 October 1970
Norway	22 October 1970
Portugal	21 February 1972
Spain	5 August 1971
USA	See note

Note

USA – A stock exchange in the USA is a recognised stock exchange for UK tax purposes if it meets the following:

"Any exchange registered with the Securities and Exchange Commission of the United States (SEC) as a national securities exchange under Section 6 of the Securities Exchange Act of 1934 is a recognised stock exchange for UK tax purposes".

The American Stock Exchange was a recognised stock exchange between 22 October 1970 and 1 October 2008, but following its split into new markets, it is no longer a recognised stock exchange in its own right.

Alternative finance investment bonds

(ITA 2007 s 564G)

The following is a list of recognised stock exchanges designated solely for the purposes of *ITA 2007, s 564G* (alternative finance arrangements: investment bonds) (formerly *FA 2005, s 48A*). The date of recognition in all cases is 1 April 2007:

- Abu Dhabi Securities Market
- Bahrain Stock Exchange
- Dubai Financial Market
- Dubai International Financial Exchange
- Labuan International Financial Exchange
- Saudi Stock Exchange (Tadawul)
- Surabaya Stock Exchange

Recognised futures exchanges

(TCGA 1992, s 288(6))

Tax year of recognition	Exchange
1985–86	[The Baltic International Freight Futures Exchange]
	The International Petroleum Exchange London
	[The London Cocoa Terminal Market]
	[The London Coffee Terminal Market]
	The London Gold Futures Market (nb no longer exists)
	[The London Grain Futures Market]
	[The London Meat Futures Market]
	The London Metal Exchange
	[The London Potato Futures Market]
	The London Rubber Market
	[The London Soya Bean Meal Futures Market]

continued

19 General

Tax year of recognition	Exchange
1985–86 – contd	[The London Sugar Terminal Market]
	The London Wool Terminal Market (nb no longer exists)
	The London Gold Market
	The London Silver Market
1986–87	The Chicago Mercantile Exchange
	The Philadelphia Board of Trade
	The New York Mercantile Exchange
1987–88	The Chicago Board of Trade
	The Montreal Exchange
	The Mid America Commodity Exchange
	The Hong Kong Futures Exchange
	The Coffee, Sugar and Cocoa Exchange Inc, New York
1988–89	The Commodity Exchange, Inc (COMEX)
	The Citrus Associates of the New York Cotton Exchange, Inc
	The New York Cotton Exchange
	The Sydney Futures Exchange Ltd
1991–92	The London International Financial Futures and Options Exchange
	London FOX
	OM London
	OM Stockholm AB

Notes

(1) Recognised futures exchange means the London International Financial Futures Exchange and any other futures exchange which is designated (for the purposes of *TCGA 1992* by order of the Board.

(2) The exchanges shown in brackets above have been part of the London FOX since January 1991. This in turn merged into the London International Financial Futures and Options Exchange in 1996.

(3) The above exchanges are accepted as recognised futures exchanges for the tax year of recognition onwards (CG56120).

Recognised investment exchanges

(*ITEPA 2003, s 702*)

Date of recognition	Exchange
22 November 2001	LIFFE Administration and Management
22 November 2001	London Stock Exchange plc
19 July 2007	PLUS Markets plc
22 November 2001	The London Metal Exchange Limited

Notes

(1) Source: The FSA Register (www.fsa.gov.uk/register/exchanges.do)

(2) The definition of 'readily convertible asset' (*ITEPA 2003, s 702*) includes an asset capable of being sold or otherwise realised on a recognised investment exchange, within the meaning of the *Financial Services and Markets Act 2000*.

Recognised overseas investment exchanges

(*ITEPA 2003, s 702*)

Date of recognition	Exchange
30 January 2002	Australian Securities Exchange Limited
23 November 2001	Chicago Board of Trade (CBOT)
23 November 2001	EUREX [Zurich]
17 May 2007	ICE Futures US Inc
23 November 2001	National Association of Securities Dealers Automated Quotations (NASDAQ)
23 November 2001	New York Mercantile Exchange Inc. [NYMEX Inc.]
29 September 2009	NYSE Liffe US
23 November 2001	SIX Swiss Exchange AG
23 November 2001	The Chicago Mercantile Exchange [CME]

Notes

(1) Source: The Financial Services Authority (FSA) Register: (www.fsa.gov.uk/register/exchanges.do)

(2) The definition of 'readily convertible asset' (*ITEPA 2003, s 702*) includes an asset capable of being sold or otherwise realised on a recognised investment exchange, within the meaning of the *Financial Services and Markets Act 2000*. The FSA has recognised and supervises a number of Recognised Overseas Investment Exchanges.

DOUBLE TAXATION AGREEMENTS

(*TIOPA 2010, Pt 2, Ch 1*; HMRC Double Taxation Relief Manual DT2140 et seq)

Countries with a Double Taxation Agreement (DTA)

Country	Authority	Coverage
Algeria	SI 1984/362	ATP
Antigua & Barbuda	SRO 1947/2865 Amended by SI 1968/1096	C
Argentina	SI 1997/1777 Amended by Protocol of 3 January 1996	C
Armenia	SI 2011/2722	C

continued

19   General

Country	Authority	Coverage
Australia	SI 2003/3199	C
Austria	SI 1970/1947	C
	Amended by Protocols SI 1979/117, SI 1994/768 and SI 2010/2688	
Azerbaijan	SI 1995/762	C
Bangladesh	SI 1980/708	C
Barbados	SI 1970/952	C
	Amended by Protocol SI 1973/2096	
Belarus	SI 1974/1269 (not superseded)	ATP
	SI 1986/224 [SI 1995/2706 not yet in force]	C
Belgium	SI 1987/2053	C
Belize	SRO 1947/2866	C
	Amended by Protocols SI 1968/573 and SI 1973/2097	
Bolivia	SI 1995/2707	C
Bosnia Herzegovina	SI 1981/1815	C
Botswana	SI 2006/1925	C
Brazil	SI 1968/572	S, ATP
British Virgin Islands	SI 2009/3013	IT
Brunei	SI 1950/1977	C
	Amended by Protocols SI 1968/306 and SI 1973/2098	
Bulgaria	SI 1987/2054	C
Burma (Myanmar)	SI 1952/751 including Protocol	C
Cameroon	SI 1982/1841	ATP
Canada	SI 1980/709	C
	Amended by Protocols SI 1980/1528, SI 1985/1996 and SI 2003/2619	
Chile	SI 2003/3200	C
China	SI 1981/1119 (not superseded)	ATP
	SI 1984/1826	C
	Amended by Protocol SI 1996/3164	
Croatia	SI 1981/1815	C
Cyprus	SI 1975/425	C
	Amended by Protocol SI 1980/1529	
Czech Republic	SI 1991/2876	C
Denmark	SI 1980/1960	C
	Amended by Protocols SI 1991/2877 and SI 1996/3165	
Egypt	SI 1980/1091	C

Double Taxation Agreements

Country	Authority	Coverage
Estonia	SI 1994/3207	C
Ethiopia	SI 1977/1297	ATP
Falkland Islands	SI 1997/2985	C
Faroes	SI 2007/3469	C
Fiji	SI 1976/1342	C
Finland	SI 1970/153 Amended by Protocols SI 1973/1327, SI 1980/710, SI 1985/1997, 1991/2878 and 1996/3166	C
France	SI 2009/226	C
Gambia	SI 1980/1963	C
Georgia	SI 2004/3325	C
Germany	SI 2010/2975	C
Ghana	SI 1993/1800	C
Greece	SI 1954/142	C
Grenada	SI 1949/361 Amended by Protocol SI 1968/1867	C
Guernsey	SI 1952/1215 Amended by Protocol SI 1994/3209, Supplementary Arrangement 2009/3011	C
Guyana	SI 1992/3207	C
Hong Kong	SI 2010/2974 including Protocol	C
Hungary	SI 2011/2726	C
Iceland	SI 1991/2879	C
India	SI 1993/1801	C
Indonesia	SI 1994/769	C
Iran	SI 1960/2419	ATP
Ireland	SI 1976/2151 Amended by Protocols SI 1976/2152, SI 1995/764 and SI 1998/3151	C
Isle of Man	SI 1955/1205 Amended by Supplementary Arrangements SI 1991/2880, SI 1994/3208 and SI 2009/228	C
Israel	SI 1963/616 Amended by Protocol – SI 1971/391	C
Italy	SI 1990/2590	C
Ivory Coast	SI 1987/169	C
Jamaica	SI 1973/1329	C
Japan	SI 2006/1970	C
Jersey	SI 1952/1216 Amended by Arrangements SI 1994/3210 and SI 2009/3012	C
Jordan	SI 2001/3924	C

continued

19 General

Country	Authority	Coverage
Kazakhstan	SI 1994/3211	C
	Amended by Protocol SI 1998/2567	
Kenya	SI 1977/1299	C
Kiribati	SI 1950/750	C
	Amended by Arrangements SI 1968/309 and SI 1974/1271	
Korea (Republic of)	SI 1996/3168	C
Kuwait	SI 1999/2036	C
Latvia	SI 1996/3167	C
Lebanon	SI 1964/278	S, ATP
Lesotho	SI 1997/2986	C
Libya	SI 2010/243	C
Lithuania	SI 2001/3925	C
	Amended by Protocol SI 2002/2847	
Luxembourg	SI 1968/1100	C
	Amended by Protocols SI 1980/567, SI 1984/364 and SI 2010/237	
Macedonia	SI 2007/2127	C
Malawi	SI 1956/619	C
	Amended by Protocols SI 1964/1401, 1968/1101 and SI 1979/302	
Malaysia	SI 1997/2987	C
Malta	SI 1995/763	C
Mauritius	SI 1981/1121	C
	Amended by Protocols SI 1987/467, SI 2003/2620 and SI 2011/2442	
Mexico	SI 1994/3212	C
Moldova	SI 2008/1795	C
Mongolia	SI 1996/2598	C
Montenegro	SI 1981/1815	C
Montserrat	SRO 1947/2869	C
	Amended by Protocol SI 1968/576	
Morocco	SI 1991/2881	C
Namibia	SI 1962/2352	C
	Extended by SI 1962/2788 – Amended by Protocol SI 1967/1489 as extended by SI 1967/1490	
Netherlands	SI 2009/227	C
New Zealand	SI 1984/365	C
	Amended by Protocols SI 2004/1274, SI 2008/1973	
Nigeria	SI 1987/2057	C

Double Taxation Agreements

Country	Authority	Coverage
Norway	SI 2000/3247	C
Oman	SI 1998/2568	C
	Amended by Protocol SI 2010/2687	
Pakistan	SI 1987/2058	C
Papua New Guinea	SI 1991/2882	C
Philippines	SI 1978/184	C
Poland	SI 2006/3323	C
Portugal	SI 1969/599	C
Qatar	SI 2010/241	C
Romania	SI 1977/57	C
Russia	SI 1994/3213	C
St. Christopher (St. Kitts) and Nevis	SRO 1947/2872	C
Saudi Arabia	SI 1994/767 (not superseded)	ATP
	SI 2008/1770 including Protocol	C
Serbia	SI 1981/1815	C
Sierra Leone	SRO 1947/2873	C
	Amended by Protocol SI 1968/1104	
Singapore	SI 1997/2988	C
	Amended by Protocol SI 2010/2685	
Slovak Republic	SI 1991/2876	C
Slovenia	SI 2008/1796	C
Solomon Islands	SI 1950/748	C
	Amended by Arrangements SI 1968/574 and SI 1974/1270	
South Africa	SI 2002/3138	C
	Amended by Protocol SI 2011/2441	
Spain	SI 1976/1919	C
	Amended by Exchange of Notes SI 1995/765	
Sri Lanka	SI 1980/713	C
Sudan	SI 1977/1719	C
Swaziland	SI 1969/380	C
Sweden	SI 1984/366	C
Switzerland	SI 1978/1408	C
	Amended by Protocols SI 1982/714, SI 1994/3215, SI 2007/3465 and SI 2010/2689	
Taiwan	SI 2002/3137	C
Tajikistan	SI 1974/1269 (not superseded)	ATP
	SI 1986/224	C
Thailand	SI 1981/1546	C

continued

19 General

Country	Authority	Coverage
Trinidad and Tobago	SI 1983/1903	C
Tunisia	SI 1984/133	C
Turkey	SI 1988/932	C
Turkmenistan	SI 1974/1269 (not superseded)	ATP
	SI 1986/224	C
Tuvalu	SI 1950/750	C
	Amended by Arrangements SI 1968/309 and SI 1974/1271	
Uganda	SI 1993/1802	C
Ukraine	SI 1993/1803	C
USA	SI 2002/2848 including Protocol and Exchange of Notes	C
Uzbekistan	SI 1994/770	C
Venezuela	SI 1996/2599	C
Vietnam	SI 1994/3216	C
Zambia	SI 1972/1721	C
	Amended by Protocol SI 1981/1816	
Zimbabwe	SI 1982/1842	C

Notes

(1) Key to coverage of agreements
    ATP Air Transport Profits
    C Comprehensive
    S Shipping Profits
    IT Income taxes only
(2) The text of many DTAs can be accessed via HMRC's website: www.hmrc.gov.uk/international/in_force.htm
(3) HMRC publishes a Digest of Double Taxation Treaties (pdf format), which can be downloaded from the HMRC website: www.hmrc.gov.uk/taxtreaties/dtdigest.pdf

DTAs signed/not in force

(1) *Bahrain* – A double tax agreement was signed on 10 March 2010. The Agreement will come into effect as soon as both countries have completed their Parliamentary procedures and exchanged diplomatic notes.

(2) *Belgium* – An amending Protocol to the Double Taxation Convention between the UK and Belgium was signed on 24 June 2009. The Protocol updates the exchange of information article of the convention to bring it into line with current OECD standards and practice, introduces a provision for binding arbitration in the event of protracted disputes, and makes other technical revisions. The Protocol will enter into force once both countries have completed their legislative procedures.

Double Taxation Agreements

(3) *Brazil* – An agreement between the UK and Brazil to avoid the double taxation of the salaries of members of the crew of aircraft operated in international traffic was signed on 2 September 2010. The Agreement will come into effect as soon as each government has completed the necessary procedures to give effect to it under their domestic laws.

(4) *China* – A double taxation agreement was signed in London on 27 June 2011. The agreement has not yet entered into force. This will happen when both countries have completed their Parliamentary procedures and exchanged diplomatic notes.

(5) *Ethiopia* – A double taxation convention was signed in London on 9 June 2011. The Convention will enter into force once both countries have completed their Parliamentary procedures and exchanged diplomatic notes.

(6) *Germany* – A new Bank Levy Agreement between the UK and the Federal Republic of Germany was signed on 7 December 2011. The purpose of the Agreement is to eliminate double charging where a bank is chargeable to the bank levy in both countries. There is also a specific measure providing for the exchange of information in relation to the levies covered by the Agreement. The Agreement will enter into force once both countries have completed their legislative procedures.

(7) *Montserrat* – Exchange of letters dated 7 December 2009 concerning an arrangement between the UK and Montserrat, amending the 1947 arrangement (as amended by the 1968 arrangement).

(8) *Singapore* – A second protocol to the 1997 double tax treaty between the UK and Singapore was signed on 15 February 2012, and will come into force when both countries have completed their legislative procedures.

(9) *Switzerland* – A 'Tax Cooperation Agreement' between the UK and Switzerland, aimed at resolving long-standing issues arising from Swiss banking secrecy, was signed on 6 October 2011 and is expected to come into force in 2013 once both countries have completed their legislative procedures. Under the terms of the agreement, existing funds held by UK taxpayers in Switzerland will be subject to a one-off deduction of between 19% and 34% to settle past tax liabilities, leaving those who have already paid their taxes unaffected. From 2013 a new withholding tax of 48% on investment income and 27% on gains will ensure the future taxation of UK residents with funds in Swiss bank accounts. This will be accompanied by a new information sharing provision which will make it easier for HMRC to find out about Swiss accounts held by UK taxpayers. The new charges will not apply if the taxpayer authorises a full disclosure of their affairs to HMRC. An amending Protocol signed on 20 March 2012 includes a joint declaration that UK taxpayers who have paid both the retention on taxation of savings and a 13% tax finality payment shall cease to have any liability to UK taxes on those interest payments. (*FB 2012, cl 216, Sch 35*; for further details see www.hmrc.gov.uk/taxtreaties/ukswiss.htm).

An updated list of DTAs signed/not in force for 2010 and earlier years is available on the HMRC website: www.hmrc.gov.uk/international/signed.htm.

Double Taxation Conventions (DTCs): Inheritance Tax

(IHTA 1984, s 158; IHTM 27161 et seq)

Country	Authority
France	SI 1963/1319
India	SI 1956/998
Ireland	SI 1978/1107
Italy	SI 1968/304
Netherlands	SI 1980/706
	Amended by Protocol SI 1996/730
Pakistan	SI 1957/1522
South Africa	SI 1979/576
Sweden	SI 1981/840
	Amended by Protocol SI 1989/986
Switzerland	SI 1994/3214 including Protocol
USA	SI 1979/1454

Note

The UK Government may enter into a DTC with the Government of any territory outside the UK. Where the deceased was domiciled in a DTC territory or owned property situate in one of those territories, the terms of the relevant DTC should be considered in relation to IHT and any tax imposed by the laws of that territory which is of a similar character or is chargeable by reference to death or gifts made *inter vivos* (*IHTA 1984, s 158; IHTM27161*).

Tax Information Exchange Agreements (TIEAs)

TIEAs in force

An updated list of TIEAs in force is available on the HMRC website: www.hmrc.gov.uk/taxtreaties/tiea/inforce.htm

Country	Authority	Scope
Anguilla	SI 2010/2677	B
	Agreement effective 28 October 2004	NR
Antigua and Barbuda	SI 2011/1075	B
Aruba	SI 2011/2435	B
Bahamas	SI 2010/2684	B
Bermuda	SI 2008/1789	B
Belize	SI 2011/1685	B
British Virgin Islands	SI 2005/1457	R
	SI 2009/3013	B
Cayman Islands	Agreement effective 16 April 2005	NR

Double Taxation Agreements

Country	Authority	Scope
Curaçao, Sint Maarten and the BES Islands (Bonaire, Saba and Sint Eustatius) (formerly the Netherlands Antilles)	SI 2011/2433	B
Dominica	SI 2011/1686	B
Gibraltar	SI 2006/1453	R
	SI 2010/2680	B
Grenada	SI 2011/1687	B
Guernsey	SI 2005/1262	R
	SI 2009/3011	B
Isle of Man	SI 2005/1263	R
	SI 2009/228	B
Jersey	SI 2005/1261	R
	SI 2009/3012	B
Liberia	SI 2011/2434	B
Liechtenstein	SI 2010/2678	B
Montserrat	SI 2005/1459	R
Netherlands Antilles	SI 2005/1460	R
San Marino	SI 2011/1688	B
St Christopher (St Kitts) and Nevis	SI 2011/1077	B
St Lucia	SI 2011/1076	B
St Vincent and the Grenadines	SI 2011/1078	B
Turks and Caicos Islands	SI 2010/2679	B
	Agreement effective 15 January 2005	NR

Notes

Key to scope of TIEAs

B Bilateral agreements for co-operation in tax matters through exchange of information

NR Non-reciprocal Agreements relating to the EU Directive on taxation of savings income in the form of interest payments

R Reciprocal Agreements relating to the EU Directive on taxation of savings income in the form of interest payments

TIEAs signed/not in force

An updated list of TIEAs signed/not in force is available on the HMRC website: www.hmrc.gov.uk/international/tiea_signed.htm

19 General

CLEARANCES

Non-Statutory Clearances

(1) Non-Statutory Business Clearances – (www.hmrc.gov.uk/cap/links-dec07.htm; HMRC Non-Statutory Business Clearance Guidance Manual (NBCG))

(a) *General* – The non-statutory business clearance service is available to businesses and their advisers about the tax consequences of transactions affecting the business in the circumstances below:

- Where there is 'material uncertainty' arising within four Finance Acts of the introduction of any new legislation; or

- On legislation older than the last four Finance Acts where there is material uncertainty around the tax outcome of a real issue of commercial significance to the business itself.

Clearance applications can be made both pre-transaction (where evidence is supplied that the transaction is genuinely contemplated) and post-transaction.

(b) *Suitability* – Circumstances where HMRC will *not* accept non-statutory business clearance applications include:

- Personal tax matters (eg Inheritance Tax or residence status);

- Employment contract matters (although applications may ask for confirmation on the tax treatment of salary sacrifice arrangements put in place);

- If the application concerns tax or NICs planning arrangements;

- Minor variations of previous applications in respect of the same person and the same transaction;

- If the application is about arrangements primarily to gain a tax or NICs advantage rather than being primarily commercially motivated;

- If there is no material uncertainty (eg the point at issue is covered in published HMRC guidance);

- If HMRC have already opened an enquiry etc into the subject matter of the clearance application or the self-assessment return for the year to which it relates, or if the 'enquiry window' has closed;

- If the application deals with matters not involving interpretations of tax law or its application (eg asset valuations or transfer pricing);

- If the application asks questions about the application of customs rules;

- Applications requesting HMRC's view on whether a particular Research and Development (R&D) project qualifies for relief in relation to R&D tax incentives;

- Applications concerning the tax consequences of executing trust deeds or settlements, and whether the 'settlements' anti-avoidance provisions apply (*ITTOIA 2005, Pt 5, Ch 5*).

Clearances

(c) *Contents of application* – HMRC publish a checklist of information required in support of a non-statutory business clearance application, and they ask that it be used as a cover sheet or its order be adhered to in any covering letter. The checklist can be downloaded (in pdf format) from the HMRC website: www.hmrc.gov.uk/cap/annex-a-checklist.pdf.

For further guidance see: www.hmrc.gov.uk/cap/links-dec07.htm#4

(d) *Submission of applications* – Non-statutory business clearance applications can be submitted to HMRC as follows.

By Post:

- Large businesses – Applications should be submitted to the HMRC Customer Relationship Manager.
- Other businesses:

    HMRC Clearances Team,
    Alexander House,
    21 Victoria Avenue
    Southend on Sea
    Essex
    SS99 1BD

By Email: hmrc.southendteam@hmrc.gsi.gov.uk

Note – In the case of market sensitive information, contact HMRC in advance: large businesses via their Customer Relationship Manager, others by telephone to 01733 317030

(2) HMRC CAP 1 (Clearances and Approvals) (www.hmrc.gov.uk/cap/cap1.htm)

With effect from 31 October 2011, CAP 1 replaced HMRC Code of Practice 10 (Information and advice) (COP10) and VAT Notice 700/6 (VAT rulings for non-business customers).

(a) *General* – Applications for a ruling under CAP 1 can be made only by non-business persons (or persons who are contacting HMRC with non-business queries) about HMRC's interpretation of recent tax legislation, and advisors acting on their behalf,

(b) *When HMRC will respond* – HMRC undertake to provide non-business pre- and post-transaction rulings on request in most cases where the taxpayer or their adviser is uncertain about the meaning of recent tax legislation as it applies to a specific issue, transaction or intended transaction and cannot find the information they need from HMRC's online guidance or telephone helplines. For this purpose, 'recent' legislation refers to enactments within the past four years. However, HMRC will give a view on earlier provisions where a query raises uncertainty about the right tax treatment and the matter is not covered in their published guidance.

(c) *When HMRC will not respond* – Circumstances In which HMRC may not give advice under this service include:

- If the application fails to provide the necessary information. (In this case HMRC will say what further information they need.)

19 General

- If HMRC do not think that there are genuine points of uncertainty. (In this case HMRC will explain why they think this and direct the applicant to the relevant online guidance.)
- If the application relates to a future transaction and HMRC are not reasonably satisfied that the transaction, as described, will indeed take place.
- If the application concerns tax planning.
- If the application relates to transactions which, in HMRC's view, are for the purposes of avoiding tax.
- If HMRC are checking the taxpayer's return for the period in question.
- If, in the case of a self assessment return, the time limit for HMRC to notify their intention to begin an enquiry into the return to which the transaction in question relates has passed.

(c) *Contents of application* – HMRC publish a checklist of information required in support of a CAP 1 application, and they ask that it be used as a cover sheet or its order be adhered to in any covering letter. The checklist can be downloaded (in pdf format) from the HMRC website: www.hmrc.gov.uk/cap/annex-a-cap1-checklist.pdf.

(d) *Submission of applications*:

There is no single point of contact at HMRC to which applications under CAP 1 should be sent, given the very wide range of tax regimes covered by this service and the number of applications received.

If the applicant has an existing point of contact within HMRC, for example a Customer Manager or their local tax office, or are already in contact with HMRC on the subject of the query, they should address their application to the contact address which they have been given.

In all other cases, applicants are asked to use the contact details and postal addresses for specialist departments or any other part of HMRC, as listed at search2.hmrc.gov.uk/kbroker/hmrc/contactus/start.jsp

(3) Post-transaction valuation checks for capital gains –
(www.hmrc.gov.uk/forms/cg34.pdf)

(a) *General* – This service allows taxpayers (including companies) to ask HMRC to check valuations required to compute capital gains tax, or corporation tax on chargeable gains. It can be used after a disposal, or after a deemed disposal following a claim that an asset has become of negligible value, but before the related tax return is submitted. If HMRC have agreed a valuation, they will not challenge the subsequent use of it in a tax return.

(b) *Contents of application* – Form CG34 must be completed for each valuation which HMRC are asked to check, and submitted together with the information listed on the form. Copies of Form CG34 can be downloaded from the HMRC website: www.hmrc.gov.uk/forms/cg34.pdf

(c) *Submission of applications* – Applicants should allow at least two months for HMRC to check valuations. Completed forms CG34 should be submitted by post as follows:

- For individuals, partnerships and personal representatives (other than those listed below and opposite)

  The Capital Gains Tax Team (Individuals and Public Bodies)
  The Crescent Centre
  Temple Back
  Bristol
  BS1 6HR

- For taxpayers dealt with by High Net Worth Units or Public Department 1:

  To the appropriate office dealing with the taxpayer's affairs

- For taxpayers dealt with by Trust Offices:

  CAR Trusts and Estates - Truro Office
  Lysnoweth
  Infirmary Hill
  Truro
  Cornwall
  TR1 2JD

- For companies:

  To the appropriate office dealing with the company's affairs.

(4) Inheritance tax (IHT) clearance service for business owner – (www.hmrc.gov.uk/cap/clearanceiht.htm)

(a) *General* – This service allows business owners (or their advisers) to make clearance applications in respect of IHT business property relief (BPR), if HMRC is satisfied that there is material uncertainty over the application of the law, and that the issue is commercially significant to the business itself. Applications can be made post-transaction, or pre-transaction if evidence is supplied that the transaction is genuinely contemplated.

HMRC will also provide a view on the tax consequences of a transfer of value that involves a change of ownership of a business (succession) where this transfer (ignoring BPR) would result in an immediate IHT charge. Clearances in these succession cases will only remain valid for a limited period of six months.

(b) *Suitability* – HMRC will not accept IHT business clearance service applications in the following circumstances:

- Applications for tax planning advice, or for HMRC's approval of tax planning arrangements;
- Applications involving minor variations of previous one for the same persons on the same transactions;
- If HMRC take the view that the arrangements are primarily to gain a tax advantage rather than being primarily commercially motivated;
- Applications where there is no actual uncertainty;
- If HMRC have already opened an enquiry into the transaction that is the subject of your clearance application, or where an enquiry into an IHT return has already been opened;

19 General

- Applications on issues not involving the interpretation of tax law or its application to particular circumstances;
- Applications concerning the tax consequences of executing trust deeds or settlements, and whether the 'settlements' anti-avoidance provisions apply (*ITTOIA 2005, Pt 5, Ch 5*);
- If the disposition of property under a will is conditional on the availability of BPR.

(c) *Contents of application*

HMRC publish a checklist of information required in support of an IHT business clearance service application, and they ask that it be used as a cover sheet or its order be adhered to in any covering letter. The checklist can be downloaded (in pdf format) from the HMRC website: www.hmrc.gov.uk/cap/Checklist.pdf.

For further guidance see www.hmrc.gov.uk/cap/clearanceiht.htm#4.

If the application involves a transaction for which there is also the disclosure of an avoidance scheme covering all or part of the transaction, explicit mention must be made of any related disclosures (eg by including a copy of the disclosure, or by reporting the allocated DOTAS scheme reference number).

(d) *Submission of applications* – Postal applications can be submitted to:

HMRC
Trusts & Estates Technical Team (Clearances)
Ferrers House
Castle Meadow Road
Nottingham
NG2 1BB

Email applications can be submitted to the Trusts & Estates Technical Team (Clearances): mailpoint.e@hmrc.gsi.gov.uk.

The following reference should be quoted: BP102/P1/08E. If the application contains commercially sensitive information, HMRC should be emailed (as above) with a contact name and telephone number and they will contact the application.

(5) General advice on specialist technical areas of taxation – (www.hmrc.gov.uk/cap/gen-advice.htm)

HMRC's website (www.hmrc.gov.uk/cap/gen-advice.htm) lists contact details for general advice on the following specialist topics:

- Non resident trusts, domicile and residence
- Charities and Community Amateur Sports Clubs
- Individual Savings Accounts and the tax deduction scheme for interest
- Child Trust Funds
- Reliefs and exemptions available under Double Taxation Treaties and the EU Interest and Royalties Directive
- Pension schemes
- Oil companies

Clearances

- Stamp Duty, Stamp Duty Land Tax and Stamp Duty Reserve Tax
- Underlying tax
- Enterprise Investment Scheme (EIS), the Corporate Venturing Scheme (CVS) and Venture Capital Trusts (VCTs) and Enterprise Management Incentives (EMI)
- Research and Development tax credits
- Controlled Foreign Companies (CFCs)
- Arbitrage

HMRC's website (www.hmrc.gov.uk/cap/#apa) lists contact details for the following:

- Advance pricing agreements
- Funding issues

Statutory Clearances

(www.hmrc.gov.uk/cap/statutory-clearances.pdf)

(1) *General* – Clearances applications may be submitted to HMRC by letter, fax or email, including in respect of the following:

Clearance category	Statutory reference
Demergers*	CTA 2010, s 1091
Demergers: Chargeable payments*	CTA 2010, s 1092
Purchase of own shares*	CTA 2010, s 1044
EIS shares – acquisition by new company*	ITA 2007, s 247(1)(f)
Transactions in securities*	ITA 2007, s 701; CTA 2010, s 748
Share exchanges*	TCGA 1992, s 138(1)
Reconstructions involving the transfer of a business*	TCGA 1992, s 139(5)
Transfer or division of a UK business between EU member states*	TCGA 1992, s 140B
Transfer or division of non-UK business by a UK company to a company resident in another EU member state	TCGA 1992, s 140D
Intangible assets*	CTA 2009, s 831
Loan relationships: transfers*	CTA 2009, s 427
Loan relationships: mergers*	CTA 2009, s 437
Derivative contracts: transfers*	CTA 2009, s 677
Derivative contracts: mergers*	CTA 2009, s 686
Targeted Anti Avoidance Rule 3 (Capital Gains)*	TCGA 1992, ss 184G-184H
Company migrations	TMA 1970, s 109B
Insurance companies: Transfer of business	TA 1988, s 444AED

continued

19 General

Clearance category	Statutory reference
Corporate Venturing Schemes	FA 2000, Sch 15, Pt X
Assignment of lease at undervalue*	ITTOIA 2005, s 300; CTA 2009, s 237
Transactions in land*	ITA 2007, s 770; CTA 2010, s 831
Offshore funds: (a) Reporting fund status (b) Equivalence and genuine diversity of ownership requirements	SI 2009/3001, reg 54(2) SI 2009/3001, reg 78
Stamp Duty Adjudication	SA 1891, s 12A

* See note (3) below

(2) *Submission of applications* – A list of HMRC contact details in respect of each category of statutory clearance application can be downloaded (in pdf format) from HMRC's website (www.hmrc.gov.uk/cap/statutory-clearances.pdf).

(3) Clearance applications under more than one of the provisions marked * above may be submitted to HMRC as a single application, by email, fax or letter, as follows:

By letter:

Non market sensitive

> Clearance and Counteraction Team, Anti-Avoidance Group
> First Floor
> 22 Kingsway
> London
> WC2B 6NR

Market sensitive

> Team Leader
> Clearance and Counteraction Team, Anti-Avoidance Group
> First Floor
> 22 Kingsway
> London
> WC2B 6NR

By Fax: 020 7438 4409

Note: If faxing market sensitive information, call the HMRC team leader on Tel 020 7438 7215 beforehand.

By Email: reconstructions@hmrc.gsi.gov.uk

For general enquiries to the unit: Tel 020 7438 7474

Statutory approvals

A statutory approval (which is different to a statutory clearance) can be required in advance for a particular tax treatment to apply on particular issues, where the tax treatment changes according to whether or not approval has been given. Statutory approvals are listed on the HMRC website at www.hmrc.gov.uk/cap/index.htm#3. HMRC contact details in respect of statutory approvals are available on the HMRC website at www.hmrc.gov.uk/cap/index.htm#12.

GIFTS OF PRE-EMINENT PROPERTY ('GIFTS TO THE NATION')

(FB 2012, cl 49, Sch 14)

	Tax reduction
Individuals	
Income tax and capital gains tax*	30%
Companies	20%

* If the individual does not express a preference, the tax reduction is first applied to the individual's income tax liability, then to any capital gains tax liability.

Notes

(1) *General* – A reduction in income tax and/or capital gains tax (individuals), or corporation tax (companies), is available where an individual or corporate donor makes a 'qualifying gift' of 'pre-eminent property' (as defined) to be held for the benefit of the public or the nation. The gift offer must be registered and accepted under a scheme set up by the Secretary of State. The relief provisions apply from a date to be appointed by Treasury order.

(2) *Individuals* – An individual can spread the tax reduction over a period of up to five tax years, ie the tax year in which the offer is registered or any of the following four tax years. The total tax reduction figure is 30% of the qualifying gift's agreed value. The relief applies to individuals, but not those acting as trustees or personal representatives.

(3) *Companies* – If a company makes a qualifying gift, a tax reduction (for the accounting period in which an offer to make the gift is registered) is treated as arising when the company's corporation tax liability became due (or the registration date, if later). The tax reduction is 20% of the qualifying gift's agreed value, although the company may choose to accept a lower percentage, if it wishes.

(4) *Capital gains* – A gain on the gift of an object under the scheme is exempt from capital gains tax or corporation tax on chargeable gains (*TCGA 1992, s 258(1A), as inserted by FB 2012, Sch 14, para 34*).

(5) *Inheritance tax* – Gifts of property under the scheme are exempt from inheritance tax under *IHTA 1984, s 25* ('Gifts for national purposes, etc') (*IHTA 1984, s 25(3), as inserted by FB 2012, Sch 14, para 27*).

Index

Accounting periods for PAYE
  monthly, 40–1
  quarterly, 41
Age-related allowances, 3–4
Aggregates levy, 170
Agriculture
  inheritance tax relief, 107–8
  special income tax relief, 67–8
Air passenger duty, 176–9
Allowances
  see also **Reliefs**; **Tax credits**
  age-related allowances, 3–4
  capital allowances
    cars, 123
    Enterprise Zones, 127–8
    industrial buildings, 124
    integral features, 123–4
    other allowances, 125
    plant and machinery, 120–2
    time limits for claims and elections, 126–7
  capital gains tax
    indexation allowance, 102–3
    personal representatives, 99
  corporation tax, 84–5
  flat rate expenses, 30–4
  mileage allowances
    cars, 22–5
    motorcycles and bicycles, 25
    vans, 25–6
  PAYE, 35–6
  pension contributions, 56
  personal allowances, 3–4
  provision of works transport, 26
  subsistence allowances, 27
Alternative finance investment bonds, 225
Alternative fuel cars, 19–20
Approvals, 242

Bank base rates, 210–1
Bank levy, 179–80
Bank payroll tax (BPT), 73, 198
Benefits *see* **Social security benefits**
Buildings *see* **Land and buildings**

Buses, 26
Business taxation
  clearance rulings
    non-statutory clearances, 236–7
    statutory clearances, 241–2
  income tax
    car hire costs, 67
    special business reliefs, 67–8
    time limits for claims and elections, 68–9
  inheritance tax relief, 107–8

Capital allowances
  cars, 123
  industrial buildings, 124
  integral features, 123–4
  other allowances, 125
  plant and machinery, 120–2
  time limits for claims and elections, 126–7
Capital allowances
  Enterprise Zones, 127–8
Capital gains tax
  allowances for personal representatives, 99
  charities, 90–1
  chattel exemption, 87
  enterprise investment schemes (EIS), 90
  entrepreneurs' relief, 87–8
  gifts to the nation, 243
  gilt-edged securities, 92–7
  identification of disposals with acquisitions, 98–9
  indexation allowance, 102–3
  interest
    overdue tax, 14–5
    repayments of tax, 15
  leases
    short lease premiums, 92
    short leases, 61–3
    wasting assets, 63, 91–2
  non-statutory clearances, 238–9
  private residence relief, 89–90
  rates, 86
  rollover relief, 89
  surcharges, 6–7
  taper relief, 88–9

Index

Capital gains tax – *contd*
  time limits for claims and elections, 99–101
  venture capital trusts, 61
Cars
  capital allowances, 123
  company car benefit charges
    alternative fuel cars, 19–20
    cars with no emission figures, 20
    diesel cars, 19
    low emissions cars, 19
    taxable percentages, 16–8
  fuel benefit charges, 20–2
  hire costs, 67
  mileage allowances, 22–5
  road fuel duty, 172
  VAT
    advisory fuel rates, 152–3
    private fuel scale charges, 153–7
  vehicle excise duty
    light passenger vehicles, 173–4
Certificates of tax deposits, 211–3
Chargeable benefits
  childcare vouchers, 28
  company car benefit charges
    alternative fuel cars, 19–20
    cars with no emission figures, 20
    diesel cars, 19
    low emissions cars, 19
    taxable percentages, 16–8
  mobile phones, 27
Charities
  capital gains tax, 90–1
  IHT reductions, 119
Chattels
  CGT exemption, 87
  IHT on pre-owned assets, 109
Children
  CGT on settlements, 64
  childcare vouchers, 28
  tax credit (CTC), 190
Civil partnerships
  entitlement on intestacy, 117–8
  gift exemptions, 106–7
Clearance rulings
  non-statutory clearances
    business taxation, 236–7
    capital gains tax, 238–9
    HMRC Code of Practice, 237–8
    inheritance tax, 239–40
    specialist technical areas, 240–1
  statutory approvals, 242
  statutory clearances, 241–2
Climate change levy, 171
Commonwealth Games participants, 4
Community investment tax relief (CITR), 64–5

Companies
  see also **Corporation tax**; **Shares**
  capital gains tax
    identification of disposals with acquisitions, 98–9
    indexation allowance, 103
Company share option plans (CSOPS), 49–50
Construction industry scheme (CIS)
  HMRC powers, deterrents and safeguards, 198
  late payments, 44
  late returns, 43–4
  payment dates, 44
  return dates, 42–4
Corporation tax
  bank payroll tax (BPT), 73
  capital allowances
    cars, 123
    Enterprise Zones, 127–8
    industrial buildings, 124
    integral features, 123–4
    other allowances, 125
    plant and machinery, 120–2
    time limits for claims and elections, 126–7
  due and payable dates, 74
  filing dates, 73
  gifts to the nation, 243
  indexation allowance, 84–5
  interest
    overdue tax, 77–9
    repayments of tax, 80–2
  loans to participators, 73
  marginal relief, 71–2
  patent box provisions, 72
  penalties, 75–6
  rates, 70–1
  time limits for claims and elections, 82–4
Credits *see* **Tax credits**

Data-gathering powers, 201
Dividends
  income tax rates, 2
  venture capital trusts, 61
Double taxation agreements
  agreements signed but not in force, 232–3
  countries with agreements in force, 227–32
  inheritance tax, 234

Electronic returns
  PAYE
    failure to use electronic communications, 38–9
    Real Time Information, 42
  VAT, 166

246

Index

Enterprise investment schemes (EIS), 90, 241
Enterprise management incentives (EMI), 47–9
Enterprise Zones, 127–8
Entrepreneurs' relief, 87–8
Errors in returns
   corporation tax, 75–6
   delivery of IHT accounts, 115
   HMRC powers, deterrents and safeguards, 197
   self assessment, 9–11
   stamp taxes, 135
   VAT, 159, 162–3
Exemptions *see* **Reliefs**

Failure to notify liability
   corporation tax, 75–6
   delivery of IHT accounts, 114–5
   HMRC powers, deterrents and safeguards, 197
   self assessment, 9–11
   stamp taxes, 134
   VAT, 160–1
Filing dates *see* **Return dates**
Flat rate expenses, 30–4
Flat-rate VAT scheme for small businesses, 146–9
Foreign exchange rates, 214–23
Fuel
   company car benefit charges
      alternative fuel cars, 19–20
      limits on chargeable benefits, 20–2
   road fuel duty, 172
   VAT
      advisory fuel rates, 152–3
      private fuel scale charges, 153–7
Futures exchanges, 225–6

Gifts to the nation, 243
Gilt-edged securities, 92–7

HMRC Charter, 197

Income tax
   business profits
      car hire costs, 67
      special business reliefs, 67–8
      time limits for claims and elections, 68–9
   cap on unlimited reliefs, 4
   capital allowances
      cars, 123
      Enterprise Zones, 127–8
      industrial buildings, 124
      integral features, 123–4
      other allowances, 125

Income tax – *contd*
   capital allowances – *contd*
      plant and machinery, 120–2
      time limits for claims and elections, 126–7
   community investment tax relief (CITR), 64–5
   company car benefit charges
      alternative fuel cars, 19–20
      cars with no emission figures, 20
      diesel cars, 19
      low emissions cars, 19
      taxable percentages, 16–8
   company share option plans (CSOPS), 49–50
   construction industry scheme (CIS)
      late payments, 44
      late returns, 43–4
      payment dates, 44
      return dates, 42–4
   enterprise investment schemes (EIS), 59–61
   enterprise management incentives (EMI), 47–9
   flat rate expenses, 30–4
   gifts to the nation, 243
   interest
      employment related loans, 29
      overdue tax, 14–5
      repayments of tax, 15
   leases
      premiums paid, 63–4
      short leases, 61–3
      wasting assets, 63
   limits on chargeable benefits
      childcare vouchers, 28
      company car benefit charges, 20
      fuel benefit charges, 20–2
      mobile phones, 27
      provision of works transport, 26
      relocation expenses, 28
      scholarships, 29
   mileage allowances
      buses, 26
      cars, 22–5
      motorcycles and bicycles, 25
      vans, 25–6
   Olympic, Paralympic and Commonwealth Games participants, 4
   PAYE
      debt recovery powers, 201
      interest on late payments, 41
      monthly accounting periods, 40–1
      penalties, 36–9
      quarterly accounting periods, 41
      Real Time Information, 42
      return dates, 36

Index

Income tax – *contd*
  PAYE – *contd*
    surcharges, 40
    thresholds, 35–6
  pension contributions
    annual and lifetime allowances, 56
    early retirement occupations, 58
    personal pension schemes and retirement annuity premiums, 56–7
    reliefs, 55–6
  personal allowances and reliefs, 3–4
  rates
    savings and dividends, 2
    taxable income, 1
    trusts, 2–3
  self assessment
    filing dates, 4–5
    payment dates, 5
    penalties, 6–15
  settlements and children, 64
  share incentive plans (SIPS), 45–6
  short leases, 61–3
  student loans, 42
  subsistence allowances, 27
  surcharges, 6–7
  termination payments, 28
  time limits for assessments and claims, 65–6
  venture capital trusts, 61
Indexation allowances
  capital gains tax, 102–3
  corporation tax, 84–5
Individual savings accounts (ISAs), 59
Information and inspection powers
  HMRC powers, deterrents and safeguards, 195
  self assessment, 14
Inheritance tax
  agriculture and business property relief, 107–8
  annual and small gift exemptions, 106
  donations to charities, 119
  double taxation conventions, 234
  gifts in consideration of marriage and civil partnerships, 106–7
  gifts to the nation, 243
  interest, 116–7
  intestate estates, 117–8
  non-statutory clearances, 239–40
  payment dates, 114
  penalties, 114–6
  pre-owned assets, 109–10
  quick succession relief, 108
  rates, 104–6
  return dates, 110–4
  taper relief, 108
Insurance premium tax, 169

Interest
  see also **Official rates of interest**
  bank base rates, 210–1
  corporation tax
    overdue tax, 77–9
    repayments of tax, 80–2
  employment related loans, 29
  income tax
    late payments of PAYE, 41
    overdue tax, 14–5
    repayments of tax, 15
  inheritance tax, 116–7
  SAYE
    basic rates, 54
    early withdrawals of SAYE, 53
  stamp taxes, 136–7
  VAT
    default interest, 167
    repayments of tax, 167–8
Intestate estates, 117–8
Investigative powers, 196
Investment exchanges, 226–7
Investments
  community investment tax relief (CITR), 64–5
  enterprise investment schemes (EIS), 59–61, 90
  venture capital trusts, 61

Land and buildings
  aggregates levy, 170
  capital allowances, 124
  landfill tax, 169–70
  leases
    CGT on premiums, 92
    short leases, 61–3
  stamp duty land tax
    interest, 136–7
    leases, 131–2
    penalties, 134–6
    rates, 129
    reliefs, 130–1
  stamp duty (pre-December 2003, 132
  statutory clearances, 242
  VAT, 149–50
Landfill tax, 169–70
Leases
  capital gains tax
    short lease premiums, 92
    wasting assets, 91–2
  income tax
    premiums paid, 63–4
    short leases, 61–3
    wasting assets, 63
  short leases, 61–3

Leases – *contd*
  stamp duty land tax, 131–2
  statutory clearances, 242
Loans
  corporation tax, 73
  interest on employment related loans, 29
  statutory clearances, 241
Low emissions cars, 19

Mileage allowances
  cars, 22–5
  motorcycles and bicycles, 25
  vans, 25–6
Mobile phones, 27
Motorcycles and bicycles, 25

National insurance
  Class 1
    employee contributions, 181–2
    employer contributions, 183–4
  Class 1A, 184–5
  Class 1B, 185
  Class 2, 185–6
  Class 3, 187
  Class 4, 187–9
  company share option plans (CSOPS), 49–50
  enterprise management incentives (EMI), 47–9
  HMRC powers, deterrents and safeguards, 198
  interest
    overdue tax, 14–5
    repayments of tax, 15
  reform proposals, 189
  save as you earn (SAYE) schemes, 51
  share incentive plans (SIPS), 45–6
National Minimum Wage
  accommodation offset rate, 193–4
  standard rates, 193

Official rates of interest
  bank base rates, 210–1
  corporation tax
    overdue tax, 77–9
    repayments, 80–2
  employment related loans, 29
  inheritance tax, 116–7
  late payment of stamp taxes, 136–7
  repayments of tax, 14–5
  SAYE
    basic rates, 54
    early withdrawals under SAYE contracts, 53

Official rates of interest – *contd*
  VAT
    overpayments, 167–8
    underpayments, 167
Olympic Games participants, 4
Options
  company share option plans (CSOPS), 49–50
  enterprise management incentives (EMI), 48–9
  save as you earn (SAYE) schemes, 51–4
Overnight expenses, 27
Overseas investment exchanges, 227

Paralympic Games participants, 4
Patent box provisions, 72
PAYE
  debt recovery powers, 201
  HMRC powers, deterrents and safeguards, 198
  interest on late payments
    late payments of PAYE, 41
  monthly accounting periods, 40–1
  penalties
    failure to use electronic communications, 38–9
    incorrect returns, 37
    late filing, 36
    late payments, 37–8
  quarterly accounting periods, 41
  Real Time Information, 42
  return dates, 36
  surcharges, 40
  thresholds, 35–6
Payment dates
  construction industry scheme (CIS), 44
  corporation tax, 74
  HMRC powers, deterrents and safeguards, 197, 198–9
  inheritance tax, 114
  self assessment, 5
Penalties
  construction industry scheme (CIS)
    late payments, 44
    late returns, 43–4
  corporation tax, 75–6
  HMRC powers, deterrents and safeguards, 197–200
  inheritance tax, 114–6
  PAYE
    failure to use electronic communications, 38–9
    incorrect returns, 37
    late filing, 36
    late payments, 37–8

Index

Penalties – *contd*
  self assessment
    errors, 11–2
    failure to comply with information notices, 14
    failure to keep records, 13
    failure to notify liability, 9–11
    false payments on account, 13
    late payments, 5–6
    late returns, 6–9
  stamp duty land tax, 134–6
  stamp duty (pre-December 2003), 134–6
  stamp duty reserve tax, 134–6
  VAT, 159–66
Pension contributions
  annual and lifetime allowances, 56
  early retirement occupations, 58
  HMRC powers, deterrents and safeguards, 198
  personal pension schemes and retirement annuity premiums, 56–7
  reliefs, 55–6
Personal allowances
  income tax, 3–4
  PAYE, 35–6
Personal representatives
  see also **Inheritance tax**
  CGT allowances, 99
  distribution of intestate estates, 117–8
Pre-owned assets, 109–10
Private residence relief, 89–90

Quick succession relief, 108

Rates
  aggregates levy, 170
  air passenger duty, 176
  bank levy, 179
  capital gains tax, 86
  climate change levy, 171
  foreign exchange rates, 214–23
  inheritance tax, 104–6
  insurance premium tax, 169
  landfill tax, 169
  National Minimum Wage
    accommodation offset rate, 193–4
    standard rates, 193
  NI contributions
    Class 1, 181–3
    Class 1A, 184
    Class 1B, 185
    Class 2, 185
    Class 3, 187
    Class 4, 187–9
  road fuel duty, 172
  social security benefits, 201–6

Rates – *contd*
  stamp duty land tax, 129
  stamp duty (pre-December 2003), 132
  stamp duty reserve tax, 134
  tax credits
    child tax credit (CTC), 190
    working tax credit (WTC), 191
  VAT, 138
  vehicle excise duty
    light passenger vehicles, 173–4
    other vehicles, 175
Real Time Information, 42
Recognised stock exchanges
  alternative finance investment bonds, 225
  defined, 223
  designated exchanges, 223–4
  futures exchanges, 225–6
  investment exchanges, 226–7
  overseas investment exchanges, 227
  recognised countries, 224–5
Reliefs
  see also **Allowances**; **Tax credits**
  capital gains tax
    annual exemptions, 87
    chattel exemption, 87
    enterprise investment schemes (EIS), 90
    entrepreneurs' relief, 87–8
    gilt-edged securities, 92–7
    private residence relief, 89–90
    rollover relief, 89
    taper relief, 88–9
  corporation tax
    marginal relief, 71–2
  gifts to the nation, 243
  income tax
    age-related allowances, 3–4
    cap on unlimited reliefs, 4
    community investment tax relief (CITR), 64–5
    enterprise investment schemes (EIS), 59–61
    individual savings accounts (ISAs), 59
    pension contributions, 55–6
    relocation expenses, 28
    special business reliefs, 67–8
    venture capital trusts, 61
  inheritance tax
    agriculture and business property relief, 107–8
    annual and small gift exemptions, 106
    gifts in consideration of marriage and civil partnerships, 106–7
    quick succession relief, 108
    taper relief, 108
  national insurance
    Class 2, 186

Index

Reliefs – *contd*
  stamp duty land tax, 130–1
  value added tax (VAT)
    exempt supplies, 141
  VAT
    de minimis limits, 149
    reduced rate supplies, 140
    zero-rated supplies, 139–40
Relocation expenses, 28
Retail prices index (RPI), 210
Retirement *see* **Pension contributions**
Return dates
  construction industry scheme (CIS), 42–4
  corporation tax, 73
  HMRC powers, deterrents and safeguards, 198–9
  inheritance tax, 110–4
  PAYE, 36
  self assessment, 4–5
Road fuel duty, 172
Rollover relief, 89

Save as you earn (SAYE) schemes, 51–4
Savings
  income tax on dividends, 2
  individual savings accounts (ISAs), 59
  pension contributions
    annual and lifetime allowances, 56
    early retirement occupations, 58
    personal pension schemes and retirement annuity premiums, 56–7
Scholarships, 29
Self assessment
  filing dates, 4–5
  HMRC powers, deterrents and safeguards, 199
  payment dates, 5
  penalties
    errors, 12–3
    failure to comply with information notices, 14
    failure to keep records, 13
    failure to notify liability, 10–2
    false payments on account, 13
    late payments, 5–6, 6–7
    late returns, 7–10
Shares
  company share option plans (CSOPS), 49–50
  enterprise investment schemes (EIS), 59–61
  enterprise management incentives (EMI), 47–9
  income tax on dividends, 2
  save as you earn (SAYE) schemes, 51–4
  share incentive plans (SIPS), 45–6

Shares – *contd*
  stamp duty reserve tax
    interest, 136–7
    penalties, 134–6
    rates, 134
Social security benefits
  non-taxable benefits, 206–8
  rates, 201–6
  taxable benefits, 208–9
Spouses
  entitlement on intestacy, 117–8
  marriage gift exemptions, 106–7
  married couples personal tax allowances, 4
Stamp duty land tax
  leases, 131–2
  penalties, 134–6
  rates, 129
  reliefs, 130–1
Stamp duty (pre-December 2003)
  exemptions, 132–4
  interest, 136–7
  penalties, 134–6
  rates, 132
Stamp duty reserve tax
  interest, 136–7
  penalties, 134–6
  rates, 134
Statutory approvals, 242
Stock exchanges *see* **Recognised stock exchanges**
Student loans, 42
Subsistence allowances, 27
Surcharges
  PAYE, 40
  self assessment, 6–7
  VAT, 161–2

Taper relief
  capital gains tax, 88–9
  inheritance tax, 108
Tax credits
  child tax credit (CTC), 190
  income thresholds and withdrawal rates, 192
  working tax credit (WTC)
    childcare element, 191–2
    rates, 191
Tax information exchange agreements (TIEAS), 234–5
Tax returns *see* **Return dates**
Termination payments, 28
Time limits
  capital allowance claims and elections, 126–7
  capital gains tax claims and elections, 99–101
  corporation tax claims and elections, 82–4

Index

Time limits – *contd*
  HMRC powers, deterrents and safeguards, 196
  income tax assessments and claims, 65–6
  special business reliefs, 70–1
Travel
  see also **Subsistence allowances**
  air passenger duty, 176–9
  capital allowances for cars, 123
  car hire costs, 67
  company car benefit charges
    alternative fuel cars, 19–20
    cars with no emission figures, 20
    diesel cars, 19
    low emissions cars, 19
    taxable percentages, 16–8
  fuel benefit charges, 20–2
  mileage allowances
    buses, 26
    cars, 22–5
    motorcycles and bicycles, 25
    vans, 25–6
  provision of works transport, 26
  road fuel duty, 172
  VAT
    advisory fuel rates, 152–3
    private fuel scale charges, 153–7
  vehicle excise duty
    light passenger vehicles, 173–4
    other vehicles, 175
Trusts
  identification of disposals with acquisitions for CGT, 98–9
  income tax rates, 2–3
  intangible property in settlor-interested trusts, 110
  settlements and children, 64

Value added tax (VAT)
  accounting schemes
    annual accounting, 145
    cash accounting, 146
    flat rates for small businesses, 146–9
  advisory fuel rates, 152–3
  capital goods scheme, 149–50
  de minimis limits, 149
  EU country codes, 157–9
  exempt supplies, 141
  forthcoming changes, 138–9
  interest
    default interest, 167
    repayments of tax, 167–8
  invoicing, 150–1
  penalties, 159–66
  private fuel scale charges, 153–7
  rates, 138
  reduced rate supplies, 140
  registration
    deregistration limits, 143–5
    distance selling, 142–3
    financial limits, 141
  surcharges, 161–2
  zero-rated supplies, 139–40
Vans, 25–6
Vehicle excise duty
  light passenger vehicles, 173–4
  other vehicles, 175
Venture capital trusts (VCT), 61, 242

Wasting assets
  capital gains tax, 91–2
  income tax, 63
Working tax credit (WTC)
  childcare element, 191–2
  rates, 191